Public Service
on the Brink

Edited by

Jenny Manson

Imprint-academic.com

Published in the UK by
Imprint Academic, PO Box 200, Exeter EX5 5YX, UK
Published in the USA by
Imprint Academic, Philosophy Documentation Center
PO Box 7147, Charlottesville, VA 22906-7147, USA

ISBN 9781845403065

A CIP catalogue record for this book is available from the
British Library and US Library of Congress

Contents

Contributors

Rodric Braithwaite was a civil servant in the Foreign Office, various embassies abroad and Downing Street from 1955 to 1993.

Dan Carrier is a journalist working for an independent newspaper group, the Camden New Journal. He is a member of the National Union of Journalists and has a special interest in how press reporting distorts political discourse.

Rebekah Carrier has worked providing advice under the legal aid scheme for over twenty years. She sees herself as fortunate to have fallen into a job which has allowed her to meet so many different people and listen to their amazing stories. Quite astonishingly, she has been able to use the law to help many of those people obtain a home or improve their housing conditions. She continues to work in both the private sector and the 'not for profit' sector, as a housing lawyer and helping to run a Law Centre in South London. As legal aid reaches its death throes, she worries about what she will do next.

Jonathan Edwards was, until 2010, a professor of medicine at University College London, working on the cause and treatment of rheumatoid arthritis. Having found providing safe and effective care increasingly difficult because of negative political and commercial forces, he retired at 60 to pursue interests in nerve cell biophysics.

Libby Goldby taught in state secondary schools from 1958 to 1993 including fifteen years as a head teacher in two different comprehensive schools. She is now a governor of a school in Haringey and is correspondent for a small educational research charity.

Oliver Huitson is an Associate Editor at Open Democracy's UK section, Our Kingdom. He completed a BA in Politics, Philosophy and Economics at the Open University in 2010 and is currently reading for an MSc in Politics and Government at Birkbeck, University of London. He works in finance in the City.

Liz Kessler is an urban designer; she trained at Oxford Brookes University, having spent many years before that working in housing and the arts. Her interest has always been in the quality of the environment and the impact it has on people's quality of life. As an urban designer she has specialised in retrofitting dysfunctional places in areas of multi-deprivation. She was employed in New Deal for Communities areas in Southampton and in Islington, London and is now working on a freelance basis primarily in Stepney, east London.

Ursula Murray works for Birkbeck University of London and tutors a range of post graduate and undergraduate courses on voluntary and community sector studies, public sector management, local government, lifelong learning and gender studies. Previously she worked as a senior manager in local government and prior to that in the voluntary sector undertaking action research projects around local economic change and women's employment and training. She has an MSc in Group Relations from Bristol UWE (2001) and completed a PhD at the Complexity and Management Centre, University of Hertfordshire Business School in 2005. Her research explored the *meaning* of the public sector using narrative and psychosocial methodologies.

Chris Richardson joined British Railways in 1961 as a trainee booking clerk. After a number of years as a Relief Station Master he moved into what became known as 'Human Resources'. He retired from a senior position at British Railways Board Headquarters in 1996.

Mark Serwotka is the general secretary of the Public and Commercial Services union—the UK's largest civil service union, with around 300,000 members in over 200 government departments and agencies and in parts of government transferred to the private sector. Born in south Wales in 1963, Mark started work at 16 in what was then the DHSS as a clerical officer, and served in the benefits service for 21 years, including seven years as a part-time worker to enable him to look after his children. During his two decades as a civil servant he held a wide range of union positions, including being responsible for employment tribunal cases. Standing as a socialist candidate and a rank and file branch secretary from the DSS Sheffield branch of PCS, he was elected to the post of general secretary in December 2000 and is almost unique among his peers, having come straight from the shop floor. Mark is a passionate believer in public services and the welfare state, as well as being a dedicated Cardiff City fan and season ticket holder. He is married with two teenage children.

David Wiggins retired in 2000 as Wykeham Professor of Logic, New College, Oxford, having previously taught philosophy at Birkbeck College, London, University College, Oxford and New College, Oxford to which he first came in 1959-60 (via a generous travelling fellowship to USA) from the position of Assistant Principal in the Colonial Office where his work concerned the implementation of the Colonial Development and Welfare Act. Philosophy apart, he was Chairman 1977-79 of the Transport Users Consultative Committee for the South East and a member of the Central Transport Users Consultative Committee. His most recent books are *Sameness and Substance Renewed* (OUP, 2001) and *Ethics: Twelve Lectures of the Philosophy of Morality* (Penguin, 2008). He has written and campaigned since the 1970s for saner public policies concerning transport and the environment.

Jenny Manson

Introduction

I have recently retired from HMRC (Her Majesty's Revenue and Customs) after a career of thirty five years.

My early delight in the job is easy to recapture. There was an atmosphere of friendliness, a rather family-like structure that everyone understood. From the first day, I was trusted to get on with the work, in the hours of my choosing if the job was done.

The initial training was long and intense. This and the working culture made it obvious what our job was — to help people struggling to understand the tax system, to chase the non-compliant, to become expert in tax legislation and to be professional in all our dealings. But things have altered greatly since then. Staff surveys have been sorry reading, putting the HMRC near or at the bottom of Whitehall departments for such things as confidence in senior managers and in the purpose of the on- going change programmes.

I have asked Revenue colleagues to what they attribute the recent catastrophic decline in morale. As one put it:

> The relative compactness of the Districts, the semi-autonomy afforded to them, plus the scope for discussion, combined to foster a feeling of togetherness. It was difficult *not* to identify with the 'firm' or to have some pride in it, as the members were truly an integral part of it.

> Another important element of this independence was that Districts were expected to 'consume their own smoke', which, at some danger to their health, they almost always did. The 'one stop shop' was one result of this policy, creating certainty for taxpayers and their advisors alike.

> It would be wrong to conclude from the above that offices had a completely free hand; accountability there was. Performance targets were set after sometimes long discussions and were challenging. For example — and by contrast with today — post was to be dealt with normally in 7 days (no misprint!), and *all* accounts submitted were scrutinised by an Inspector. Nowadays such attainments are almost beyond comprehension, and certainly out of reach. Perhaps we took our achievements for granted?

> It was clearly the case that the plethora of small units could not be sustained. It is also apparent that there was need of increased

specialisation, against a background of orchestrated and continuing campaigns of evasion and avoidance, and to cope with the sophisticated legislation and tactics which trailed in their wake.

Districts themselves expanded, seemingly exponentially. Groupings grew, and indeed still do; surely some form of gastric banding is called for? The trail of consequences from these aggrandisements is both predictable and apparent, representing a mirror image of the ethos engendered by the smaller groupings. Staff find it difficult to identify with the 'firm': indeed many are not sure who or what this is. They feel powerless to have any say in what is done or how it is done. They have developed, perhaps by way of self-protection, a form of tunnel vision. They are hurt and embarrassed by having to associate with HMRC's diminishing reputation and only vestiges of pride remain.

At one time taxpayers could contact a local office confident that they would be able to talk to someone who knew about their affairs and who could, as necessary, address their concerns. Pretty straight forward. Now, and I do speak from personal experience, taxpayers have to contact a huge marshalling yard, only to be shunted into a siding and left there indefinitely. These are called 'contact centres' but perhaps 'lack of' should be inserted initially? They are of course very big, and they are probably very cheap to run, given the conditions afforded to the inmates, but they are simply not working mainly because they ignore the very individual and sensitive nature of the commodity we are dealing with. Such a set up might work for domestic goods, garden appliances and the like, but clearly is not suited for matters which are at the core of people's personal and financial sensitivities No doubt, the poor taxpayer is consoled by being called a 'customer'? ... No, I don't think so either!

This sort of view is echoed by countless Revenue officials. Like so much of the public service, and also I believe private business, we were subjected to a series of initiatives. Some were intended to be work-related, things like 'lean' management and later Pacesetter, others to encourage a better service to the public (now called our customers) so for example, a customer centric strategy replaced earlier customer centred workshops. Increasingly from the 1980s onwards this familiar and not necessarily unhealthy attempt at process improvement was absorbed into (dressed up as) a sequence of missionary statements. Just in the last few years, there has been for example the HMRC strategy, a programme called Purpose, Vision and Way, One HMRC One Deal and in July 2011 a Vision week.

This experience is common throughout the public sector. Speak to many public servants about their job and they will say:

I know what my job is and I want to do it as well as I can. Indeed I would love my work if I could get one day's peace to get on with it. But I am beset at every turn by unintelligible, time wasting and fruitless management initiatives, constant change, ill-judged targets, wr〈 headed 'commercial' exemplars and continuous and misgu〈 restructuring.

I have to watch as, instead of my 'customer' (actually patient, pupil, taxpayer) getting a better deal from me, the only beneficiaries seem to be those who can lobby for special treatment.

The idea for this book preceded the coalition government in the UK and the cuts in public services, the talk of 'austerity' programmes, here and abroad. But much about the direction and the flavour of the cuts in 2010 onwards further exposed the difficulty of defending the idea of public service being *for* the public.

For example, the presentation of the deficit-cutting budget of June 2010 highlighted the question: why is it that the public service, set to bear the brunt of the 'pain' (used in an almost gleeful way) by way of service, pay and pension cuts, is so undefended?

The questions we address in this book are why, how and when did public service fall into disrepute and what is the reason for the current sustained attack?

People in the public sector do not take the good things for granted. In most jobs, there is interesting work, historically stable employment and, in more senior positions, good pay and pension expectations. There are comforts such as good holidays and flexi-time and most importantly, for those outside senior management there is still some independence and control over the working day and the task in hand: you are answerable to the public and not to a narrow interest group.

But to go higher you now have to toe the new lines and give up the real work for a lot of phoney stuff, strategic planning and leadership roles. There is little emphasis on real people management, although as with all workplaces, sometimes brave personnel management is needed to tackle issues of work-shy sickness and other forms of absenteeism. Instead increasingly managers are sent on endless courses on such esoteric subjects as 'leadership skills' rather than given practical support to deal with poor performers.

Of course some things that go wrong are the fault of the workers or of out-dated practices. There are inefficiencies and poor practice (as there are in all organisations). But there is a strongly held belief in the purpose of public service. Polly Toynbee wrote on the *Guardian* in August 2010 about her experience of working in low-paid jobs while researching her book, *Hard Work*.

I was struck time and again at how even agency workers — outsourced and not a part of the schools, hospitals, nurseries or nursing homes where they worked — strove to do their best, often against the odds, with the wrong equipment, inept managers or rules that were obstacles to kindness. They were more frustrated by waste or hindrances to good work than by their own rotten terms and conditions. Most took a pride in their jobs that went under-recognised.

The contributions to this book cannot be dismissed as special pleading by 'Luddites'. There is unanimity of view between the retired and the younger contributors (Dan Carrier, Oliver Huitson and Rebekah Carrier). Worrying though is the indication in the articles (for example Professor Jo Edwards on the NHS) that younger staff have to 'talk the talk' to get off the lowest rungs.

Public servants have noticed the more 'apparatchik' approach in the new joiners and it may be significant that this phase in the history of public service (the last four decades or so) has coincided with a dip in conviction (or any) politics.

This may be an often rehearsed and old debate. But as Professor David Wiggins notes in his piece, 'If all this has been heard a thousand times before, then what was the answer to the complaint?' So far he points out that the only answer is a counter- complaint against the complainant.

Many of the contributions refer to the experience of new public management (NPM) and of managerialism. NPM is used to describe the wave of public sector reforms throughout the world since the 1980s. A publication by the UN research institute for social development (UNRISD) in 1999 notes the usual features of NPM on the international stage:

> Key elements include various forms of decentralizing management within public services (e.g., the creation of autonomous agencies and devolution of budgets and financial control), increasing use of markets and competition in the provision of public services (e.g., contracting out and other market-type mechanisms), and increasing emphasis on performance, outputs and customer orientation.

Ursula Murray and David Wiggins give their view of the impact of the 'creed' of NPM.

Managerialism is defined as 'the application of managerial techniques of businesses to the running of other organizations, such as the civil service or local authorities' or as 'a belief in or reliance on the use of professional managers in administering or planning an activity'.

In the public service, managerialism is associated with the puzzle that lessons are never learnt from the failures. Are these repeated examples of 'sunk cost error', the tendency to continue an endeavour once an investment in money, effort, or time has been made? As Stuart Sutherland wrote in his book *Irrationality*: 'The willingness to change one's mind in the light of new evidence is a sign of rationality not weakness.'

People in post long for a pause to build on previous changes, good or bad. In my HMRC career, such consolidation is what we called for so that the service to the public could improve and the current structures (whatever they were) bed down a bit.

Another feature of the endless programme of 'Change Management' is the tendency to overlook internal expertise, instead bringing in expensive management consultants from outside. I guess that they have one advantage — they dare question the direction things are going in — a luxury often denied to insiders. Oliver Huitson gives his conclusions on how ineffective and costly this exercise has been.

One result of managerialism is a huge auditing apparatus. To quote Professor Tessa Rajak, in universities 'accountability is translated into interminable monitoring, peer reviewing, quality assessment, reporting, evaluation, targets, aims, objectives, obsession with standardization of grading and outcomes in the interests of a spurious fairness'. In his piece David Wiggins attributes this partly to a modern tendency to excessive faith in 'management and IT, each reinforcing the other in costly fantasies of system, quasi-omniscience and quasi-omnipotence'.

People standing a little way back see the danger. In an interview with Brian Cox for the *Radio Times* in March 2010 the playwright Stephen Poliakoff said 'We have to roll back this managerial culture' and described it as happening all over the Western World at the expense of 'contemplation.'

Anecdotal evidence suggests that though absurdities have bedevilled private organisations too, pragmatic experience counts for more in the private sector. So, for example, restructuring tends to be aimed at the *work* of the organisation rather than meeting some textbook design. That sort of reform can be very valuable. I have witnessed the enthusiasm of colleagues for sharing ideas about how to short cut processes. But a simple 'suggestions' cardboard box is now dressed up in today's HMRC in the expensive programme called Pacesetter which involves a weekly, seemingly devout, ritual in front of a white board. The NAO concluded that Pacesetter cost a total of £115 million between 2005–06 and 2010–11.

The public sector is largely voiceless except through its very effective unions, who speak up mainly in the more limited sphere of workers' rights. I got a strong sense of the enforced silence of public *servants* when I was a local councillor for the London Borough of Barnet. My concurrent experience as a civil servant gave me an insight into the unfairness of attacks by politicians on their officials, often used as cover for their own failures.

In late 2011 there were uncomfortable examples of this. Accusations were made against Brodie Clark by Theresa May and he was unable to defend himself until he had resigned from the UK Border Agency. This was followed by what was widely considered the extreme bullying of Anthony Inglese, the General Counsel and Solicitor of HMRC, by the Public Accounts Committee (the PAC). That meeting of the PAC in November 2011 revealed something staff of HMRC have been concerned about for some time — that there was almost nobody in a senior position with expertise in tax. For years tax inspectors were told that 'blue sky thinking' was what promotion depended on not tax knowledge.

In the past in HMRC there were reporting systems which were easily understood, devoid for the most part of jargon and individual to each member of staff. Reports then were based, substantively, on one's achievements initially and after that one's suitability for advancement etc was appraised. So then one needed to demonstrate that one could actually do the job. The shift to needing to 'talk the current talk' to secure progression, that is essentially to self-promote, has been very damaging to a department unusual in Whitehall in requiring specialist knowledge at all levels. The subsequent PAC report in December 2011 and the demand for judicial intervention has thrown open the debate about how HMRC should be run amid the disaster of excess managerialism.

Perhaps surprisingly to outsiders, some staff in HMRC see the criticism of senior officials by Parliament in the last two years for making deals with powerful business rather differently than the politicians and press commentators (who have to be applauded for their efforts to get the truth): To quote a colleague again:

> It is only those who owe society most in terms of tax, who can afford to pay for these avoidance schemes. Having parted with their money, they, and particularly their advisors are reluctant to concede. Cases, in cartloads, are trundling down the litigation trail. To break the impasse, and to release staff resource, some compromises have been made, otherwise the whole appeal process would implode. Sadly, and usually, unfairly, staff, particularly lately, have been slated, by the media, for taking this course. The avoiders themselves and their well rewarded advisors, seem to be immune from criticism, but it is their greed and reluctance to yield that has created the problem in the first place.

> It is also the case that the resource consumed in countering these schemes means that less time can be devoted to looking after the needs of other taxpayers ... yes the poorest once again.

> So we have seen, progressively, and it seems remorselessly, the development of a virtual industry which flourishes by seeking to contrive that the wealthiest pay less tax than Parliament intended,

meaning that the poorer pay more and get a worse service. Yet at the same time, a bespoke service is provided to those who have the most. All this is doused with regular media criticism, to produce a toxic mix.

Usually however public servants can only speak out anonymously. For example, there are the occasional unsigned articles in the *Observer* (described as the secret diary of a civil servant). On 11 July 2010 this mole wrote: 'I can't escape the feeling that all our dynamism and creativity — so long targeted at the problems in our society — have been turned inward. Vast systems have been built to freeze spending and implement cuts'.

The risk is that independent-minded and truthful people, who refuse to acknowledge the emperor's new clothes, are replaced by the toadies described by Jo Edwards in his piece on the NHS. In my experience many of the most skilled and dedicated people have left public service, voluntarily or under some compulsion (if say the only job offered is to 'lead' on the latest initiative which is seen as nonsensical and even destructive). Others have held on to their sanity by trying against the odds to do the actual job, letting opportunity for promotion go and enjoying the camaraderie of like-minded colleagues.

John Sellers, a former Parliamentary Counsel, wrote to me in July 2010, when, after many years of outstanding service, he concluded that, post-'modernisation', there was no longer really a place for him:

> The current vogue appears to involve replacing the oxygen of individuality with the carbon monoxide of conformity. It's like having gone to sleep in the Promised Land and woken up in captivity in Egypt! It is no consolation to be told that it has been done on the basis of the best possible management consultancy advice.

The contributors to this book tend to laugh about the language of managerialism but there is a suspicion also that there is something more sinister behind the jargon. Use of jargon and pretentious language is of course not the preserve of public services. The Dark Angels programme (for creative writing in business courses) is attempting to make business language natural and authentic.

Oliver Huitson writes in his contribution that there is a political agenda in the language directed at public service 'reform'; in particular his findings suggest the cover up of privatisation in the language of devolution of power and alternative providers.

Another worry expressed by many people I speak to in the public sector is that the language denotes a fervent belief in things which look and sound like business, and that heretics are silenced: so John Sellers says now that a position in the senior civil service can no longer be viewed as simply a job. 'Rather, it has to be embraced as a quasi-religious experience!'

Nigel Hawkes, a freelance journalist, wrote an article in the BMJ on 8 May 2010 with the heading 'Message to new government: ban buzzwords'. Those he describes for the NHS are stakeholder, world class, service user, key worker, frontline, investment, 'our NHS', clinical governance and passionate. Many of these reverberate for all of us – and it is funny.

But then jump forward to an item on the BBC Radio 4 *Today* programme of 7 October 2011. This was a report on a cost cutting project given the name 'NHS reinvestment'. The reporter said that Health Service managers were expressing a concern that government was not being straight with the public as in some cases the cuts were endangering patient care. The health minister Simon Burns could only describe these as 'challenges' (and say that the cuts were the fault of the Labour government).

HMRC has always been a political football because tax is used as an economic tool and at the same time taxation levels are politically so sensitive. The change of language in the old Inland Revenue from taxpayer to customer was presumably an attempt to pretend that this was not a taxing department.

An effective campaign against cuts by ARC (the Association of Revenue and Customs), titled 'Defeat the Deficit', seems to have restricted the current cuts but if you read the press releases you might think there is an increase in staff levels. Instead there is another form of 'reinvestment', in this case moving £917 million and the equivalent staff around in the department.

The Treasury chief secretary Danny Alexander stretched language a bit further at the LibDem conference on 18 September 2011 with his talk of an additional 2250 tax inspectors to fight tax evasion. As far as I know these are neither new staff nor inspectors (a term historically restricted to staff who have undertaken specialist training in business tax). These are the same redirected civil servants and the funding comes from that same pot, the c£900m 'reinvestment'.

What is happening to people working in the public services is dwarfed by what is happening to the most vulnerable people in our society. John Goodchild, a psycho-analytic psychotherapist describes austerity programmes as a way of making sure that the poor suffer pain for the pleasure that they never had so that the rich can continue to have guilt-free pleasure from not joining in the suffering.

Many public servants are in very low paid employment though, and this gets forgotten. In this austere time there have been nasty, undermining, ill-focused attacks on public sector pay and the suggested extravagance of public sector workers (the specious use of false information for this is illustrated in Dan Carrier's piece).

Polly Toynbee wrote in the *Guardian* on 24 August 2010:

> Time and again public employees hear of their demise in the news, trashing their endeavours without even token regret or thanks for years of service, only raw glee and spurious charges of wastefulness.

As Rodric Braithwaite notes in his contribution the current cabinet secretary and Head of the Home Civil Service, Gus O'Donnell, has felt the need to defend the civil service. He wrote in an article in the *Guardian* on 19 November 2010 announcing a new system of Civil Service Awards.

> While entertaining, the tired old caricatures of the civil service stand in stark contrast to the modern reality, epitomised by the recipients of these awards... The hackneyed stories of civil servants on Premier footballer-style salaries, living and working in luxurious conditions in Whitehall, enjoying a job for life, and retiring on fat cat pensions, are becoming increasingly absurd.

On pay and staffing he writes: 'It is not the lure of pay and pensions that draws most people to the civil service. The median salary of a civil servant is £22, 850 a year ... The average pension is £7000.'

The number of civil servants has not grown, in fact, 'quite the reverse. We will soon have the smallest civil service since the beginning of the second world war'. But he writes 'the civil service will continue to draw on the dedication and quality for which it is internationally renowned'.

There is a vindictive and punitive element to the attack on the public service by government which is explored in the book. To some public sector workers it came as a shock when the attacks did not stop with New Labour (thought to be a natural ally) but in fact in some ways the managerialism got worse.

For example an evening standard headline just before the May 2010 election announced that Gordon Brown pledged himself to 'punish failing schools' (often schools struggling in areas of high deprivation). Perhaps as a result of this sort of approach, a poll on 21/4/10 showed that only 29% of public sector workers were going to support Labour compared to 40% supporting the Liberals and 23% the Tories.

There is some recognition of this gap between the New Labour government and the public service from the advocates of Blue Labour. Maurice Glasman in an interview with the *Observer* on 25 April 2011 was quoted as saying that:

> Both Blair and Brown were recklessly naïve about finance capital and the City of London and relentlessly managerial in their methods.

But Progress (the New Labour pressure group) wrote of the Purple Book which they circulated at the time of the Labour Party Conference that among the key themes needed for Labour to win the next election is for it 'to have a credible programme of reform for public institutions'. The key message from Progress in October 2011 was that 'Public service reform must not be an afterthought'.

And Neil Lawson, chair of Compass, another Labour Party pressure group, tapped into the anti-state mood when interviewed by the *Big Issue* in August 2011 about the 'Big Society' theme. He is quoted as saying that David Cameron's idea 'shows the Labour Party became too connected and synonymous with the growth of the big state'.

As for the coalition government, they have reiterated the same themes, as if these are new. In November 2010 David Cameron spoke of 'a once-in-a-lifetime opportunity to transform our public services'. In February 2011, he wrote 'our public services desperately needed an injection of openness, creativity and innovation' and promised to release public services from the 'grip of state control' and in March 2011 he said that he could announce today that 'we are taking on the enemies of enterprise' by reducing the 'ridiculous rules and regulations' that bureaucrats impose.

None of this was enough for the CBI who on 17 June 2011, complained that the government had allowed its radical plans for public service reform to be derailed. 'In most areas we are seeing public services cling on to existing ways of doing things with vested interests fighting modernisation at every turn and campaigning against change' — according to the deputy director general Neil Bentley.[1]

Not enough also for the *Sun*: in its leader on 4 October 2011 commenting on George Osborne's Tory conference speech:

> But there is still massive waste and incompetence in Whitehall, the NHS, welfare and local government which could provide billions to put tax cuts in workers' pockets, and crucially, make a job pay better than benefits.

> Despite Mr Osborne's savings, the State has got even bigger since the Coalition took over and now spends more than half of everything Britain earns.

The size of the public sector can be a double-edged argument. David Cameron estimated in advance of the strike on 30 November

---

1 The CBI spokesman was concerned about proposed amendments to the NHS Reform Bill: 'The forces of inertia in the NHS unions triumph on health reform ... Patient services will only be improved if the NHS is opened up to far greater competition and dependence on hospital care is reduced.'

2011 that the cost in lost output would be around £500 million. That puts the contribution of public sector workers to the economy in a year into mega billions.

But the anti-Big State agenda is easy to tap into as Will Hutton wrote in the *Observer* on 1 November 2009 in a piece headed 'Inefficient, expensive, poor service, dangerous ... that's our private sector':

> What has been wrong with too much of the public sector is not the fact of being owned by the state, or bureaucracy. It is a loss of a sense of purpose. Too many dumb, clunky targets: too much preoccupation with narrow cost saving and too little concern with greater purpose.

Again Will Hutton writing in the *Observer* on 12 June 2011:

> For much of my working life, the state has been the subject of consistent and ever more vitriolic attacks from the political right. But [he says] we are living through a watershed as the state's crucial and indispensable uses become obvious to all.

Like many observers, Will Hutton thinks that current anti-state attitudes 'have been inflamed through the baleful rise of US conservatism and the import of its ideas to Britain'.

The contributors

Included in this book are accounts of public service from people both inside and outside of the public sector. In common is a belief in the importance and value of public service, an enthusiasm for getting things right and for the opportunity of sharing such varying experiences.

Ursula Murray, an academic in the field of public sector management, discusses what lies behind bringing the private sector into the heart of public service delivery. Her experience was largely in local government: she describes this as an unloved relative of the NHS. Her postscript is concerned with the uncertain role of the voluntary sector given the uneven playing field of government contracts.

Ursula's points find an echo in all of the other contributions: for example her description of the excessive reduction of service to narrow parameters of budget and process.

There are two contributions from the civil service. Mark Serwotka, General Secretary of the Public and Commercial Services Union (PCS) looks back to his career in what was then known as the DHSS. Mark writes that he fell into the job at an early age with very little sense of vocation but as time passed he found that he loved and was dedicated to the work. He attributes the decline in services to privatisation and the cult of individualism.

Sir Rodric Braithwaite writes about the Foreign Office. His career included the post of Ambassador to Moscow in 1988 to 1992. Rodric quotes from Sir Ivor Roberts whose valediction on leaving the embassy in Rome in 2005 was unacceptable to the then Labour government. The following year the Permanent Secretary at the Foreign and Commonwealth Office banned the century-old practice of valedictory telegrams from British envoys. Sir Ivor in his turn quotes Rodric, then working in the UK, as saying that the Foreign office had been reduced to a 'demoralized cipher'.

While accepting there was never a golden age, Rodric shows that until the early 1960s, governments respected the genuine sense of dedication of their civil servants and were not afraid of there being an elite in this service — after all, Rodric argues, there is a recognized elite in other spheres such as music. Business methods have not worked; financial profit is not the main motivator in the public service.

Libby Goldby writes about secondary education. Again she writes of high ideals and great satisfaction in her early years though she provides a very balanced view of the good and less good aspects of education in the 1970s and early 1980s. But the clamp down by central government and the business models have in Libby's view led to a greater inequality between schools and a more divided society. She writes about her concern about Free Schools in a postscript.

Chris Richardson's pleasure and pride in his career in the railway colours his piece on Britain's railways. The ingenuity and odd characters stand out from the early history and the good worker/manager relations in the periods after the Second World War. Chris's conclusions on privatisation are not those of Oliver Huitson, but no-one can doubt the difficulties in running a national railway, from the account of the various periods of its administration and from Chris's own experience of the different forms of management.

Professor David Wiggins writes about university education. His chapter starts with the reprint of a talk he gave at the University of York in 2005. He describes the effect of 'subversive external forces' on scholarship. As a philosopher he looks also at what is behind 'the processes by which practical reason is parted from its proper object and replaced by a rationality of abstractions which is incapable of registering or preserving within it any trace of the deliberated reasons why an end was proposed or adopted in the first place, or of the context for which it was endorsed'.

Professor Jonathan (Jo) Edwards retired as a Professor of Medicine in 2011. He had found that his job had become virtually impossible to do. Jo uses three worrying illustrations of the 'incompetence that goes with muddled motivation'. He then attempts 'to tease out the tangle'.

His conclusion is disturbing: notably that to get on you have to be a toady to nonsensical management. Jo's analysis goes to the fundamentals of social tides and the real function and quality of money. His postscript looks at the NHS Reform Bill: 'everything goes round and round in circles. Moreover for providers to be commissioners creates a clear conflict of interest ...'.

The campaign against the NHS Reform Bill has engaged a very wide range of expertise and a lot of what has been said applies to other branches of the public sector too. There is a concern that the real value of *managers* is lost in the furore about wasteful restructuring costs.[2]

Rebekah Carrier is a lawyer and a legal aid practitioner. She argues that legal aid should be a welfare state service and explains her fears that its dismantlement is nearly complete and that she and her colleagues will lose their (scant) livelihood. Her story of Anna's case will reverberate forever. Her history of the changes, the interchange with other bodies and the dominance of processes (such as 'matter starts') will be new material to many readers but the phenomenon will be familiar to all.

Liz Kessler writes about her experience of working as an urban designer in the New Deal for Communities (NDC) programmes intended to transform neighbourhoods of multi-deprivation into environments that local people could enjoy and be proud of. Her contribution is illustrated with photos of the improvements she managed to achieve despite the obstacles of a management culture. She was both an insider and an outsider as she spent some time working for a local authority while remaining an employee of NDC.

Unfortunately her time there (which continues although in a different capacity and area) coincided with the worst of managerialism both in local government and in the NDC. Her frustration speaks for

---

2   For example Jon Restell, the chief executive of Managers in Partnership in a letter to *The Times* of 18 May 2011 wrote that: 'Management is essential if we are to meet the challenges facing the NHS. Unfortunately, the Government has spent the past year in a state of management-denial. It has denigrated managers, including many clinicians who undertake managerial duties. It has ordered the dismissal of thousands of managers.

'We fear that patients, clinicians and taxpayers will pay a high price. Patients' needs are again being subordinated to yet another structural re-organisation. Short-termism is rife, with too few people to manage some budgets, contracts and savings programmes properly. We are also seeing cases of the NHS making staff redundant and then having to re-hire them because it still needs their skills. This makes a mockery of the intention to save money and increase efficiency. The Government needs to act. It should build the management capacity needed by patients, clinical staff and the taxpayer.'

many others—for example she notes how employees on the ground care passionately about the wellbeing of the residents they serve but are powerless in the face of tiers of management processes.

In her postscript Liz examines the effect of privatisation of local authority services in her sphere: in particular contracts stifle initiative and so called 'localism' tends to result in areas of deprivation being further disadvantaged.

Oliver Huitson writes about the Private Finance Initiative (PFI) using the MOD as a case study (it may be new to many that the indebtedness and budgetary chaos at the MOD were largely caused by PFI deals and the use and cost of management consultants) and about the wider use of private consultants and the revolving doors between Whitehall and the consultancy firms. He also gives his account of the effects of the privatisation of British Rail and looks at other forms of more hidden privatisation. Oliver's financial expertise backs the increasingly negative perception in the parliamentary committees of how the private-public partnership has been played out in practice.

Dan Carrier examines the motivation behind the press coverage of public sector workers. He talked to the London FBU representative Ben Sprung, Geoff Martin press officer of the RMT, Unison officer George Binette, John Gaston the press officer for the College of Social Work and the then NUJ president Jeremy Dear.

Dan gets to the heart of the dilemmas faced by public workers trying to do a good job and be properly recompensed (and to be treated fairly). The picture that emerges is alarming. Dan finds political will behind the vitriol and the false information. To take another example of this, in *More or Less* on Radio Four, Tim Harford demolished a report from the think tank Policy Exchange on 9 May 2011 which was, as intended, widely reported. The report suggested that the pay gap between the public and private sector had increased to 43% and that public sector pay was 'hugely out of control'.

Actually the supposed gap was 7% not 43% after taking into account that the staff were better qualified, older and more experienced. Then the numbers had to be readjusted since the figures were two years old and had preceded the current cuts. The spokesman from Policy Exchange accepted the points but still said it has been right to publish their report of a gap of 43% knowing that it would be headline news in, for instance, the Daily Telegraph.

Incidentally the figures are now skewed further since the lower paid workers tend to be those whose jobs have been privatized.

Dan has given particular attention to social workers. No one in government defends them from the damned if they do (take children from abusive parents) and damned if they don't media attacks. Already in September 2010 experts in the field endorsed the idea that there is a failure in the UK to give social workers support and gratitude for a difficult job in the Radio 4 'Bringing up Britain' series introduced by Mariella Frostrup. This was in addition to the usual criticism made by the experts of the predominance of processes. Social work is not ring-fenced (in theory or in practice) from the current public service cuts.

Dan adds a note on the Leveson enquiry, stressing the responsibility of reporters for fair and accurate copy.

The way forward

I hope that this book will encourage more analysis of the supposed *value* of constant change in the structure of public service. The late Tony Judt, an academic based in America, looked back at a gradual shift in political theory towards 'economism' (judging all in monetary terms) and away from 'moral sentiments' (an Adam Smith term) in public policy considerations.

More recently, the social psychologist Timothy Wilson in his book *The Surprising New Science of Psychological Change* asks politicians to look for evidence and not rely on 'common sense'. For example he argues that the key to altering behaviour is not via economic incentives.

Signs are that the main political parties will find that the endless talk of incompetence and waste in the public sector, as a cover for more uncomfortable political realities, will begin to lose its electoral appeal as the private public partnership unravels (see for example the popular opposition to further NHS reform).

Ideally a rethink will build on a still widely held belief in the ethos of public service and will encourage more trust in workers in the public sector so that they can continue to take pleasure in their work and can hold on to the enthusiasm to work for the common good.

PART I
The Civil Service

Mark Serwotka

Saving Public Services

To say that I started working in the public sector because of a deep desire to help people, driven by an acute awareness of a public sector ethos, would be a wonderful thing. But it wouldn't be true.

I started in the civil service at the age of 16, working as a Clerical Officer in what was then known as the Department of Health and Social Security (DHSS). My reason for starting there was simple: I lived in Aberdare, an area of quite high unemployment, and I had the minimum requirements (5 O-levels) for the civil service at the time and there was a department in the village.

While there was little sense of vocation when I started, the fact I was still working there 21 years later demonstrates the real affinity for the job that I developed very quickly. I loved working in the DHSS even though it was often tough, emotionally-draining, hard work. I was helping the most vulnerable people around, and by working in Aberdare I knew a lot of the community I was serving.

The DHSS, became the DSS (losing health), and later the Department for Work and Pensions (DWP). I noticed a number of changes in my 21 years and there have been many since. I want to look at those changes: organisational, cosmetic, social, and industrial. They reflect a process—a clear yet often unspoken political project—that has transformed the notion of public service.

My union represents staff in the DWP and across the civil service: in the criminal justice system, tax collection, and in fields as diverse as air traffic control and the coastguards—but in this chapter I want to focus on the area I worked in for over 20 years: welfare. Many of the processes I will describe have happened across government and will be familiar to those working not just in the civil service, but in local government, education, the health service and in other areas of the public sector.

The delivery of welfare

My very first job was working on disablement benefit which was common in the mining villages around Aberdare. Sickness or Invalidity

benefit has since become Incapacity Benefit and now Employment and
Support Allowance—and may soon be integrated into a new Universal
Credit.

The name changes are not just cosmetic, they reflect the dramatic
changes that have affected the labour market and the debate about
welfare in the 30 years since I started work in the Aberdare DHSS
office. The heavy industry of steel and coal, ship-building, car
manufacturing has either disappeared or substantially declined. The
jobs have largely not been replaced.

In 1979 the Conservatives won the election with the aid of the now
iconic campaign poster headed 'Labour isn't Working' with a snaking
dole queue. It reflected the public concern that unemployment had
reached a post-war high and was over one million. By the mid-1980s
the Conservatives had been an abject failure on the issue that helped
propel them to power: unemployment reached 3.5 million and
hundreds of thousands were destined never to work again.

It was in this period that we saw the emergence of the hate
campaign against welfare that we see today. Barely a day goes by in the
tabloids without some sort of exposé about 'welfare cheats',
'scroungers', 'layabouts' to give the impression that anyone not in work
is feckless, lazy and ripping you off.

The origins of this lie in the period of the 1980s, when the
Conservative government of Mrs Thatcher was busy laying waste to
swathes of the labour market. Norman Tebbit famously said the
unemployed should 'get on their bike' to look for work. Not long after
Peter Lilley was singing ditties to Conservative Party conference about
the evils of single mothers.

While the victims of the Conservative industrial policy were being
increasingly demonised by politicians and the press, it was not until
1995 that any legislative changes were made. The Jobseekers Act
brought in significant reforms to how we deal with unemployment in
this country.

To understand the impact of the Act though we have to go back to
the debates fifty years earlier when the welfare state was being created.
One of the key figures of the founding of the welfare state was William
Beveridge, a Liberal politician, whose ideas would be implemented by
the post-war Labour government. Beveridge had witnessed the poverty
and despair that followed both the First World War and the Great
Depression in the 1930s. Back then there was an entitlement condition
for unemployment benefit known as the 'actively seeking work
principle'. When it was dropped, Beveridge said: 'May it never rise
again from its dishonoured grave.' He described it as 'a humiliating
and futile experience'.

Beveridge believed in a system of social insurance. People would collectively pay a contribution while they were in work to give them rights to benefits when they were unable to work: whether through unemployment, ill-health, disablement or old age. The welfare state gave people rights, while the 'actively seeking work principle' treated people with suspicion. The 1930s was a decade scarred by mass unemployment ended only by the horror of the Second World War. The generation that followed vowed to 'win the peace' — to condemn mass poverty and unemployment to the history books. Britain developed the NHS, the welfare state, comprehensive education and council housing. Funded through progressive taxation we became a more equal society. Until the 1980s.

As inequality grew, so did division. The Conservatives started talking about an underclass, with horrible echoes of the *untermenschen* term used in Nazi Germany. It is therefore no surprise that this divisive politics disinterred the corpse 'actively seeking work principle' from its 'dishonoured grave', as Beveridge had called it.

The Jobseekers Act meant the unemployed had to prove they were looking for work. The Conservatives had caused mass and enduring high unemployment yet they were actively promoting the fiction that claiming benefits was a personal failure, due to the individual's laziness, stupidity or selfishness.

Another punitive element came in shortly afterwards. The government introduced Project Work in April 1996, with a compulsory work element of up to 13 weeks for those unemployed for two years or more. For the first time civil servants would be compelling claimants to work full-time, for only an extra £10 payment on top of their Jobseeker's Allowance. When it was debated in Parliament, it was condemned by then deputy Labour leader John Prescott as 'workfare, chain gangs', while another Labour MP described it as 'taking us back to the days of the workhouse and workfare'.

This changed the nature of the relationship between the people claiming benefits and those of us working at the benefits offices, soon to be rebranded as jobcentres and jobcentre plus. We were no longer simply there to help, work out what people with us needed and were entitled to, but instead we now had to police their behaviour — interrogate them on a fortnightly basis.

Despite the protestations from their own MPs at the time, in government Labour intensified the demonisation of welfare claimants, adding more and more conditionality to claiming benefits. They also brought in a largely new component with the introduction of the private sector into the welfare state.

Working in welfare today

In the 21 years I worked in the DHSS it changed out of all recognition, but it has changed even more violently now.

It would be dishonest of me not to admit that the offices were a bit grotty looking when I started. People took a ticket, like at a supermarket deli counter, but our job was to help. Whether it was income support or sickness benefit, we served everyone and dealt with their issues. Now there are different 'business streams' and you have to have an appointment just to get in the office. If not you're directed to a call centre. We had all services under one roof but now they only deal with Jobseeker's Allowance.

It might sound ironic that I favour the grotty offices of old and regret the business-speak that pervades the department today, when I describe the supermarket deli-style ticket system of old. But it is not necessarily the visual surroundings that define the system: it is the ideology behind it. Jobcentres are indisputably much nicer looking offices now, but there was a better system before and a better service.

How can I relate this to you — perhaps a reader who has never worked in or had to visit a jobcentre? Think about a guest house versus a modern large hotel. The guest house might be a bit twee and the decor a bit old-fashioned, but there's a warm welcome and a homeliness about it. Modern large hotels with their spacious and ultra-modern glass fronted and ceilinged arboreal lobbies might look better superficially, but there is something mass-produced, cold and remote about them. You are dealt with as a customer, not a guest (a fellow human being).

I left in 2000 when I was elected General Secretary of the union, but I regularly meet people I used to work with and they tell me, 'There's never been a worse time and it's getting worse'. The management is more hardline, it's all about quantity not quality, which saps morale when you are being forced to fail to deliver the service you want to provide to people.

That same year I left we had a long-running dispute with management about the removal of screens in the new jobcentre plus offices. The increased policing role that benefits staff now had to play inevitably brought them into conflict with the people they were serving — sometimes desperate people who could not make ends meet, people who had substance misuse problems, people with mental health problems. By now the Labour government had also nodded through cuts in lone parent and incapacity benefits too.

In November 2001 a man walked into Leyton jobcentre in east London demanding a payment. His benefit had been stopped because he had failed to sign on. Staff advised the man that he was not entitled to payment and had to call the police when the man became aggressive. Before the police could arrive the man pulled out a knife and stabbed a security guard in the chest. This is not the only example — many staff will have been abused or spat on at some point, and they will often know a colleague who has been physically assaulted. Frustrated and desperate members of the public have attacked offices and staff with baseball bats, crowbars and glass bottles.

The department's permanent secretary described us as 'anti-public' and 'anti-claimant', and throughout the dispute they portrayed us as walling ourselves off from the public and not wanting to deal with people. Nothing could have been further from the truth, but our members were now on the frontline of the government's unjustifiable assault on those on welfare.

During the dispute some union representatives went to lobby their local MP over the issue of safety in jobcentre plus. They were surprised to find that his constituency office was screened. The MP explained that the screen was needed because he and his staff had recently been assaulted. The MP in question was Ian McCartney, then minister in the DWP. So it was made even clearer that, on a lesser but significant scale, our members were indeed the frontline troops in this unnecessary war on welfare.

The irony is that despite portraying us as 'walling ourselves off from the public' during the dispute, shortly after it management came forward with their 'reducing footfall strategy'. The strategy was to divert people away from the shiny new jobcentre offices, which have become appointment-only, and to expensive hotlines to call centres. This move precipitated the closure of many of these relatively new offices and the transfer of thousands of workers from public-facing jobcentre assistants into remote voices at the other end of a telephone.

When the DSS (the Department for Social Security which took over from the DHSS in 1988) became the Department for Work and Pensions (DWP) the entire focus changed from welfare in the wide sense — people's health and social security — to work. The whole focus was about getting people into work, accompanied by a plethora of targets. No one is against getting people into work, but that became the sole focus and with it came more conditionality. And as the post-finance sector crash occurred in 2008 there were harrowing echoes of the 1980s, as against a backdrop of rising unemployment a government, this time Labour, sought to blame the victims for the government's own economic mismanagement and absence of a labour market policy.

The direction of travel was now becoming very clear and it impacted on the job. Staff now have much less discretion to deal with people than when I worked there.

Call centres, known as jobcentre contact centres, are a new horror both for the public and our members working there. They are the 'dark satanic mills' of the 21st century. People's toilet breaks are monitored, logged and time-limited. This is the 21st century, working for the government. It may not be a factory or a steel foundry, but they're very difficult jobs, low paid, and oppressive: the turnover rates are huge.

The advent of call centres has meant the disempowerment of staff is complete, and it's a much less personalised service for the public too. Staff are tapped on the shoulder if they take more than four and a half minutes on a single call. If they do so too often they can be disciplined. Remember the people on the other end of the line might have learning difficulties, have poor hearing, or have English as a second language. It is a far cry from my experiences, when we took as long as it took—that might be two or three minutes if the enquiry was simple but it might be half an hour or more.

As a union we are often accused or derided for representing 'producer-interest', but our members care about the services they provide. Their producer interest goes beyond their own pay, pensions or terms and conditions. While those things are important, and I discuss them below, it is ludicrous to assume that people who have chosen to work in the public sector are self-interested. These are people working with and providing services for some of the most vulnerable people in our society. No one can leave their workplace content at the end of their working day if they feel they have not done the best they can by those people.

In 2011 our members helped expose a new government target for benefit processors to meet: the number of claimants they should recommend for sanction. At first the minister denied the target existed and said the allegation it did was 'claptrap'. Within two days, he was publicly scrapping the target.

That same year our members working in contact centres took industrial action, fed up at the way they were being treated and frustrated because they were unable to deal with claimants in the way they would like. The situation is terrible, enquiries are left unanswered and desperate people virtually hung up on to satisfy an arbitrary target.

The dispute is ongoing as I write, but the tragedy continues to unfold in new and devastating ways. The government is now proposing that all benefit claims will be made and processed through online accounts over the web. According to the 2009 Digital Britain report, 10 million adults in the UK have never used the internet. I do not know for sure but I believe it's a fair assumption that those people will disproportionately be the people who might need welfare.

Privatisation

It was Conservative government minister Peter Lilley's Project Work that first allowed the private sector a foot in the door of welfare. He told his party's conference in 1996:

> For the first time, we will be involving the private sector in helping people move into jobs. Private firms will compete with Government Teams. They will be paid by results.

This opened the floodgates. The private sector is now embedded in the delivery of welfare. Lord Freud, an investment banker appointed as a welfare adviser by the Labour government and now a welfare minister in the coalition government, described welfare as 'an annual multi-billion market'. Welfare was no longer the social insurance that slays Beveridge's 'five giants' of squalor, ignorance, want, idleness and disease, but a commodity to be traded on the market and some of the biggest multi-national companies on the planet are keen to be involved.

Now there is payment by results, contractors are cherry-picking which cases they deal with. When I did the job you did all the cases, some quite complex and you could spend all day on one case, but then you might get several quick ones. These contractors are looking to shift people as quickly as possible to make a profit—whether they push them into something suitable or not.

Fed up with seeing our members jobs privatised or cut so that money could be paid to private contractors, my union commissioned research from Cardiff University into the effectiveness of jobcentre plus against private and voluntary providers. They found, in 2008, that: 'whenever jobcentre plus has been allowed the same flexibilities and funding as private sector companies or charitable organisations it has been able to match, if not surpass, the performance of contractors'.

A couple of years later, the National Audit Office evaluated the Pathways to Work scheme which was part run by jobcentre plus and partly by contractors. Their findings are even more clear: 'contractors have universally underperformed against targets set by the department ... Jobcentre plus achieved better job outcome rates for mandatory customers compared to external providers in areas led by them.'

Parliamentary select committees, charities and other academic studies have all reinforced these findings. Yet the coalition government announced that its Work Programme, the successor to Labour's Pathways to Work and the Flexible New Deal, will be wholly run by 'social enterprises, charities and businesses'. It would be impossible for me to overstate the demoralising effect that has on loyal in-house staff. They have met every target asked of them, they have outperformed external contractors and their reward is to have their skills and dedication totally overlooked. But it gets worse, because the reality for many of them is the job now faces being privatised or cut, so they can very often no longer continue to work for a successful employer doing the job they love — or at least once did.

Rewarding staff

I hope that I have shown the demoralising impact of creeping market methods on staff, how their autonomy and discretion have been eroded through automated systems and a rigid target culture.

Civil servants are also being used as a political football. In 2004, and to cheers from the Labour benches, then Chancellor Gordon Brown announced that he would cut 100,000 jobs. New terms were invented to deride the contribution of the people I represent and who work hard in a range of public service fields. Brown created a false division between the 'front line' and the 'back office' — as if the two were distinct and as if one does not rely on the other in a necessary and symbiotic relationship. Some in the media went further, referring to 'pen-pushers' and 'bureaucrats'.

Brown eventually cut 78,000 jobs from the civil service. The impact on public service was clear in a number of areas. The shift from face-to-face contact in jobcentres to hotlines connected to call centres is just one example. In the year following Brown's announcement over 7,500 jobs were cut in the jobcentre plus business stream alone. By the beginning of 2008, 30,000 posts were lost in the DWP — just as the recession hit. The department panicked, introduced a moratorium on job losses and office closures (as explained many jobcentre plus offices, revamped at great expense, had been closed after just a few years' service). It also made an emergency statement to parliament in October 2008 saying they would hire an extra 2,000 staff. By the following month the crisis overwhelming jobcentres meant they had revised that figure to an extra 6,000 staff. These staff though were appointed on fixed term contracts, without the job security and some of the rights of the staff they would be joining. Nevertheless my union recruited them and has managed to negotiate some of what eventually became 15,000 fixed term staff into permanent jobs.

But the damage done by job cuts is evident in other ways. For 2005/06, the welfare minister told parliament that 85% of jobcentre customers were satisfied with the service. Today, the Institute of Customer Service informs us that figure is 57% — an appalling indictment of the management of such a vital resource. Further job cuts are taking place in the department even though unemployment remains at similar levels to 2008, when the service was struggling to cope—hence the new proposal to make people claim online. It is beyond parody, it is tragedy.

Despite media reports of generous salaries and pensions, administrative assistants in the department start on barely over the minimum wage. In 2009, about half of the staff in the department earned less than £20,000 and 25% less than £15,000.

Average civil service pay is lower than in both the rest of the public sector and the private sector. Our members do not expect a champagne lifestyle but they are currently facing a two year pay freeze—meaning their pay will fall further behind.

A lot is also said about public sector pensions normally preceded by the ubiquitous phrase 'gold-plated', but the reality is that an average civil servant in my union can expect a pension of just £4,200 per year, which equates to about £80 per week. They have recently been told that they must now pay higher contributions and work longer in exchange for a reduced pension. Understandably, when faced with an assault on their jobs, pay and pensions, they have voted to take strike action.

Conclusion

When I started working, I was told by my manager 'you're there to help the public in difficult circumstances'. Today, until our members exposed it, welfare staff were being told 'you're here to hit your target on sanctioning claimants'. How did we get to this situation?

There have, I believe, been two processes over the last generation that have interacted to leave us where we are today:

- Privatisation—an almost maniacal belief that the private sector is inherently more efficient than the public sector, and that in no sector of our society should the profit motive be considered inappropriate: whether that's the running of prisons or probation or in health assessments for the disabled. The market reigns. This has resulted in a 'private good, public bad' instinct across the major political parties and allowed public sector workers to be punch bags.

- Individualism—Thatcher's oft-quoted phrase 'there is no such thing as society' went on 'only individuals and their families'. This was a deliberately divisive policy which has led to a less caring society in which people are now blamed for their own situation regardless of circumstance. It allows politicians and media to portray the unemployed as feckless, the incapacitated as lazy or dishonest. Once these people have been dehumanised it is much easier to remove any belief that they have rights. It is the antithesis of the collective social insurance principle upon which Beveridge and Bevan founded the welfare state.

The central theme that binds these processes is neoliberalism—the term given for the deregulated, privatised and liberalised markets that are today so clearly failing to deliver for the majority of people.

But while the market might be effective at delivering a range of chocolate bars to consumers with relative affordability, it cannot extract profit directly from assisting people back to work or paying benefits to carers, pensioners or the disabled. To do so, the government creates market-like processes to reward success against various targets. So the labour of my members becomes a 'cost' and the people in need of assistance become a 'target'. It is a nasty and brutal vision and one that has damaged much of the public sector.

It's the mark of a civilised society to support people when they are in need, whether they are ill, disabled or unemployed. Welfare was established to provide a decent existence. Coming from the South Wales valleys I saw the importance of the social security system before my eyes every day. When the Work and Pensions Secretary Iain Duncan Smith said, in October 2010, people from Merthyr Tydfil should 'get on the bus' he echoed the words of Norman Tebbit a generation earlier, swapping only the mode of transport. The reality was that both their governments ensured there weren't enough jobs no matter how far you pedalled or how far you rode.

My union has recently published a short campaigning pamphlet 'Welfare: an alternative vision', taking head-on the ill-founded prejudices about welfare and making the case again for the collective security it provides.

Collective endeavour—whether public services, trade unions or community organizations—were undoubtedly huge forces for progress in the 20th century. It is essential that we make the case for collective security and action again for the 21st century.

Rodric Braithwaite

Why We Need an Elite
Public Service

Until somewhere in the 1960s the British civil service was highly regarded both at home and abroad. It consisted of a small elite of policy makers, and a much larger number of people who provided government services directly to the public. Most people never met a senior civil servant: their dealings were and are with people in tax offices, employment exchanges, council offices and the NHS.

On the whole governments used to be satisfied with the service they received from their bureaucrats. It was after all the British civil service which successfully delivered a far-reaching social revolution on behalf of the incoming Labour government in 1945. Since then the regard has seeped away. There are a number of reasons for this. One was the decline in the deference which ordinary people were prepared to pay to any kind of established institution, and the growing populism which accompanied it. Another was the increasingly comprehensive and complex matters for which government was assuming responsibility.

Economic and political failures in the 1970s—the stand-off with the unions, the three day week, the winter of discontent—meant that many people came to believe that government itself was failing in important ways. Both political parties were implicated. But the civil service was also held responsible. Some of the reforms and privatisations which came in under Thatcher were botched. But at the time many people saw them as necessary and broadly successful.

And it was about that time that politicians came to believe that the shortcomings of the public service could be remedied by applying the fashionable new management theories. These may or may not have worked in business. But they were largely inapplicable to the entirely different culture of public service. Successive governments tinkered in increasingly intrusive ways with the way the service was run. Those who manned it became increasingly demoralised, especially when they were told by ministers with underdeveloped leadership skills that, in the words of John Reid, a former Home Secretary, they were 'not fit for purpose'.

Those who defend the old system may—understandably—be accused of nostalgia for a golden age, when government was run in an orderly fashion, when civil servants were devoted to their vocation and spoke truth unto power, and when government and parliament observed the written and unwritten rules and practices of the British constitution without question. Of course that golden age never existed in reality. Government has always been a messy business, muddled, sometimes inconsequential, and occasionally corrupt. That was certainly true of the British system at the end of the 18th century, where recruitment and promotion depended on patronage, and when many offices were open for sale.

But things did change with the Northcote-Trevelyan report of 1854, which recommended the creation of a permanent, unified, and politically neutral civil service. Recruitment was by examination, appointments were made on merit. A clear distinction was drawn between the 'administrative' class, which formulated and implemented policy, and those responsible for the more routine business of delivering those policies to the public. Officials were paid a decent salary, and that helped to end corruption. Britain was not alone in making these reforms. Prussia, Sweden, Holland, and of course France set up similar mandarinates. They were seen as an essential element in the creation of a modern state.

On the whole this system gave ministers and the public the services they wanted. It depended to a significant extent on a genuine sense of dedication among officials. However implausible it seems to the outsider, officials were motivated not by the desire to make money, but by a desire to give the state their service. In return they got respect, job security, a good pension, and for some of them, the possibility of state honours. The failure in recent years of one expensive management consultant after another to understand the simple facts of the culture and motivations of the British civil service underlay their sometimes grotesquely inappropriate recommendations for change.

One reason why most of those involved in the system were reasonably content for over a century may be that at first senior politicians and senior civil servants came from much the same backgrounds: privately educated, sometimes related by family, sharing a common view of domestic politics and of Britain's place in the world.

The rise of the labour movement in the last part of the nineteenth century introduced people into political life who did not share the social or political assumptions of those who had hitherto run Britain. The new people—outsiders like Lloyd George as well as the new

Labour politicians — did not automatically buy the proposition that civil servants were politically neutral, or that they would work as loyally for them as they did for the country's traditional ruling class. They introduced their own political advisers from outside the service — men such as Tom Jones, who worked for Lloyd George — in order to keep an eye on it, and to ensure that their policies were not subverted.

Even so, the post-war Labour government expressed few doubts about the fitness for purpose of the British civil service. That may have been because some of them, including the Prime Minister, came from the traditional ruling classes. Others, such as Bevin and Morrison, had considerable experience of running large organisations. And almost all of them had served in government during the war, and knew how to manage the people who worked for them.

That seems to have changed with the arrival of the first Wilson government in 1964. Able though the new ministers were they had, unlike the Labour ministers of an earlier generation, little practical experience of affairs, and were only too prone to believe that they would be outsmarted by the people who were supposed to be working for them. They brought with them a prejudiced conviction that all civil servants were 'Conservative' — with a capital C. Their prejudices and their lack of confidence were captured in the memoirs of Richard Crossman, Marcia WIlliams (Baroness Falkender) and Joe Haines. It was perhaps the first time that an incoming government had assumed that the civil service as a body was prejudiced in favour of its predecessor, though similar damaging misjudgements were later made by the Conservatives in 1970, by Labour in 1974, by the Conservatives in 1979, and by Labour again in 1997. The hostility of Labour to the established civil service was perhaps understandable. The hostility of Tory governments after 1970 was less so, but can perhaps be explained by the fact that the new leaders of the Conservative Party, Edward Heath and then Margaret Thatcher, did not come from the social background which had previously dominated it.

The essence of the relationship between ministers and senior civil servants was that senior officials gave knowledgeable advice, and ministers exercised political judgement and took the decisions. Contrary to the myth propagated by that excellent satire *Yes, Minister*, officials preferred ministers to be decisive, even if they did not wholly agree with the decision. If their disagreement was sufficiently strong, they could resign. Many argued that it was their duty as public servants to execute the will of their political masters, however much they disliked the decision itself. They were not wrong: any decision to resign from office is likely to be morally more complex than outsiders are prepared to recognise.

Even when they came from similar backgrounds, the relationships between ministers and senior officials could be scratchy, tinged with a mutual suspicion and—on the side of the officials—even a certain arrogant disdain for what they saw as the intrusion of grubby politics into what they believed should be (but in the circumstances of real life never can be) a clear-cut process of rational decision making. These frictions, which are common to any organisation, were manageable and on the whole they were managed.

From the 1960s onwards attitudes to the civil service began to change. In 1966 Harold Wilson set up the Fulton commission to look into 'the structure, recruitment and management of the Civil Service'. The commission reported in 1968. Its main findings were that the generalist senior civil servants lacked professionalism, that they spent too much time making policy and not enough time managing, that the division between the administrative class and the rest was stultifying and obstructed the promotion of talent, that specialist officials were not given proper responsibility or authority and that the service as a whole was weakly managed.

The recommendations of the report were very influential, and led to many changes in the structure and management of the service. But although some of the strictures in the report were justified, many were based on a misunderstanding of what the different bits of the service were for.

The division of the service into classes was indeed stultifying, and could deal unjustly with the ambitions of individuals. But it reflected a reality, which Northcote and Trevelyan identified, and which has not gone away: the reality that the function of public policy making is qualitatively different from the delivery of services to the public. In all political systems the number of senior policymakers is necessarily rather small. They constitute, in fact, an elite: a word which has acquired almost entirely negative and anti-democratic overtones in Britain, even though in very many walks of life—medicine, sport, the performing arts, and so on—we much prefer to be served by elites. So Wilson's government, and all those that have succeeded it, have tried to blur the lines between the classes of the civil service. This has inevitably led to a confusion of thought and function.

Fulton concluded that some of the varied work of the civil service 'has no counterpart in business or, indeed, anywhere outside the government service'. In that he was quite right. Public service is intrinsically different from business. In business the criteria of success are simple—shareholder satisfaction, profit maximisation. The aims of the public service are far more complicated and far less easily measured. They include the need to satisfy ministers that their policies are being properly implemented and the need to satisfy parliament that money is being properly expended. This means that government is subjected to all sorts of contradictory pressures, and a range of differing accountabilities, of which business is wholly free. And though officials have a primary duty of loyalty to their ministers and to the government of the day they also have, some would argue, a separate and intangible duty of non-political loyalty to 'the Crown', a peculiarly British conception of the state which transcends party politics and changing governments.

One important consequence of all this is that 'management' cannot mean the same thing in the public service as it does in business. Senior officials do not bear the ultimate responsibility for the management of their departments. Their decisions, including their management decisions, can be, and regularly are, over-ridden by ministers or parliament for reasons that have nothing to do with simple management objectives. In a democracy, this is entirely right and proper. But it does mean that the methods, motivations, and incentives that may work in business cannot be blindly read across into the public service.

This is why attempts to bring businessmen into Whitehall have usually ended in tears, except in the peculiar world of arms procurement. The culture is so different, and so frustrating, that the businessmen usually leave again after quite a short time. This is not of course true in France, where senior civil servants often make the transition into business (though there is much less traffic the other way), not least because they often went to the same 'grande école' as their new business colleagues; or in America, which does not have a parliamentary system and whose political culture is vastly different from the British system.

The failure of later governments, reformers, and management consultants to realise these fundamental subtleties has led to much confusion, waste, inefficiency, and lost morale. But Fulton's criticism of the lack of professionalism of the senior civil service, like his implied criticism of its elitism, reflected a more general feeling that senior officials were drawn from too narrow a background. Most senior civil servants came from private schools, or at least from Oxbridge, and therefore did not 'represent' the people they were supposed to serve: a meaningless proposition, since it is MPs who are supposed to represent the people, not technocrats. Moreover the civil servants were supposedly out of touch with practical life and with developments in science, technology and management, and were obsessed instead with the arcane and sterile complexities of bureaucratic procedure.

The criticism has rumbled on. Some of it was of course justified: all organisations need to pull themselves together, learn from change, and reform themselves from time to time. But much of it still reflects a failure to understand the process of policy making, and the core skills required to do it properly: the ability to master information, to analyse it, to present it clearly, and to base recommendations on it that accord with the policy objectives that the government is trying to achieve. This requires a clear mind and a high degree of specialised professionalism. A clear mind can be trained even by a generalist course at university. But the professionalism that policymakers need cannot be learned in a college: it has to be acquired by experience on the job and the mentoring of more senior colleagues. Numeracy and a broad knowledge of statistics accounting are useful additional skills for a senior civil servant. He needs to know enough of these things to manage effectively the accountants, statisticians, and other specialists who work in his department. He doesn't need to do them himself.

Fulton was right, however, to point out that the management of the civil service was unduly rigid and half-baked, and that financial accountability was inadequate at the working level. Some of this was a reflection of the fact that the civil service is accountable to parliament through ministers. In business, mistakes have financial consequences which can often be written off. In public life they have political consequences as well. It is one of the duties of civil servants to ensure that the financial and procedural rules have been properly followed so that their ministers will if necessary be able to defend themselves successfully against a hostile parliament. In public life you cannot simply write off financial losses: you have to explain them. This leads inevitably to a climate of caution in which the spirit of entrepreneurial policymaking can hardly flourish. Ministers do not thank officials who launch enterprising policies which end up in a major parliamentary row.

A number of sensible changes were pushed through, often quite simple ones. Up until the 1970s, officials could authorise expensive travel simply by certifying that it was 'necessary and in the public interest' — an obvious invitation to abuse. Thereafter senior officials were given a limited travel budget and told that they and their subordinates could travel wherever they liked until the money ran out. Others measures were absurd. In the 1980s the Treasury insisted that the Foreign Office charge for its commercial services — in itself a sensible measure — but then subverted the process by insisting that the proceeds be returned to themselves. The Treasury still undermines officials' sense of financial responsibility by micromanaging even the limited financial autonomy they have been willing to concede to other departments. A system of Treasury control which had been invented by Henry II and reinforced by Gladstone and his candle ends was on the way to strangling initiative among all but the most buccaneering public servants.

Fulton's reforms failed to solve many of the problems they were meant to address. So the Tories turned in the 1970s to their friends in the management industry. Consultants, often with little relevant knowledge or qualifications, flooded into Whitehall to advise on personnel management, financial accountability, output measurement, objective setting, and many other aspects of official life. These were all areas where improvement was possible and necessary. But the recommendations the consultants produced were often hopelessly ill-adapted to the task in hand. Assuming that civil servants were motivated by the same desire for financial profit as people in industry, the consultants recommended all sorts of unworkable bonus schemes. They recommended that senior civil service salaries should be comparable to those earned in industry. They proposed that competition for senior posts be opened to the public, without considering the evidence that outsiders, especially businessmen, who had been brought into the service in earlier years had almost all departed early in an aura of frustrated dissatisfaction, having delivered little or nothing of use.

These grossly expensive absurdities reached their height under the Labour government which came to power in 1997. Few of the new ministers had ever managed anything, which may have been one reason why they were so attracted to the enticing but fraudulent mantras of management jargon. Seven years later Ivor Roberts wrote in his final despatch from Rome of the unending 'Cultural Revolution' imposed on the Foreign Office by the Cabinet Office and the Treasury. Much of the 'change-management agenda', he said, 'is written in Wall Street management speak already ... discredited by the time it is introduced. Synergies, best practice, benchmarking ... roll out, stakeholder ... fit for purpose, are all prime candidates for a game of bullshit bingo, a substitute for clarity and succinctness.' His despatch was suppressed by a Labour Foreign Secretary who lacked the self-confidence to face up to—or face down—his criticism.

Similar complaints could be heard all over Whitehall. Less colourfully expressed, they were equally well-founded. The natural consequence of what officials perceived to be a longstanding campaign of denigration of civil servants, the portrayal of them as a bunch of unprofessional parasites, was that morale declined and so, to some extent, did professional standards. Ministers increasingly began to complain of the quality of the work that was put up to them.

With the arrival of the Coalition government in May 2010 there has been some attempt to repair the damage. Ministers have spoken in defence of the service. Since 11 November 2010 the principles behind the Northcote-Trevelyan reforms—a politically impartial Civil Service, recruited on merit through fair and open competition—have been set in legislation. Ministers have spoken critically of the breakdown of recognised conventions for the conduct of business under the last government, of the proliferation of management targets and special advisers, and have begun to speak about the people who work for them with a modicum of appreciation. Morale has perked up a bit as a result, though it has been dashed again by the climate of austerity which is likely to rule in the public services for the next few years.

Gus O'Donnell, the Cabinet Secretary, has done much valuable remedial work behind the scenes. He is right too to emphasise the sense of service which actuates most public servants: that motivated most of us to join the service in the first place. His attempts to explain to the public how and why the service functions have been less convincing. This is partly because he, too, feels it necessary to elide the distinction between the administrative branch of the civil service and the executive branch. In an attempt to deflect criticism of the high salaries paid to public servants, he has argued that the median salary of a civil servant is about £23,000 a year, and the average pension is about £7,000.

But that is only true if you lump together all branches of the public service. Those in the top four ranks of the civil service, from Cabinet/Permanent Secretary down to Deputy Director, earn far more than this: O'Donnell himself, the most highly paid, earns between £235,000–£239,999. The public deals with the lower paid civil servants, but what it resents is the high pay of the senior civil servants, whose functions it neither understands nor appreciates. Eliding the distinction simply increases the degree of public resentment.

Defending the existence of a bureaucratic elite gives rise, of course, to a genuine political problem. But it is not the only area where the problem arises. Dislike of elitism led the previous government to press music academies to lower their standards so that they could provide access to students from deprived areas of society. The aim is of course beyond reproach: in our society as it is presently organised, much talent goes unnoticed or rewarded. But conservatoires do not exist to train second class violinists. And bureaucracies do not exist to employ second class civil servants. If we want to be properly served, in government as in the arts, we need to go for the best. The issue cannot be brushed under the carpet. So ministers and senior civil servants need to face up to it, and defend it robustly.

This leads on to the perennial question: what is to be done? The answers are not all that difficult.

First, ministers need to recognise that they have a personal responsibility for the good management of their departments and the people who work there. The snide slagging off that John Reid and, in his day, Richard Crossman indulged in shows how little some ministers know or understand about what managing a great department of state involves. It is a basic function of management to motivate the staff, a function to which some ministers appear to attach little importance.

Second, ministers need to understand the difference between the motivations which apply in business, where it is comparatively easy to reduce the objective to, say, the maximisation of profit and shareholder satisfaction, and in government, where the objectives and motivations are quite different. 'Professionalism' in the public service is very different from 'professionalism' in business. Once they understand these differences, politicians of all three parties will not ignorantly assume that what works in business (sometimes) will also work in the bureaucracy. 'Bullshit bingo' is not the answer to anything, though it does serve the modestly useful function of making consultants rich at the taxpayers' expense.

Third, even if it is politically awkward, they need to defend the idea that the job of senior civil servants is not to 'represent the people', but to bring their knowledge and experience to bear on the task of serving governments, of whatever political persuasion, efficiently, impartially, and honestly. These people are necessarily an elite, and there is no point in denying it.

Fourth, every effort must be made to recruit into this elite from every part of British society: it is almost axiomatic that the present system of education and recruitment fails to tap existing talent to the full. This is not at all easy to do — post code selection is not the answer — but it is essential for the broad purposes of social justice, as well as for the narrow objective of recruiting the best candidates for the serious business of running the country.

Many of the same arguments apply to the vast majority of public servants who are not part of the policymaking elite, who are in much more regular contact with the general public, and who are often not given the support they deserve and need from their ministerial bosses. Ministers regularly seek — and inevitably find — comparatively junior scapegoats when things go wrong, for example, in the child protection services. People who are often trying to do their best in difficult circumstances are thrown to the lions of the press for reasons of political expediency. This too is not a way of motivating people, or of recruiting the best people into branches of the profession which can be thankless as well as essential.

In conclusion, no one would deny that all institutions, and that includes the public service, need to change constantly to adapt to changing circumstances and new tasks. The public service of course suffers from inherent weaknesses and professional distortions which need to be constantly corrected. But the basic principles that were laid down by Northcote and Trevelyan are as valid today as they were when they were first formulated. Necessary change must continually bear these principles in mind as government adapts to the demands of the twenty first century.

PART II
The Academic Debate

Ursula Murray

Local Government and the Meaning of Publicness

Current analysis of public spending cuts suggests that the £81 billion reduction announced in the 2010 budget for the next four years up to 2014/15, will result in a reduced public sector workforce of 850,000. The Local Government sector experienced 11.8% or £ 3.8 billion cuts during 2010-11 alone and can expect a further 26 % reduction in government support by 2014/15 (Audit Commission, 2011). These devastating cuts to public services are ostensibly to reduce the financial deficit.

However, the unstated policy aim appears rather to be the bringing about of a smaller state. There is a sustained attack on the very idea of a *public* sector underpinned by a simple narrative which repeatedly stresses inefficiency, wastefulness, fat cat pensions and salaries. A powerful message has become embedded over three decades that the public sector is parasitical, unproductive, a monopoly and that staff are overpaid or superfluous. While the public sector is certainly not perfect, much of this stance is open to challenge. But any media coverage assumes it is a good and unproblematic thing to bring the disciplines of a valorised private sector into the heart of public service delivery. With the 2010 Coalition Government in power, we are now witnessing a rapid intensification of this process of commercialising, marketising and privatising public services. The UK is a pioneer at the forefront of a global process of outsourcing public services and embracing the idea of a smaller state.

The purpose of this chapter is not to combat the individual misrepresentations about the role of the public sector but to drill deeper into addressing some of the more philosophical underpinnings of why a public sector exists and why 'publicness' (Newman and Clarke , 2009) matters and should be defended. In other words to counter some of the fundamental thinking which seeks to undermine and contract the public sphere. The relative ease politically with which the assault on public services is taking place forces us back to thinking about the basic *meaning* of public services. Only in this way will we begin to understand the task involved in sustaining the idea of publicly funded services in a society shaped by neo-liberal economic thinking, individualised ways of living and the unchallenged influence of corporate power over the democratic political process itself. Under the pressures of the moment there is little time to 'think' so this chapter aims to provide the reader with grounds for such thinking and insight into what the hollowing out of our public institutions means.

As a former senior manager in local government in the 1980/90s and now as a lecturer in social policy, I have found particular readings helpful in unravelling the confusions and dilemmas which surround the lived experience of these changes. As the pressures mount on institutions and on ourselves as individuals, we need to gather ideas which will help to support our resilience and sustain our commitment to the idea of publicness as a different moral sphere.

Current social policy shifts

The Open Public Services White paper (Cabinet Office, 2011) seeks to further open public services to private and third sector providers. It notes that 40% of spending by local authorities already goes on contracts to the private and voluntary sectors. This White Paper has prompted concern that this reform agenda ignores the transaction costs of creating these new markets (Evison, 2011) and that this drive to make public service provision more 'diverse' is merely easing the path of the private sector (Butler, 2011). An analysis of NHS services similarly indicates that 31% is already managed by the private sector (of which almost 10% are GPs). By 2016 this would have risen to 64% under the original proposals of the current Health Bill to hand over commissioning of health care to GPs by 2013 (McCabe and Kirkpatrick, 2011). Despite modifications to this Health Bill the expectation is still that involvement of the corporate sector in managing commissioning will still grow as pressure to make budget savings in health intensifies.

Similarly, the award of seven year long contracts as part of the Department of Work and Pensions 'Work Programme' in April 2011, saw the letting of eighteen primary contracts valued at £3 to £5 billion of which only one contract was awarded to the public sector and two to the voluntary sector (Butler, 2011b), despite evidence to suggest the private sector is less capable than Job Centres at getting people into work.[1] Altogether 90% of contracts were let to the corporate sector

---

[1]   There is a further analysis of the work programme in Mark Serwotka's contribution to this volume.

including companies such as Ingeus Seloitte and A4E. The assumption however is that 300 voluntary sector bodies like Mencap and CABs will become involved in the running of the programmes. This then will mark the development of a new role for the voluntary sector as a major subcontractor for the *private* public service sector. Finally, it has been announced that the civil service pension scheme is to become an enforced new 'mutual' (Codrea-Rada, 2011). This also represents a further strand in the governments strategy to bring about a 'smaller state' embedded in the Localism Act (2011) with its proposals to 'spin out' one million public sector employees into new mutuals without any secure 'lock' to prevent these ending up in the hands of the corporate sector

More generally in local government the scale and impact of a front loaded programme of four years of cuts has devastated support services for young people and for children outside statutory provision. Libraries are also the focus of cuts, rationalisation and marginalisation which has prompted strong anti-cuts campaigns reflecting the still powerful and popular identification of the welfare state with specific local services, if not local government as a whole.

Local government always seems unloved and unvalued relative to the NHS. This has encouraged the coalition government and predecessor administrations to make sure that local government takes the brunt of the cuts, safe in the knowledge that the voting public is for the most part unengaged with their local councils. Yet in reality the wide ranging roles of local government and local political histories of how services were fought for are very deeply woven into the fabric of our daily lives. These services are a constant and mainly progressive presence. Life without recycling and waste management, street trees and parks, school meals and play schemes, social services or swimming pools etc., is unimaginable – until their survival is threatened.

In the early mid 1970s I shared a room at work with a political economist. One day he remarked that the discovery of North Sea oil was 'the worst thing that could have happened to the British economy, it will prop it up for another 40 years'...! And as he predicted, North Sea oil aided and abetted by the rise of London as a global centre of finance capital after deregulation in 1989, *has* indeed shielded us from the facts of our precarious economic position which followed from the loss of an empire. It has meant that the illusions of an imperial mindset still rule us and we still have to properly face up to the fact that the UK no longer has the resources of half the world to support its lifestyle. This economic 'elephant-in-the-room' has been obscured by the 2008 recession.

The coalition government's commitment to high risk austerity budgets has been criticised by economists such as Skidelsky (2011) Blanchflower (2011) and Elliot (2011) for rapid and unnecessary public sector job and service cuts driven by political interest in creating a smaller state and which undermine our economic recovery. The scale and speed of these cuts will actively impede the deeper thinking that we need to creatively rethink public services over the longer term. The likely outcome of austerity will be an intensification of the inequalities mapped by Dorling (2010) and the social problems reaped by unequal societies outlined by Wilkinson and Pickett (2009), with especially negative consequences for women for whom the welfare state is key in enabling greater autonomy. To defend *and* maintain public services with fewer resources will involve hugely challenging innovation (Cottam, 2009) in public service delivery. It calls for a new sceptism about choice and competition and ideas which appear innovative but lead to fragmentation. We need a revaluing of taxation and as a society of what we think care of the vulnerable means if we are to maintain the welfare state at a time when it hovers on the brink of being dismantled.

Aims of the chapter

Over the rest of this chapter I will discuss some of the concepts and theories which I have found helpful in understanding publicness. It is thus a springboard to both thought and action in trying to make sense of the changes we are now living through. It will start with some reminders of previous attempts to roll back the state in the 1980–90s and my own experience of this working in local government. I then unpick 'public choice theory' which has so powerfully undermined more collective ways of thinking. An assertive counter discourse to this exists around the value of bureaucracy as necessary to reconciling conflicting interests and as a robust defence against corruption.

Economists and business schools have been widely seduced by public choice theory and the new public management norms, whereas social policy theorists (and public service practitioners) have mainly critiqued them. To illustrate this conflict of ideas I will consider the contested definition of a 'new public service ethos'. Exploring this points towards the need for a more psychosocial understanding of the role of public institutions as 'containers of social anxiety' (Hoggett, 2005; 2006). Finally, there is a need to imagine new ways in which an expression of publicness can continue to arise if familiar structures are hollowed out. How will commitment to the idea of the welfare state (Bell, 2010) and to *publicly* funded services continue to resonate and demand our allegiance? As Eagleton (2003:128) drawing on Aristotle emphasizes, by 'politics' we mean ethics and how we live together. He adds 'if you want to be good you need a good society'.

A collapse of 'meaning'

What can be learnt from the experiences of the past three decades which can help steer us through the present turbulent times? The eighteen years of the Thatcher-Major governments from 1979 to 1997 were a similar period of economic crisis but also social unrest. The early privatisation of public utilities and roll out of compulsory tendering of local authority public services was also accompanied by the 'New Public Management', which became a modernisation model (Hood, 1992). This introduced competition and market thinking into public services via adoption of private sector methods such as business units and a pervasive measurement culture of new quality and audit systems.

In the years following the 1984 miners strike, key local authorities became the frontline of conflict seeing themselves as a 'defensive shield' for their communities against aggressive central government cuts. I worked as a senior manager during this period in one such London Borough and witnessed a sustained commitment by local politicians, trade unions and service workers to work together to counter this push to privatise local services. Yet like many women in these roles I had spent the previous decade challenging and campaigning against the technocratic and gendered way local authorities interpreted service provision and roles. This was what Hoggett, (2000:195) describes as the attempt to recapture the loss of the ethical vision in public services in the 1970s and with it the idea of a welfare state as a 'gift relationship' (Titmus, 1971:11) which he classically represented in the image of the blood transfusion service in which people freely donate blood to the 'unknown stranger' in an 'unspoken shared belief in the universality of need' (ibid: 238). The welfare state was a huge achievement of the post war Labour movement at a time of real austerity. But at the same time it was also inevitably a contradictory formation as it was a post war compromise between capital and labour and one which was blind to class and gender divisions.

My position was therefore classically one of being '*in and against the state*' (London-Edinburgh Weekend Return Group, 1979). Inevitably the tensions between means and ends were ever present. As a senior manager responsible for the tendering of local services in compliance with and under the duress of compulsory competitive tendering (CCT) legislation, I was deeply concerned about whether my integrity was being compromised. So the question of moral and ethical choices—

doing what was 'right' in the circumstances and seeking to live with
integrity—*were* in constant discussion. This pervaded our day-to-day
decisions as we struggled to contest the weight of the new orthodoxies
of the three 'E's': economy, efficiency and effectiveness and the
competition driven business model of the New Public Management
ethos. It was a 'dilemmatic space' (Honig,1996) which, in the tumult of
constant change, staff sought to make sense of unresolved political
conflicts.

After nine years in a senior management role, I was brought face-to-
face with how far I could continue to reconcile the pressures of the ever
more conflicting and contradictory demands of working in local
government. I was holidaying in Greece in 1995 in a 'summer camp'
environment where someone organised a *'passion evening'* in which
anyone could take a seat as speaker on some issue on which they felt
passionate. I had spent years passionately involved in different
ventures to radicalise and reform the welfare state. Working in
collectives, my research had supported the launching of numerous
innovative campaigns and the setting up of new services to meet unmet
needs. This had been followed by nearly a decade in senior
management from the late 1980s in local government in which I was
actively engaged in preventing privatisation of public services.
Although my role was quite technical in focus, it was imbued with
political meaning and a collective energy. As I sat under the stars that
night my immediate thought was I would speak on this. Speakers came
and went and I heard about the intricacies of organic sewage farms, or
why not voting was a crime by an Argentinian now living in London.
But gradually I became I aware that I could not speak.

Intellectually, I still remained very committed to the idea of public
services but under the weight of managing all the contradictions
implicit in my role, I realised that I had lost my passion. The
entrenchment of the new public management was the reality
increasingly shaping my day-to-day life. Later, I had a dream about
searching through the tangled chaos of a jumble sale, in which the
clothes were impossible to separate out. I was searching for a *'lunch box
with a pink lid'*. The meaning of this dream for me lay in a search for a
more nourishing work environment. My workplace was draining away
my feminist and 'feminine' energies. I had ceased to be able to 'think'
and felt increasingly cut off from a capacity to reflect in any of the
former collective ways. Underlying my 'truth-in-the-moment' this
warm summer evening I sensed, but could not yet understand, that the
emotion of loss about the meaning of public service was trying to make
itself present. My inner compass was at work and so the question of the
meaning of public services emerged for me in a very personal way at

this point. I felt driven to think more and reflect on this sense of disorientation and confusion after a decade on the 'front line' and in 1997 moved towards a research environment to do this. This time to 'think' eventually re-connected my energy and replaced my sense of confusion with a renewed sense of the meaning of public services.

Key questions

My research took the path of a narrative exploration of making meaning in the public sector, drawing on my own lived experience of the radical 'reformation' of the British welfare state over the previous three decades. The 1980s to mid 1990s had been characterised by highly contested views about the growing commercialisation of public services, turbulent social movements and by a profound sense of loss. But with the economic boom of the New Labour years from 2000 onwards and significant increases in public investment such public debates became blurred and marginalised. Stuart Hall (2004) describes the confusing triangulation involved as a 'double shuffle'; one in which neo-liberal economics remained very much the dominant stance but coexisted with a secondary social democratic range of initiatives such as Sure Start centres.

Some of the questions which my research posed about the meaning of public services (Murray, 2005) are now highly transferable to the present moment as these ideological debates have re-emerged. These research questions included: Has something been 'stolen' and if so what is it? Does it matter whether we send our public services 'off to the market'? Does the public sector remain a particular kind of moral community in a way that readily translates into a distinct public service ethos? What will sustain and mobilise the meaning we invest in public services as the traditional taken for granted structures of the public sector continue to erode? Can public services remain meaningfully 'public' outside the formal boundaries of a public sector and could new or transformed meanings be possible?

Amongst the conclusions that I came to in 2005 was that:

> Harassed by government into driving down costs and into using the private finance and partnerships to do so, local authority politicians and managers have opted for the route of quick and easy outsourcing to the corporate sector. As a consequence, a handful of corporate monopolies are being brought into being, which are exercising day-to-day authority over a widening area of public service provision and which is now extending its reach towards enrolling parts of the voluntary sector as a sub contractor (Murray, 2005:277).

This conclusion rightly anticipated that we were heading for a monoculture of public service control by a handful of corporate players. It was both prescient and accurate. But as the economy continued to boom and resources were effectively siphoned off to improve public services, such warnings had little purchase. The voluntary sector organisations likewise seemed uninterested in the implicit dangers of a contract culture enabling its own growth but also allowing for corporate, global multinational companies to take control of the public sector. As a society we turned a blind eye to the same risks and concerns which have underpinned the implosion of the finance sector (Elliott, 2011) and which is now evident in the collapse of the Southern Cross Care Homes scandal (Wilby, 2011).

Ultimately we are talking about how as a society we understand and want to differentiate between public and private. While concern for efficiency, economy, and effectiveness has a proper place in meeting the social reproduction of communities, it is still widely accepted that 'it is not like shopping' (Clarke, 2007). It is not the same as managing a supermarket to which politicians continually turn for advice on how to modernise and manage public service delivery. A private sector ethos, as Jane Jacobs (1992) pointed out, operates with its prime obligation being orientated towards making a profit for shareholders. She argued that the public and private sector work domains constitute two contradictory different 'moral syndromes': that of the 'commercial' and that of the 'guardians'. In her view the role of bureaucracies is to serve the public openly and above board, whereas this may be quite inappropriate in the commercial world. She suggests that combining fundamentally different moral practices does not work and that confusing the different spheres can only result in 'monstrous hybrids'.

Is this the world of the new private public service sector? Will a blurring of sector roles as some have argued, give rise to the institutionalisation of 'secondary corruption' (Hodgkinson 1997:17) in which covert, unaccountable forms of influence become endemic, impacting on the independence of judgment by public officials? To misquote a Cafavy poem: 'the barbarians are inside the gates'. The 2011 revelations around the role of the media in relation to the police and politicians and the now widespread revolving door syndrome would seem to confirm this.

Public choice theory

Tony Judt (2010: 91–210) describes the ideological shift from a post war consensus on the need for a welfare state to the 1970s embrace of Hayek and other economists and their concern to shrink the state. Business Schools have largely taught the neo-liberal management theories and norms of a market orientated 'business model' on MBA's which have duly colonised public and voluntary sector management thinking. Public choice theory was one such powerful conceptual template which is now the dominant mindset.

Finlayson (2003:110) argues that the influence of 'public choice theory' was crucial to the growth of 'contracting out' and 'internal markets' alongside the earlier selling off of the assets of the public sector. It is conceived of as a neutral objective method of political study in which economic theories of decision-making can be applied to non-market choices. The behaviours and rationality assumed by utilitarian and individualistic models of economic choice are put to use in making sense of those choices in the public sector as though they were the same as purchases in a supermarket. Bureaucratic action is understood as a private choice made by individuals and thus, he argues, 'economic theory colonises political science' (Finlayson, 2003a:29).

This theory ultimately underpins the move via the 'New Public Management' of the 1990s towards the pervasive measurement of inputs, outcomes and league tables for schools, hospitals and universities. Likewise Le Grand (2005), the social market theorist and New Labour government health policy-maker, argued for an NHS run on payment by results. What is startling about Le Grand's and other such commentaries on the need to introduce choice into public services is the complete absence of any discussion of the nature of the tasks involved. It is a wholly managerial and economistic discourse.

Rustin (2000:122) also emphasises how under New Labour the 'modernisation' of the public sector became infused with the aim of creating regimes which mimicked as far as possible the competition and discipline of markets through intensifying the place of measurable turnover and profit (evidence-based outcomes), the context of inter-institutional competition (league tables), and the power of management to undermine 'producer privileges' of protected and safeguarded conditions of employment. In his view, the benefits of all of this for capital are threefold: firstly, in reducing the power of public sector labour and using it more intensively; secondly, in opening up the large opportunities for profit making and capital accumulation in provision of prisons, education and health; thirdly, in the ideological shift of a sector based on values opposed in many ways to the market and remote from the disciplines of measurement, to one of conformity, reward and punishment.

Finlayson's (2003) likewise suggests this sort of approach is very damaging for democratic politics because public choice theory treats problems as managerial rather than political. It is a system of control and rule rather than a plan for political change. Crucially, he points out 'it has nothing to say about what we actually want a public service to do' (2003a:31). While in itself it cannot decide political direction, the

norms of the 'New Public Management' has encoded within it, value
judgments about public services (ibid:30), which shift the overall
management stance into narrow notions of efficiency and undermine
their fundamental underpinning, politically and organisationally. It
entrenches the values of the market rather than public service indirectly
through the roles that we take up as workers and as users. In this way
the individual behaviours of 'public servants' are being re-shaped as
we come to see ourselves as 'business managers' (Finlayson, 2003:114),
rewarded in our everyday roles for being 'purchasers' or 'contractors'.
Personal achievement in a personal appraisal may come by
demonstrating effective contracting out. Overall policy and delivery are
split, and politicians are distanced and separated from responsibility
for the specific nature of the public realm.

This thirty year incremental expansion of the role of the private
sector has brought with it the loss of collective notions of what
constitutes the public interest. Finlayson, (2003a:36–39) summarises the
different costs attached to this. Firstly, it denies the need for political
decisions by replacing participation in politics with participation in the
market. Secondly, consumerism in itself is not enough to shift the
distribution of power. In spite of the rhetoric of 'choice', taking away
bureaucratic systems of power is not the same as giving power to the
user. Thirdly, he argues that contradictions will always arise in the
different dimensions of our lives and that it is politics that can
articulate them and establish a new way of ordering—it is the glue
which binds the increasingly blurred spheres of state, individual,
society and economy. Public reason, he argues, is to reason in public
and by a public. It is an attempt at the public level to think about what
is best for all as well as ourselves (ibid:38).

The values of bureaucracy

This highlights the dilemmas that underlie the simplicities of the
'choice' agenda. We have to balance our individual needs and
perceived rights against our relinquishing those same rights so as to
avoid damaging more vulnerable others in society. It is why managing
the most basic public services continually raises complicated moral
judgements in finding the balance between the particular interest and
the universal need. The management of public services means engaging
with a wide range of day-to-day dilemmas and attempting to reconcile
multiple conflicting viewpoints and meanings: hence the role for
bureaucracy.

Bureaucracies stem from a modernist view of the world and
rational-legal forms of authority. Contrary to popular sentiment,
bureaucracies have a positive role and function in society as du Gay

(2000; 2005) has argued. Bureaucracies are also widely present in private companies and larger voluntary bodies for good reason. Public sector bureaucracies take on roles which define the balance between the particular and the universal, the individual and societal needs. Of course *bureaucratic* ways of working can become problematic in the public sector but it is grossly inaccurate to caricature the British welfare state in this way (Crouch, 2003:58) or as inevitably inflexible and unresponsive.

Du Gay seeks to rehabilitate this negative understanding of bureaucracy as outmoded and inefficient, and emphasises this important but usually ignored distinction between bureaucracy and bureaucratic. In his argument, a bureaucracy is a unique kind of moral institution for the organisation of public affairs which is committed to norms of impersonality, neutrality and objectivity — all essential to the continuous contestation of public purpose and a means of containing moral ambivalence. But it is not bureaucracy *per se* which is responsible for hierarchy or instrumentalism. In Scandinavia 40 years ago, a progressive social democratic movement humanised and decentralised the welfare state within a public sector form, far more than was the case in the UK (Crouch, 2003:60). Furthermore, it can be argued that the network-based, contractual, inter-organisational partnership world of the 'New Public Management' merely constitutes a different form of rationality. It is just as much an assertion of power and hierarchy, albeit more hidden, through the way centralised command is concealed by these new forms of decentralisation (Clegg, 1990).

This kind of authoritarianism — whatever the service improvements and benefits from increased funding under Labour — helped pave the way for the current assault on the state (Rutherford, 2011: 4). It has meant that the dominant mode of regulation in our society has now become contractual (Jordan, 2011: 3-4) which is expressed in target setting regimes that undermine older, relational approaches in which accountability had to be negotiated. Jordan also argues that 'the emphasis on individuals, their choices, aspirations and achievements obscure the collective processes at work' (ibid:17).

A public service ethos

In its approach to the 'modernisation' of public services, New Labour governments of 1997–2010, came to advocate that it does not matter who provides the service as long as the ultimate ownership remained in public hands. This blurring of sector roles is now set to intensify with a corporate sector openly and vigorously pressing for the outsourcing of public sector contracts and a government legislating to enable 'any willing provider' to deliver them including the take over of commissioning roles. The growing homogenisation of management styles, the commercialisation and the blurring of sector boundaries, all call into question the very idea of whether the public sector still operates with a unique underpinning philosophy that shapes a different ethos.

Hoggett (2005; 2006) argues that organisations primarily involved in a public purpose do still have two unique characteristics: these are the continuous contestation of public purposes and secondly how they act as a receptacle for containing social anxieties. In relation to the first characteristic, he emphasises that government and the public sphere which supports it, is as much a site for the enactment of particular kinds of social relations as it is the site for the delivery of goods and services and concludes that:

> to reduce it only to the latter is to commodify such relationships, to strip them of their moral and ethical meaning and potential meaning which is inherent in the very concept of citizen but marginal to the concept of consumer (Hoggett, 2006: 77) .

In contrast to the apparent simplicities of government targets, the actual reality of managing a library or swimming pool is as much one of grappling with complex policy issues as to *who* has access to what level of resources in an increasingly diverse society. So public organisations and those who work for them are always intimately concerned with equality and value conflicts in society that are inherent and irresolvable. In Hoggett's view, the ethic of care to an individual has to be constantly balanced against an ethic of justice to those potentially present, which can only be kept in mind in an abstract sense. A business approach alone will elide such complex value questions. He identifies four distinct sets of administrative values underlying effective bureaucracy—keeping it visible and accountable, keeping it lean and purposeful, keeping it honest and fair, keeping it robust and resilient. The present emphasis which concentrates on 'lean and purposeful' has in his view reduced the question of public services to mere service delivery (2005:169).

Hoggett (2000:147) also considers that it is easy to denigrate public sector workers rather than seek to understand how they are often caught up in a contradictory logic responsible for both 'care and control, equity and rationing, and empowerment and exploitation' in which there will always be tension between users and workers who face each other in a relationship of 'conflictual interdependence'. He returns to the work of Lipsky (1980:41), who coined the phrase 'street level bureaucrat' in relation to public officials like teachers, nurses, police officers, housing, planning, and benefit officers and points out that politicians with an eye to electoral appeal are often far from clear what they want. They may indulge in a collusive contract with the electorate by deriving some of their legitimacy from not confronting the electorate with realities in a 'contract of mutual indifference' (ibid quoting Geras, 1998). Public servants are frequently pushed into classic scapegoat roles — blamed for things that neither citizens nor governments will properly address such as social care. As Lipsky argued, 'a typical mechanism for legislative conflict resolution is to pass on intractable conflicts for resolution (or continued irresolution) to the administrative level (1981:41). As a result, the unresolved value conflicts re-emerge at the level of operations as impossible tasks, adding to the already considerable ethical complexities of day-to-day roles. It remains to be seen whether the outcome of debate about the Dilnot Report on social care (Rowntree, 2011) will avoid this.

In sharp opposition to this way of thinking, Le Grand (2003:29) ignores such ethical complexities with which public servants grapple on a daily basis. He argues that far from public service workers being seen as 'knights', they should just as easily be 'knaves' and connects an often-perceived insensitivity or arrogance as arising from being in a monopoly supplier position. In his view, competition and user choice have the moral virtue of increasing fairness and respect for service users in a way that other systems do not. He argues his case around the benefits of public managers being necessarily interested in the financial health of an institution. Fear that users would be damaged if the financial health of an institution declines, suggests for him that the spirit of caring is being retained.

Being clear about financial constraints is important and clearly does have a key role to play. But reducing health care management to such narrow parameters is also deeply concerning. In my own experience, managers for whom 'the budget is the budget is the budget' are dangerously out of touch with their own feelings and with the painful predicaments facing service users.[2] This can permeate the technocratic norms of procurement, commissioning and contracting as key workers with these skills move back and forth across the blurred public/private boundary with ease, applying seemingly common business values, whether it is hotel facilities management or local hospital. This underlines how a public service ethos is not a fixed thing. It is constantly influenced by social, technical, political processes and

---

[2]   See, for example, Liz Kessler's contribution to this volume for evidence of how much the narrow parameters of budget and process can obstruct constructive and innovative work.

reworked by individuals in a day-to-day contestation of ideas and processes

Traditionally a public service ethos was deemed to stem from a deep recognition in society of underlying interdependencies and human well being best addressed outside market relations. The argument for and against the public sector having an intrinsically different set of core values was put to a key Parliamentary Select Committee on Public Administration in 2002. The then still emerging private public service sector presented a very specific argument. The case was put by the founder and chair of Capita, one of the earliest and now most important private public services providers (see Aldridge and Stoker, 2003) and subsequently published by the think-tank 'The New Local Government Network' (NLGN). It proposed that all service providers, whatever the sector, can and should be prepared to advance a 'new public service ethos'. They based this around five criteria: a performance culture, a commitment to accountability, a capacity to support universal access, responsible employment and training practices, and a contribution to community well-being (ibid:17). These five points reflect good practice in terms of quality and human resources management. A well-run private company with motivated staff could achieve these just as a poorly managed public sector organisation could fail.

The Select Committee (2002) adopted this perspective represented in the NLGN pamphlet, endorsing its well-argued position that private companies providing public services should develop an appropriate *new* public service ethos. It accepted the view that there was no reason why a public service ethos cannot be upheld by private service providers, but suggested that it needed to be reinforced by building it into contracts of service and employment to prevent it being 'put under strain by the profit motive'. The chair of the Select Committee, writing subsequently, also rejected as a myth any equation of a public service ethos with a public *sector* ethos (Wright, 2003).

The trade union representative viewpoint put to the Parliamentary Select Committee in 2002 on defining a public service ethos argued that a public service ethos was represented by acts of 'kindness'. This statement contrasted strongly with the coherent list of systematic recommendations put forward by the representative of the private public service sector. Mere 'kindness' in this context seemed nebulous and unconvincing in comparison and it did not impress the chair of the Committee. But I want to argue here that the trade union viewpoint did in some way point in the right direction and takes us away from the instrumental language of Aldridge and Stoker and the Select Committee. In the end it did place human relating and questions about intimacy, authenticity and the non-commercialisation of human feelings (Hoschschild, 1983) at the centre of what is meant by any public service ethos. It is noticeable for example how it is the kindness of ancillary staff in hospitals which is often remarked upon by patients. The utilitarian cross-sector 'new public service ethos (Aldridge and Stoker, 2003:17), fails to consider how and why emotional and ethical dilemmas are integral to day-to-day public services roles.

However, the desire to do 'good things' can equally be accompanied by dysfunctional relationships in altruistic environments. It underlines how the lived experience of public service workers can be paradoxical and muddled. A more relational approach to the idea of a public service ethos is adopted by Hoggett, Mayo and Miller (2006) who emphasise that encounters in 'post bureaucratic' organisations are more fluid and traditional authority relationships are weakened, intensifying ambiguity and heightening reliance on deploying a personal authority. They write:

> Rather than an essential public service ethos, that can be enshrined in abstract principles, in practice public service workers constantly have to negotiate boundaries between such general principles, their own values and the particularist requirements of service users and different kinds of communities ... From the perspective of lived practice, what constitutes justice is therefore not abstract and immutable but has to be worked through often case by case. (Hoggett et al., 2006:767)

The crucial difference in the way Hoggett thinks about public services compared to Le Grand is its avoidance of the technocratic which displaces the ethical, emotional and political issues. In addition he brings to bear a wider psychosocial literature on thinking about public services in which the concepts of 'social defences' and the 'containment of social anxieties' are central.

Containment of social anxieties

Health services and local council services of many kinds deal constantly with fundamental human anxieties and in Hoggett's view (2006: 180) such institutions play a vital role in 'containing' some of the most troubling feelings that we as citizens experience and for whom anxiety is one of the most powerful affects. He also points out that a systemic and psychoanalytic way of thinking is still largely ignored by researchers and policy makers in the broader field of public and social policy. Analysis of the complicated emotional life and politics of welfare services which draws on a psychosocial approach is exemplified in the work by Cooper and Lousada (2005), Hoggett (2000, 2006) and Obholzer and Roberts, (1994).

Most people working in public services can tell stories that are suffused with emotional turmoil and ethical dilemmas.[3] Also one cannot help but encounter power struggles and conflict when working close to the policy and political domains. Public consultations between different political, professional and user interests can be very fraught. Yet the administrative and cultural legacies of the public sector still reinforce a style of talking and thinking in which the 'emotional labour' (Hochschild, 1983) involved in many public services is comprehensively ignored. There is still little importance attached to reflecting on the emotional impact of the kind of work described in the following example.

The care of strangers

Donal tells me about the time when a woman came into his environmental community centre in west London and slipped past reception. The woman was drunk and demanding 'giz us a job'. He talked with her about volunteering and eventually she left. Later someone comes to tell him there is a woman in distress (the same woman), this time in the park, lying half naked by the sundial. His choice is to call the police or to go and talk to her. He tells me how Annette, a young administrator, steps forward and offers to talk to her. She finds out that the woman has just lost her children into care. She returns leaving the woman fully dressed, albeit not for long. Donal reflects on the duty of care to strangers who are drunk and effectively waste their time. An environmental centre is not a hospital or social services: it is not part of their job description to 'care', but they do. We ponder about what in Annette's background enabled her to step forward and respond with kindness and empathy. I also point out that he has told me before how each new generation of local kids trash their facilities, until with time and painstaking effort he and his colleagues draw them into the work of the centre so that their destructive energies are calmed. He could call the police, but deliberately chooses not to do this, because the vandalism would put their parents in council tenancies at risk of eviction. He tells me, children who have vandalised the project will return next day 'expecting to be received with open arms' and they are welcomed back.

This story draws attention to how many public service frontline and management roles deal on a daily basis with vulnerable people and experience their dependency, failure, fear, shame and even death. Workers may respond to such raw emotion with a generosity of spirit, kindness, compassion and intimacy as in this story above. But if this kind of situation is encountered more regularly or causes irritation and fear, then an absence of care or empathy or a seeming arrogance can

---

[3]   See, for example, the story of Anna in Rebekah Carrier's contribution to this volume.

easily take over. A feature of institutions designed to enhance human welfare is how they can be suffused not with the altruism of their overriding purpose, but overwhelmed by the 'social defences' which people evolve which can then result in quite inhuman practices (Young, 1994:163). A 'social defence system' (Menzies, 1960/1988) may arise in order to avoid experiencing the unpleasant feelings which the vulnerability of others arouses. People who work in the public sector are not somehow kinder, nicer or more altruistic than people who work in the private sector: they just often work in a more challenging environment than the private services sector and this emotional labour needs to be properly processed if it is not to generate perverse individual and organizational responses.

This is still a rarely understood aspect of the welfare system. It sits uneasily with the desire for certainty among politicians and their unwillingness to recognise that social failure can never be entirely removed. A transfer of work from the public sector to the private or voluntary sector does not prevent this same kind of destructive dynamic occurring. The impact of working on a daily basis with vulnerable people and the raw feelings and emotions aroused will not disappear. But the private sector is more likely to cherry pick the easier and more profitable work, leaving the difficult to resolve work for a residual public sector or voluntary sector services to handle.

The evidence of human dependency contrasts sharply with an ethos of self-sufficiency and aspiration for individual autonomy that characterises government policymakers. Recognising these key needs and the kind of difficulties and dilemmas which result is therefore a key argument for maintaining a public sector with an institutional memory of how to accommodate these issues. However, the mainstream literature on public services has placed little emphasis on the complex relational dynamics that can arise in public service work. A simplistic way of thinking dominates and underpins much of the impetus for blurring the arguments that take account of the separate sectors and their different contributions. Lost from sight are the unavoidable constraints of life and the need for continuity, reciprocity and mutual recognition (Rustin, 1999:112–118).

Re-imagining publicness

This brings us back to the meaning of the public realm and different definitions of publicness. Newman and Clarke (2009) sound a cautionary note about reading off the meaning of publicness in a simplistic structural way. They offer a subtle, nuanced reading of public sector modernisation in which publicness is being disassembled but also reassembled around the relationship between public services

and public *values* (ibid:132). They draw out the complex and
contradictory processes of change emphasising that it is emergent and
unstable and in which conflicts must be managed, contradictory
imperatives balanced, and new and old agendas reconciled. They
suggest:

> Public services have had a critical role in producing publics and
> mediating publicness. Their reform has certainly undermined some of
> its established and institutionalised versions. But public services remain
> a focus of collective aspirations and desires — perhaps all the more so in
> times of growing inequality division, anxiety and uncertainty (Newman
> and Clarke, 2009:184–185).

They believe public services can be reconstructed in ways that both
reflect and summon emergent publics because they hold the possibility
of decommodifying goods, services and above all relationships and can
enact principles of 'open access, fairness and equitable treatment'
(ibid:184). In their view they have the potential to make people feel like
'members of the public' offering a sense of 'belonging, connection and
entitlement' (ibid:185). So how the public experiences their encounters
with public services and of being treated with respect and fairness
matters greatly. Like the earlier significance of kindness these qualities
'speak to the mundane qualities of publicness that people value and
desire' (ibid:185).

Stuart Hall (2004) considers the 'public' to be a social dimension and
not a separate domain. The idea of an autonomous 'public realm' is, he
suggests, untenable. Feminism demonstrated how the apparently
private domain of the family was saturated by questions about the role
of the public: that the 'personal was political'. In his view 'the public' is
about the material and institutional expression of interdependence and
is not reducible to the individual. The welfare state brought about an
institutionally recognised set of alternative criteria determining how
social provision was not to be governed by money but by a different
form of social assessment. In Hall's view, the 'public good' is a
principle of social organisation about why, when, and how we should
govern market rationality. Economic access to public goods is,
therefore, not separable from what we mean by the 'public'. It is not a
question of wanting to suspend all markets but of what areas of life
should be governed by such criteria. He argues the NHS embodies a set
of values over market relations and institutionalises this in a place and
in the relations between professionals and people. In his view, the
citizenry know this, know they are governed by some ethic and are not
governed by the criteria to pay. In this way he considers it
institutionalises *a lived* public ethic.

Similarly, Caroline Steedman (1986) reflecting on growing up in the 1950s points out, 'I would be a very different person now if orange juice and milk and dinners hadn't told me in a covert way, that I had a right to exist, was worth something' (ibid:122). She was reflecting on how she had been shaped by huge historical labels like charity, philanthropy and state intervention but understood this in precisely these kind of 'mundane ways'.

This is a signal to pay attention to emotional life in the politics of public service provision as well as to traditional questions of social justice. Hoggett points out that there is no future for public welfare unless people are moved to combine in solidarity around some shared vision. He argues that 'It is not facts that move people but illusions' and a 'mobilising fiction' (2000:139–141). It is this that is the agent of change and the crucial tool in all liberatory struggles. In politics, he suggests, it is not whether the idea of community is true or not; the question is whether it has the power to effect a transition from what is to what might be. In his view, it is the fictional or playful quality of any vision that matters otherwise an unreflexively held dogma takes over. In this he emphasises the avoidance of a symbol becoming concrete or a thing-in-itself and that it is important that the symbolic retains an 'as if' quality. He considers the idea of 'universal provision' is just such an illusion or 'mobilising fiction', which is both absurd *and* absolutely necessary. We have to re-discover this narrative in a new way. The old story is not dead but under modernity in its present form it is losing its potency. If we defend this 'mobilising fiction' in traditional ways it will not survive.

Holloway (2001:61) likewise speaks of the potency of 'fictions' by which we live but also of the fear that if the present one is understood in a different way it will lose its power, but equally if it is only defended in traditional ways it will not survive.

Understanding our resistance to the changing welfare state and public services over the past two decades in these terms is quite rare and yet is key to the kind of action which can ultimately prevent the disappearance of publicly funded services. In 2011, we have seen that campaigns against the privatisation of forests and libraries have had the power to mobilise because they are loved and have a deeply rooted place in people's psyches. So we have to reflect on how new social movements can challenge why the 'Right' have so easily colonised the territory of the 'Left' with the potent but empty rhetoric of 'big society' or the new mutualism. Does this lie with a rediscovery of lost roots, of a 'good society' based around tradition and virtue as Cruddas (2011), Rutherford (2011) and Glasman (2011) have argued in different ways? Others have dismissed this as an exercise in misplaced nostalgia. It also somewhat ignores the lessons of the social movements of three decades ago, in which women especially sought to change and democratise public services for the better. None-the-less there is a sense of starting to grapple with the need for a revitalised civil society in which a re-imagined sense of a public sphere once again shapes our ethics.

Conclusions

The Introduction raised a number of questions. Has something been 'stolen' and if so what is it? Does it matter whether we send our public services 'off to the market'? Does the public sector remain a particular kind of moral community in a way that readily translates into a distinct public service ethos? What will sustain and mobilize the meaning we invest in public services as the traditional taken for granted structures of the public sector continue to erode? Can public services remain meaningfully 'public' outside the formal boundaries of a public sector and could new or transformed meanings be possible? Definitive answers to some of these questions are still unclear but some broad conclusions can be drawn from this review of theories about our dilemma.

- That very extensive colonisation by the private sector *is* taking place although this is also being resisted and any future settlement is uncertain and unstable in what is an experiment with a potential for large scale failure.

- That a new world of subcontracting public services to the corporate sector *is* being incrementally put in place. It has the potential for an Orwellian enslavement of public sector and voluntary sector workers in a new kind of technocracy managed by a handful of private public service companies operating in a global market.

- That the public sector represents a *different moral sphere* underpinned by different social relations. It also undertakes a societal role of containing social anxiety in routine, mundane and day to day ways. In the absence of embedded public sector institutions this will seek other and perhaps more disturbing outlets

- That even if public sector institutions are extensively outsourced and hollowed out, resistance to new norms will inevitably follow and work practices be contested. New social movements and networks will seek to 'imagine the public' in new ways and struggle to articulate different *public* values afresh and embody them in new social relations.

- That what is understood as 'public' has always been a contested issue reflecting different forms resulting from political and cultural change. While there has never been a golden age we are at a fault line in which 'territory' secured with the inception of the welfare state in terms of social justice *is* being fundamentally rolled back.

- That if outsourcing continues at the present speed the struggle for *public values* will of necessity move out of the familiar institutional forms of the public sector and take place in new constituencies of interest—in the community and voluntary sectors but also in the private public service sector.

- That a different politics is needed which confidently rebuffs current attacks. One which uses the theories and ideas discussed in this chapter to re-assert the essential nature of shared public values.

POSTSCRIPT: The voluntary sector's ethical dilemma.

Having grown its workforce by 40% between 2001–2010, the voluntary sector now faces a £3 billion decline in funding over the next five years and down from £12.8 billion in 2007/08. There is now a real ethical dilemma for organisations between seeking to survive in a market economy and staying true to their independent ethical values. Some now consider parts of the voluntary sector will 'become more truly voluntary, with the benefits of social cohesiveness that this can bring. Other parts will just get closer to the state'(Cook, 2011). But this analysis somewhat ignores the changing nature of what is meant here by the 'state'. With multi nationals now winning public services contracts, the voluntary sector may easily now become a sub contractor to a private public service sector organisation: one who may even have other roles in the economy which are ethically unacceptable.

The Work Programmme and Social Enterprises

In April 2011, the Department of Work and Pensions let eighteen primary contracts for the new 'Work Programme' (WP), valued at £3 to 5 billion. As already noted, only one contract was awarded to the public sector and two to the voluntary sector—despite all the evidence of the existing capability of Job Centres to get people into work and of voluntary sector organisations to work with ' hard to reach' groups. The contracts went instead to very large multi nationals and the voluntary sector was assured that 300 voluntary sector organisations would be involved as subcontractors in delivering these contracts. Six months on and many specialist charities have been given no business as yet from their partner prime contractors who were happy to co-opt them as partners. This has sparked complaints that charities have been used as 'bid candy' and several charities have pulled out of the Work Programmme, believing the contract terms to be financially unsustainable and voicing concerns that 'specialist voluntary sector role will be annihilated' (Butler, 2011c).

The voluntary sector more generally is being encouraged to move to a business orientated social enterprise model to fund its work. For many, this will require capital to be borrowed to get them off the ground and driving them into debt (Alcock Tyler, 2011). Alongside this, there is a programme to promote the 'spinning out' of one million public sector jobs as autonomous 'mutual organisations' — for example childrens centres and hospitals. New legislation in the pipeline includes the Public Service (Social Value) Bill which would establish a new 'social value' criteria in the award of contracts in order to facilitate a role for social enterprise and mutuals in the externalising of NHS and local government services. However, the positive rhetoric about the success of selected former NHS social enterprises ignores the fact there is no long term public 'lock' which exists on such outsourcing. Rather than a decentralisation of control, the consequences could eventually be fragmentation of the NHS and ultimately enabling an easier route to full privatisation. As Toynbee (2011) points out, Central Surrey Health run by nurses and one of the new Pathfinder social enterprises, 'failed to win their first genuinely competitive contract, losing out to private group Assura. The Surrey nurses could only raise a £3m bond, while the winners reportedly raised a£10m bond' She adds 'so much for social enterprise and NHS staff security when up against big capital'. In another example of loose definition of social enterprise, Circle Health took over the running of Hinchinbrooke Hospital in 2011 and is referred to as a social enterprise. Yet it is funded by some of the world's largest hedge fund managers (Observer, 2011)!

What can these examples can tell us?

The dilemma facing a voluntary sector organization is whether in becoming a subcontractor to the private public service sector, rather than being in a partnership with a local council service, such an organisation now risks becoming a pawn in the dismantling of the welfare state over the longer term. The intentions are very different to that of a voluntary sector grown by New Labour largely as a community based provider in a mixed economy of public welfare providers with new forms of governance.

All the new public services legislation in the pipeline consistently promote this idea of voluntary organisations becoming an alternative provider to the public sector under the governments 'any willing provider ' strategy. At the same time many medium sized voluntary organisations who have provided local services are now actually folding. Awareness is also growing in the aftermath of the Work Programme awards, that the interests of the Coalition Government lie primarily in a market led system of public service delivery in which contracts will inevitably flow to the large scale and increasingly multinational corporate sector. US health companies have circled the NHS for many years lobbying for precisely the strategic changes now taking place.

Has the sector finally begun to lose its 'political innocence' (Kendall, 2010)? This remains to be seen. National structures if anything, seem to be moving closer to a working relationship with the corporate sector. The constant reference to a role for voluntary sector organisations in all the new tendering processes (which increasingly exclude the public sector from bidding), mask the risks in this process of privatisation taking place. The role promoted for charities confuses the public and leaves the voluntary sector compromised as a 'Trojan horse' or short term 'bid candy'.

However, it is important to remember that the voluntary sector is an alliance of differing interest groups (Alcock, 2010). It includes large charities and medium sized community based organisations drawn into the contract culture as an alternative service deliverer. The national structures of the voluntary sector largely speak for these groups. Yet most of the community based voluntary sector is still unfunded, 'under the radar', or locally funded and orientated. So independent voices do still exist in the voluntary sector. While public sector trade unions frequently view the voluntary sector with suspicion, local alliances of community groups and trade unions do exist with joint local campaigns against cuts seeking to protect public and voluntary sector services and jobs. Local Councils who have been placed in the unenviable role of implementing government austerity budgets, also have a key role to play in forging, engaging with and nurturing such alliances: ones which should aim to re-awaken awareness of the value of retaining 'public' control and renew commitment to retaining local democratic accountability rather than a market driven ideology.

References

Alcock, P. (2010) A strategic unity: defining the third sector in the UK. *Voluntary Sector Review* 1 (1) pp. 5-24.

Alcock Tyler, D. (2011) 'Why push us into debt?' *Third Sector* 13th December.

Aldridge, R. and Stoker, G. (2003) *Advancing a New Public Service Ethos*, New Local Government Network, London (Ch 2 p 15-22)

Bell, D. (2010) 'Welfare state expresses an ideal of the good society' *Society Guardian* 3rd November http://www.guardian.co.uk/society/joepublic/2010/nov/03/welfare-state-ideal-good-society

Blanchflower, D. (2011) 'Those who call for austerity are calling for the second great depression' *The New Statesman* http://www.newstatesman.com/blogs/david-blanchflower/2011/06/economy-wing-fiscal-mpc

Butler, P. (2011) 'The reform agenda is fast losing allies' *Society Guardian* 13th July

Butler, P. (2011b) Cuts: are charities getting a fair share of the 'back to work' business? *Society Guardian* 1st April http://www.guardian.co.uk/society/patrick-butler-cuts-blog/2011/apr/01/are-charities-getting-a-fair-share-of-welfare-business?INTCMP=SRCH

Butler, P. (2011c) 'There is little charity in the work programme ' *SocietyGuardian* 11th October

Cabinet Office (2011) *Open Public Services White Paper* 11th July. http://www.cabinetoffice.gov.uk/resource-library/open-public-services-white-paper

Clarke, J. (2007) 'It's not like shopping: relational reasoning and public services', in M. Bevir and F. Trentham (eds) *Governance, Citizens and Consumers: Agency and resistance in Contemporary politics*: Basingstoke: Palgrave Macmillan.

Clegg, S. (1990) *Modern Organizations: Organization Studies in the Postmodern World*, Sage, London

Codrea-Rada, A. (2011) 'Is the government right to spin out civil service pensions?' Public Leaders Network 13th April http://www.guardian.co.uk/local-government-network/2011/apr/01/private-sector-artnerships-social-enterprise

Cook, S. (2011) 'Editorial: Forward or back, it looks the same' *Third sector* 13th December

Cottam, H. (2009) 'Public service reform: the individual and the state' *Soundings* Issue 42

Crouch, C. (2003) *Commercialisation or Citizenship*, Fabian Society, London

Cruddas, J. (2011) 'A country for old men' *New Statesman* 7th April

Dorling, D. (2010) *Injustice: why social inequality persists.* Polity Press, Bristol

Du Gay, P. (2000) *In praise of bureaucracy*, Sage, London

Du Gay, P. (ed) (2005) *The values of bureaucracy*, Oxford University Press, Oxford

Eagleton, T. (2003) *After Theory*, Penguin, London

Elliot, L. (2011) 'Insights from ecologists show ways of preventing economic disaster' *The Guardian* 18th April

Elliot, L. (2011)'The strategy of stagnation' *The Guardian* 30th May http://www.guardian.co.uk/business/2011/may/30/strategy-of-stagnation

Evison, J. (2011) 'Southern Cross landlords to take control of homes' *The MJ* 11th July

Finlayson, A. (2003) *Making sense of New Labour*, Lawrence and Wishart

Finlayson, A. (2003a) Public choice theory: enemy of democracy' *Soundings* 24, Autumn, 25-40

Geras, N. (1998) *The Contract of Mutual Indifference: Political Philosophy after the Holocaust*, Verso, London

Glasman, M. (2010) 'Labour as a radical tradition' *Soundings* 46 Winter

Hall, S. (2003) 'Labour's double shuffle' *Soundings* Issue 24, Autumn Lawrence and Wishart and also (2005) 'The Review of Education', Pedagogy and cultural studies Vol 27, No 4, October December, 319-335

Hall, S. (2004) Debate on the meaning of the Public Realm. *Soundings,* London

Hood, C (1991) 'A public management for all seasons' in *Public Administration,* Vol 69.1.3-19 RIPA

Hochschild, A. (1983) *The Managed Heart. The commercialisation of human Feeling,* University of California Press, Berkeley

Hodgkinson, P. (1997) 'The Sociology of Corruption', *Sociology* Vol 31. 1, 17-35

Hoggett, P. (2000) *Emotional life and the politics of welfare,* Macmillan Press, Basingstoke

Hoggett, P. (2005) 'A Service to the Public: the containment of ethical and moral conflicts by public bureaucracies' in P. du Gay (ed) *The Values of Bureaucracy*

Hoggett, P. (2006) 'Conflict ambivalence and the contested purpose of public organizations. *Human Relations* 59: p175

Hoggett, P., Mayo, M and Miller, C. (2008) *The Dilemmas of Development Work* Bristol Policy Press

Holloway, R. (2001) *Doubts and Loves* Canongate, Edinburgh

Honig, B. (1996) 'Difference, dilemmas and the politics of home'. In S. Behabib (e Democracy and Difference: Contesting the boundaries of the political. Princeton, NJ: Princeton University Press p257

Le Grand, J. (2004) *Motivation, Agency and Public Policy,* OUP, Oxford

LEWRG: London-Edinburgh Weekend Return Group (1979) *In and Against the State,* Pluto Press, London

Jacobs, J. (1992) *Systems of survival: A dialogue on the moral foundations of commerce and politics,* Hodder and Stoughton, London

Joseph Rowntree, (2011) What *does the Dilnot report propose?* Joseph Rowntree Foundation http://www.jrf.org.uk/blog/2011/07/what-does-dilnot-report-propose?gclid=CImem-6AiKoCFUwc4QodRG5O0A

Jordan, B. (2011) *Why the Third way failed* Bristol, Policy Press

Judt, T. (2010) 'The unbearable lightness of politics' in *Ill fares the land.* London. Penguin Ch3 pp 91-119

Kendall, J. (2010) 'Bringing ideology back in: The erosion of political innocence in English third sector policy' *Journal of Political Ideologies,* 145:3. 21 -258.

Menzies Lyth, I. (1988) *Containing anxiety in institutions: Selected Essays, Vol 1,* Free Association Books, London

LGIU (2011) 'Reaction to the Open Public Services White Paper *The MJ* 11th July

Lipsky, M. (1980) *Street Level Bureaucracy: Dilemmas of the individual in public Services,* Russell Sage Foundation, New York.

London -Edinburgh Weekend Return Group (1979) *In and Against the State,* Pluto Press, London

McCabe, C. and Kirkpatrick, I. 'The NHS braces itself for privatisation' *Society Guardian* 12th April http://www.guardian.co.uk/society/2011/apr/12/private-sector-involvement-nhs

Murray, U. (2005) 'A Narrative exploration of meaning in the public sector' Unpublished PhD thesis: University of Hertfordshire Complexity and Management Centre.

Newman, J. and Clarke, J. (2009) *Publics, Politics & Power: Remaking the public in public services* London, Sage

Obholzer, A. and Roberts, V. Z. (eds) (1994) *The Unconscious at Work,* Routledge, London

Observer Business Leader (2011) 'Circle Health: the social enterprise run by the world's largest hedge fund managers' *The Observer* 13th November.

Pollock, A. M. (2004) *NHS plc: The privatisation of our health care,* Verso, London

Rustin, M. (2000) 'The New Labour Ethic and the Spirit of Capitalism', Soundings 14, Spring 2000.

Rustin, M. (1999) 'Psychoanalysis: The Last Modernism' in D. Bell *Psychoanalysis and Culture,* Tavistock Series, Duckworth, London

Rutherford, J. (2011) 'Poor law Britain' *Soundings* Issue 47 Spring

Skidelsky, R. (2011) 'Britain's economy is stagnant. Osborne needs Plan B' *The Guardian* 21st June http://www.guardian.co.uk/commentisfree/2011/jun/21/economy-stagnating-osborne-plan-c

Steedman, C. (1986) *Landscape of a Good Woman,* Virago, London

Steiner, J. (1999) 'Turning a Blind Eye: The cover up for Oedipus' in D. Bell (1999) *Psychoanalysis and Culture,* Tavistock Clinic Series, Duckworth, London

Thomson, E.P. *(1963) The making of the English Working Class.* London Gollanz

Titmuss, R. (1971) *The Gift Relationship,* Allen and Unwin, London

Toynbee, P. (2011) ' This shocking NHS Bill is without sense or mandate ' *The Guardian* 7th October.

Wilkinson, R. and Pickett, K (2009) *The Spirit Level: why more equal societies almost always do better.* London, Allen Lane.

Young, R. (1994) *Mental Space,* Process Press, London

Whitfield, D. (2001) *Public Services or Corporate Welfare,* Pluto Press, London

Wilby, P. (2011) 'Rampant private equity will mean more Southern Crosses' The Guardian 10th June

Wright T. (2003) 'Defining the ethos', *The Guardian,* October 1st

Oliver Huitson

The Public Private Partnership
The Privatisation of Governance

The supposed superiority of the private sector in delivering public services has complex roots but in its most current guise it can be roughly traced to the collapse of the post-war Keynesian paradigm, the increasing primacy of the individual, the emergence of public choice theory and the ascendancy of neoliberalism. Gone was the pragmatic, practical world of uncertainty and imperfect markets and in its place the elegant completeness of efficient market theory. Only the market, free of government interference, can efficiently allocate resources. It's a world of rational, exclusively *self-interested*, profit-maximising agents employed in markets operating at, or approximating to, perfect efficiency and competition. Public service is a defunct concept. State provision is by nature bloated and inefficient, it lacks the discipline of the market, it fails to respond to price signals and, in the absence of competition, costs and prices remain high. The conclusion was clear: privatise everything, keep regulation to the minimum and let the magic of the market do its work. The Chicago school doctrine went global.

The theory suffers from a fatal flaw, however, that of making practice fit the theory rather than theory the practice, a perverse world where numerical tidiness trumps any relation to the world as it actually operates. Away from the textbooks, markets are often *in*efficient, competition is frequently lacking, agents are far from rational, state providers can be remarkably effective and, as highlighted so dramatically in 2008, human behaviour cannot be accurately modelled via risk algorithms. The whole intellectual edifice on which mainstream economic doctrine was based is now tumbling down and taking most of the Western economy with it.

In public services the consequences have been particularly dire, where privatisation has created a series of grossly inefficient cartels bathing in taxpayers' money. So unsightly has the situation become, and so reviled by the public, that privatisation is now an unword, replaced by the soothing sounds of 'choice', 'empowerment' and a friendly 'range of providers'. What has been lost in the process is the fundamental spirit of public services, the idea that costs should not always be minimised, nor revenues maximised, the idea that civility comes at a price, and a price worth paying.

The shocking case of Southern Cross, blown into the headlines in 2011, crystallised the moral bankruptcy of treating everything as a tradable commodity. In May, following the exposure of major abuse in the Winterbourne View hospital by Panorama, the extent to which private care homes had taken over was beginning to dawn on the public. Just months later, Southern Cross, the biggest private provider, would collapse. It could no longer afford the rent on its properties — properties sold off and leased back by its private equity owners, Blackstone, to prepare the firm for resale. While the nation reeled at the crisis unfolding in elderly care, Blackstone had made around £500m in profit. In modern Britain, even the elderly and the dying are fair game for asset stripping.

This chapter will look at four areas: the Private Finance Initiative, the privatisation of British Rail, procurement at the Ministry of Defence and, finally, the growing reliance on private consultants and the 'revolving door' phenomenon. In examining the merits of the private sector in public provision, the recurring question is no longer whether the system 'works', but rather who it works *for*.

Private Finance Initiative: The Scandal that Refuses to Break

The Private Finance Initiative is a way of funding public infrastructure projects with private capital. As opposed to standard procurement, under PFI arrangements private consortiums raise the finance needed, construct and maintain the buildings required and lease them back to the government for a yearly fee, typically on 30 year contracts. In the UK, PFI has been heavily criticised yet this is barely covered in the media. The latest Treasury Committee report[1] was not a story, despite once more exposing that the PFI scheme is expensive, inflexible, prone to sub-standard building quality and theoretically unsound. The public should be enraged that they are paying hundreds of billions of pounds for a scheme so riddled with failures in both theory and practice. Parliament knows PFI to be a sham, as the MPs report shows, but will it do anything to halt it?

In Opposition, George Osborne described Labour's PFI model as 'discredited'. (Over £260bn of PFI commitments were accrued by the

---

[1]   Treasury Committee report on the Private Finance Initiative, August 2011

time Labour left office for buildings valued at around £60bn.) Yet Osborne has taken forward 61 PFI projects worth £6.9bn in just a year. What happened to the Coalition's message that spending on the national credit card is the road to ruin and a theft from future generations?

The following from the PFI report could hardly be more damning [my **bolds**].

> The cost of capital for a typical PFI project is currently over 8% — double the long term government gilt rate of approximately 4%. The difference in finance costs means that **PFI projects are significantly more expensive to fund over the life of a project** ...

> We have not seen clear evidence of savings and benefits in other areas of PFI projects which are sufficient to offset this significantly higher cost of finance. Evidence we studied suggests that the out-turn costs of construction and service provision are broadly similar between PFI and traditional procured projects, although **in some areas PFI seems to perform more poorly**. For example we heard that design innovation was worse [and] building quality was of a lower standard in PFI buildings. **PFI is also inherently inflexible, especially for NHS projects**.

The cost of private finance may now be a full *double* the cost of government borrowing, but it has always been considerably more expensive and for obvious reasons: corporations are a much higher lending risk than governments. The tightness of credit post-2008 is not a new phenomenon afflicting an otherwise sound model, it has merely exacerbated an already glaring fault.

In evidence submitted by Mark Hellowell the seriousness of the problem is made clear: for just one project, the Royal Liverpool and Broadgreen University Hospital NHS Trust, the higher cost of financing alone will add £175m to the cost of the project as compared to standard procurement: 'the government could have secured 71% more investment by borrowing on its own account'.[2] PFI financing, the report concludes, is now 'extremely inefficient'. It has never been otherwise. The original case for PFI, that private efficiencies would drive value for money, bears not even a passing semblance to reality. The MPs report, to its credit, goes a long way to confirming just how deep the fantasy goes.

Part of the rationale for the enormous fees paid to PFI providers is that risk is transferred from public to private; if the project fails, the private provider shoulders the cost. That the taxpayer has paid substantially for this risk is not disputed. The problem is that risk has

---

[2]   ibid, p. 17

rarely been transferred: it is still the taxpayer who picks up the pieces. On the efficiency of PFI risk transfer, Professor Helm told the Committee that 'it is quite hard to think of many other aspects of the British economy that are more inefficient than that risk allocation'.

Construction risk is the single area where risk has at times been transferred successfully. Andy Friend, for example, cites failures at the National Physics Laboratory project which saw his firm, John Laing Plc, 'book £68m of losses'. The PPP (public private partnership) for upgrading the London Underground, in comparison, saw the public book losses of £1.7bn when Metronet folded, coupled with £710m to bailout, and buy-out, the second partner—Tube Lines.[3] Where heavy losses are concerned, public is always the preferred option. Not only is it unrealistic to expect genuine risk to transfer to the contractor for a public project—'the government is ultimately accountable for the delivery of public services'—but even if risk transfer were the goal PFI is still not necessary; the report finds turnkey contracts could transfer risk equally well, and without the 30 year contract.

On building quality, the Royal Institute of Architects stated that 'the quality of the buildings delivered through PFI schemes remained poor in many cases'. Why? To 'maintain the contractor's preferred levels of profitability'. Citing a study by the Audit Commission in 2003, the report states that though building costs between PFI and non-PFI schools were largely similar, 'it did find that the quality of PFI schools was significantly worse than that of the traditionally funded schools'.

The problems don't stop there. Contrary to notions of private efficiency, the report finds that 31% of PFI projects are delivered late and 35% run over budget. MPs found PFI 'inherently inflexible'; there was 'little evidence of the benefits of these arrangements, but much evidence about the drawbacks, especially for NHS projects'.

On competition, due to the excessive costs of failed bids—£2m per school and £12m per hospital—PFI is highly uncompetitive. In a third of the projects the NAO assessed, there were only 2 serious bidders. The section on 'assessment bias' is fascinating. In blunt terms, the figures are openly rigged on multiple fronts. Expressing their 'surprise' and 'concern', the MPs criticise this widespread 'bias to favour PFI'. In particular, it is assumed that a full 25% of PFI revenues will be paid in corporation tax and hence offset against cost. As for reality, the FT found that 'more than 90 PFI projects have been moved offshore' and

---

3   'Metronet costs taxpayers £1.7bn', *BBC*, Feburary 6th 2008

cites HSBC Infrastructure's PFI deals where just £100,000 tax was paid on £38m of profits; a rate of less than 0.3%.[4]

Finally, on value for money, it is found that the financing costs of PFI are now 'significantly higher' than standard procurement:

> We have not seen evidence to suggest that this inefficient method of financing has been offset by the perceived benefits of PFI from increased risk transfer. On the contrary there is evidence of the opposite.

What then is the attraction to overpriced, late, poor quality, inflexible and uncompetitive procurement? The report suggests PFI has been favoured for its accounting benefits, keeping government borrowing off the balance sheet. Due to changes in accounting methodology in 2009, PFI projects are now on departmental balance sheets but, crucially, not the National Accounts depicting deficits and debt. If our PFI obligations were all brought on to the balance sheet it would add an additional 2.5% GDP, or £35bn, to the national debt.

Whilst this is clearly an attraction, PFI should be considered in the wider milieu of 21st century England: public services are significantly geared towards private profit. PFI is now an enormous industry dominated by the big construction firms, banks and accountancy firms. Indeed, so lucrative has it become that there is now a thriving secondary market trading in PFI equity, the average profit margin on which was found to be over 50%.[5]

> As infrastructure funds increase their offshore portfolios of PFI assets, they will use their power to influence decisions affecting the future management and provision of key public facilities.[6]

There is far more keeping PFI rumbling on than just 'Enron accounting' perks. Westminster, once again, seems to have forgotten exactly who it is supposed to represent.

The Great Train Robbery

The most spectacular failure of privatisation has been, without question, the railways. Fares have grown to such heights that it is now cheaper to fly around Britain than to use the train. Despite the promised efficiency of the private sector, we now have the highest fares in the world. The story of the trains is important in two respects: it not

4   Nick Shaxson, 'FT: over 90 UK PFI projects moved offshore', *Treasure Islands*, June 20th 2011

5   Rob Cave, 'HM Treasury 'in dark' over 'excessive' PFI profits', *BBC*, 14th June 2011

6   Professor Dexter Whitfield, 'Democratic erosion, profiteering and tax havens: PFi equity sales exposed', *Left Foot Forward*, June 15th 2011

only exposes the failures of free-market orthodoxy, but in addition it poses a serious challenge to the nation's representational model; we now have a system run for the benefit of a handful at the expense of millions. How could this happen?

Despite even Margaret Thatcher baulking at the idea, in 1993 the privatisation of the rail network was begun in earnest by the Major government. The policy was heavily pushed by the Adam Smith Institute (ASI), an aggressive corporate lobbying group. Like nearly all such 'think-tanks', their sources of funding were, and remain, secret. ASI's guide to the failures of the nationalised model could be lifted from any privateer discussing any service imaginable:

> State-owned rail networks in many countries have suffered from under-investment ... More traffic then switches from rail, as passengers find the alternatives faster or cheaper ... Congestion becomes more common, and pollution rises. It is no wonder that state rail companies are usually under-invested. So many of them have developed into national monopolies, notorious for inefficiency and bad industrial relations ... In the United Kingdom prior to privatization, British Rail was significantly overmanned, the workforce exploiting its monopoly power to demand large and continuing taxpayer subsidies.[7]

Considering the realities of privatised rail the passage has a rich irony, yet this mentality has been the staple economic orthodoxy for three decades and is applied equally to rail systems, health, prison services, schooling, utilities; no matter what the service, private is best. The state is inefficient, wasteful, it has no incentive to reduce costs or offer good service, it fails to innovate, offers no choice and, due to its lack of efficiency, must charge high prices to cover its bloated costs. The private sector, conversely, are as ruthless in their pursuit of savings as they are innovative in their services. To survive in a competitive market they are forced to find efficiencies everywhere, stripping back costs and driving down prices as they compete for customers. With the state bureaucracy swept away and replaced with the dynamism of the private sector the public could look forward to cheaper rail fares, better service, more choice and less government subsidy to boot. In 1996, the *Mail* confidently announced that 'privatised railways will save taxpayers at least pounds 6bn over the next 15 years'.[8] As has become clear since 2008, however, the gap between free-market theory and reality is substantial. Whatever the public were promised, what they got was a little different.

---

[7] 'Track to Success', *The Adam Smith Institute*, 2002
[8] Christian Wolmar, 'Today our chronicle of the absurdities of rail privatisation ends', *The Independent*, 22nd December 2006

Firstly, on rail fares, the impact has indeed been dramatic though not quite in the fashion intended: fares haven't fallen, they have risen astronomically. For many journeys they have more than *trebled*. In 2009, it was reported that for the first time ever a single rail fare within the UK had broken the £1000 barrier: a first-class walk-on return from Cornwall to Scotland had reached £1002.[9] To put this into perspective, at the time of writing that sum could buy a round-the-world plane ticket, and still leave over £250 in change. In 1995, the last year that nationalised pricing was still in operation, a first-class walk-on return from London to Manchester cost £134. Today, the journey will cost you £399; for the same money, you could fly to Los Angeles and back. Even the Conservative Transport Minister, Philip Hammond, has admitted the trains have become 'a rich man's toy'.[10]

Similar to the methods employed by the privatised energy providers, train firms have brought in extremely complex fare systems to mask the realities of their pricing. According to Passenger Focus, 'so complex is the fare structure that the current National Fares Manual (No. 91) valid from September 2005, lists over 70 fare types, governed by 760 validity conditions, on 102 A4-sized pages'.[11] On one route, London to Manchester, at least thirty-four different fares were found.[12] Though you may find a cheap rate buried in the corner of a website, in practice cheap fares are only available to very savvy travellers booking a long time in advance. For the average user the system is a labyrinthine nightmare and a recipe for being ripped-off. Gerry Doherty, who heads the TSSA rail union, said:

> The rail companies are modern day highwaymen. They will rob the passenger of as much cash as they can get away with it at any moment … Ticketing is deliberately confusing so passengers end up paying for a dearer ticket at all times.[13]

Comparing British rail fares to those of other major European countries (whose rail systems are mostly nationalised) highlights just how extreme our fares have become. Whether for short, medium or

---

9   Jonathan Prynn, 'First £1000 rail fare in history of British train travel', *The Evening Standard*, 6th November 2009

10   Simon Hoggart, UK train travel like the Orient Express? That's rich', *The Guardian*, 15th September 2011

11   House of Commons Transport Committee, 'How fair are the fares? Train fares and ticketing', 10th May 2006

12   Dick Murray, 'How train firms take us for a ride', *This is Money*, 19th May 2006

13   Sean Poulter, 'More than half of rail ticket staff fail to quote cheapest train fares (and that could cost passengers more than £100-a-time)', *Daily Mail*, 25th February 2011

long distance travel, a report by Passenger Focus found that most European states cluster fairly close together in price level. At around *double* those levels you'll find Britain. In the medium distance category, for example, British fares are a full 1.59 times higher than the next most expensive country, Switzerland, and 3.19 times higher than the cheapest—Spain. For longer distance journeys (41–80km) the average European fare is about £11. In Britain, it's £25.[14] Our privatised trains are not just expensive, they are extortionate. If British rail users paid the same fares as in France—around four times cheaper—they would stand to make annual savings of £4.6bn.[15]

Nor is it the case that eye-watering fares actually deliver a better service or luxurious surroundings, far from it: our trains are not just the most expensive but also the most *crowded* in Europe.[16] This won't come as a surprise to anyone who has managed to lever themselves into a rush hour London train, the intense, sweltering dens where trains are found loaded to twice their capacity.[17] Perhaps the oft-cited increase in passenger numbers since 1997 owes more to a swelling population than the opulence of our train franchises. Even Parliament now reels at the cost of train fares. In 2006 the House of Commons Transport Committee, a cross-bench group of MPs, wrote a withering report on the fare system, stating that:

> The industry has demonstrated beyond doubt that it can neither be relied upon to produce a simple, coherent and passenger-friendly structure of fares, nor is it capable of maintaining reasonable ticket prices. Prices for Open fares are now exorbitant … Passengers are being held to ransom by a system that is deeply flawed.[18]

Indeed, economists at UBS have confirmed British fares are now the highest in the world.[19] For a scheme alleged to *reduce* fares there is clearly still some room for improvement. On to the privateers' second claim then, that government subsidies would reduce. What happened to the *Mail*'s '£6bn of savings'?

Prior to privatisation, total government subsidies tended to fluctuate between £1bn–£2bn a year, and in the final year before

---

14   'Fares and ticketing study', *Passenger Focus*, February 2009
15   'Fares rip-off costs UK rail passengers £4.6 billion a year', *RMT*, June 26th 2011
16   ibid
17   'Rail overcrowding 'worsening' in London and the South East', *BBC*, 11th August 2011
18   House of Commons Transport Committee, 'How fair are the fares? Train fares and ticketing', 10th May 2006
19   'British train fares are highest in the world, but London slips down…', The Independent, 20th August 2009

privatisation took hold, it was just £431m. Having implemented the voodoo magic of the Adam Smith Institute, subsidies would explode. In 2006, total government subsidy was £6.3bn—it has more than tripled.[20] Each year, we are wasting around £3bn–£4bn in additional subsidies and, when compared to France, over £4bn in inflated fare prices. Something has gone badly wrong for the British public here. But for the train companies involved the picture is much less downbeat.

Overall data on money paid to our train operators can be difficult to find as the government, for obvious reasons, makes very little effort to offer transparent, accessible data. A Catalyst paper in 2005 reports that subsidies to the train operating companies (TOCS) have never been below £1bn, while other estimates cite the current subsidy in the region of £2bn a year. In what is becoming a staple theme of our 'corporate socialism' model, there have been some generous rewards for failure: in 2002, Connex South East were bailed out with £58m because, according to the Chair of the Strategic Rail Authority, they had 'got their numbers wrong'. By 2005 with the aid of billions of pounds of taxpayer subsidy, the TOCs had paid out £890m in dividends to their shareholders.[21]

The problem was highlighted again in 2011 when, only days after passengers learned they would be facing price-hikes of 8%, the highest rise since privatisation began, Stagecoach announced that it was returning £340m to its shareholders, including an £88m windfall for the company's two founders.[22] With billions in public aid, the train operators provide the most expensive train fares in the world for journeys on the most overcrowded carriages in Europe, and all the while they are funnelling hundreds of millions of pounds into the pockets of their executives and shareholders. What went wrong?

At the heart of the failure is basic economics of the common sense variety, something lacking in the discipline's mainstream for the last thirty years. When comparing public to private the economies of scale afforded to a state provider have been routinely underplayed, at best, while the additional costs imposed by the market system tend to be ignored. The fragmentation of our rail system saw a unified state monopolist shattered into around 25 train operating franchises while 'in maintenance alone ... it is estimated that around 2,000 firms are involved'.[23]

20 'Rail privatisation', ASLEF, January 2009
21 Jean Shaoul, 'The performance of the Privatised Train Operators', *Catalyst*, 2005
22 Dan Milmo, 'Stagecoach to hand £340m to shareholders', The Guardian, 19th August 2011
23 Brendan Martin, 'British Rail Privatisation: what went wrong?', *Public World*, May 2002

To even compete with the state, let alone undercut it, it's worth considering the additional costs that must be balanced by efficiency savings and innovation: there are now thousands of companies involved, each funding their own HR departments, marketing departments, sales teams, legal teams, PR departments, compliance staff, accountants, technical staff, and they will each be paying for separate sets of premises. There are now thousands of senior managers and executive boards, all of whom require private sector remuneration levels. The replication of overhead costs is staggering.

But they still need to find more money: they need to pay bonuses and they need to pay shareholders — hundreds of millions of pounds. Change and strategy can no longer be managed in one organisation but must be negotiated between thousands of firms with competing interests: each wants the most revenue for the least work, the least liability and the least risk. The internal frictions actually reduce flexibility and increase costs. It is precisely because the NHS is a unified entity that it is able to deliver one of the most efficient health systems in the world, despite the embarrassing propaganda of the Conservative party and their donors from the health industry. In a report by Unison, administration costs for Britain's monolithic NHS were just 12%. In the US, with its fragmented market system, administration costs are 30%.[24] For a natural monopoly, such as rail, in what possible world could these additional market costs be offset by efficiencies?

Fragmentation has had another serious, indeed fatal, consequence: safety failures. When the system was privatised the track maintenance was to be carried out by Railtrack, a commercial company created for this purpose. Railtrack held contracts not only with the TOCs but with a large body of maintenance firms; it was a jungle of conflicting roles and interests spread amongst a complex web of sub-contractors. Following privatisation came a string of fatal train crashes at Southall, Ladbroke Grove and finally Hatfield in October 2000, where inter-company wrangling caused a rail to remain unfixed despite it being known to be faulty. That piece of rail would kill four and injure seventy. The safety record of the private model lay in tatters.

Railtrack's panicked response would bring the network to a standstill as widespread speed restrictions were imposed; it simply didn't know what other problems were lurking on the tracks. Facing spiralling costs and compensation payments, Railtrack went from turning a profit to booking £534m in losses. The same year, however, it

---

[24] 'Why we love the NHS', Unison, August 2009

still managed to pay a dividend to shareholders of £137m.[25] With public opinion behind them, Labour finally caved in to the inevitable and Railtrack was effectively nationalised, becoming Network Rail in 2002.

Besides its poor record on safety, the system also lacks a critical element of any functioning market: competition. As was acknowledged in the House of Commons Transport Committee report in 2006, 'most routes are operated as virtual monopolies. As a result, prices can be held in check only by regulatory intervention'.[26] There is no such thing as a pure market in trains and nor, by virtue of the physical requirements of the system, could there ever be. At the outset regulated fares were capped to RPI (retail price index) minus 1% however, in 2003, Labour would increase the cap to RPI *plus* 1%. From a promise that private efficiency would drive down fares in real terms, Labour had sanctioned the train firms to *increase* them year on year— something they have taken full advantage of.

Piling on the misery, the Coalition government has revised the formula yet again: from 2012, regulated fares will increase by RPI plus 3%.[27] Passengers are now looking forward to fare rises of 8% while pay levels remain frozen and the economy tanks. Instead of competition driving down price, we have a political class working hand in hand with the regulator and train firms to ensure prices keep rising.

Having delivered the highest fares in the world, the most crowded trains in Europe, a tripling of government subsidies and a string of crashes, privatisation has been a catastrophe for the public. Indeed, this has been the consistent view of the British public ever since privatisation began. In 1999, following the Paddington crash, even two-thirds of Tory voters wanted full nationalisation of the rail system.[28] By 2009, an RMT poll showed 70% of the public are still of the same opinion.[29] Westminster, by contrast, is firmly committed to letting the plunder continue: all three major parties support the private model despite its multitude of failings. Though hard to believe, the situation appears to be getting even worse. On top of the Coalition upping fare increases to RPI plus 3% the recent McNulty Review takes the journey even further into ideological madness.

---

[25] Christian Wolmar, 'Forget Byers: the scandal was the original sell-off', ChristianWolmar.co.uk, July 8th 2005

[26] House of Commons Transport Committee, 'How fair are the fares? Train fares and ticketing', 10th May 2006

[27] 'Rail fares to jump 8% as inflation rises', *The Telegraph*, 16 August 2011

[28] Alan Travis & Matt Wells, 'Nationalise Railtrack, says public', *The Guardian*, 26th October 1999

[29] '70% back renationalisation', *BBC*, 14th September 2009

Commissioned by Labour but published under the Coalition in 2011, McNulty's report has little trouble spotting the problems of fragmentation or the costs it imposes. Nor does he struggle to see the advantages of Europe's nationalised systems which operate at a fraction of the costs incurred in Britain, an efficiency gap of 40%.[30] But, in line with directions from the Department for Transport and Westminster, he manages to overlook one obvious solution: re-nationalisation. Instead, the report suggests combating fragmentation with *more* fragmentation, more devolution and decentralisation, while adding new cross-industry bodies and, most outrageously, 'managing' peak-demand by putting prices up still further. Meanwhile, a union-commissioned report finds re-nationalisation could save the public £1.2bn a year, and '£300 million alone could be saved by taking train operating companies into public ownership'.[31]

Rail has become a good barometer of our democratic health. What is painfully clear to the British public, the rail unions, the press and academics is that privatisation has failed. Modest improvements in punctuality and modernised carriages are certainly welcome, but with a doubling of fares and a tripling of government subsidy there can be little doubt a nationalised British Rail would have delivered all this and much more besides. The only problem with nationalisation, it seems, is that there's no money to be made from it. There is something profoundly wrong with a political system that allows a handful of firms to plunder the nation for billions of pounds a year, where a heavily-subsidised public service is run for the few at the crippling expense of the many. And not one of the major parties is prepared to stand with the public on the issue. Our privatised rail is another ugly symptom of democratic failure; rail is not just run by the private sector, but *for* the private sector. And it's the public, as ever, paying the price.

MOD: The Ministry of 'Fantasy Projects'

The Ministry of Defence faces a spending 'black hole' estimated at £38bn. Even by the standards of Britain's crippled state this is an eye-watering shortfall. Only the NHS comes close to the MoD's reputation for procurement, a record of failed projects seemingly unhindered by either common sense or financial literacy. The MoD shares some other common features with the NHS: a penchant for PFI, the jewel of private efficiency, and an infatuation with management consultants. Both of which have been instrumental in delivering high-cost, low-value

---

[30]   Department for Transport, 'Realising the potential of GB rail', May 2011
[31]   'Nationalised rail may save £1.2bn a year', The Guardian, September 28th 2011

'solutions'. Not only have substantial profits been sucked into the defence, consultancy and financial firms involved but, from a public interest perspective, the results have been farcical.

Tasked with procuring a fleet of passenger and mid-flight refuelling tankers, the Future Strategic Tanker Aircraft (FSTA), the MoD recently brought to a close a project of such profound incompetence and waste that it verges on the surreal. The overall cost came in at £12.3bn for planes that were six years behind schedule and unfit to even fly in war zones. Underpinning this Heller-esque shambles was its procurement structure: PFI.

Finally signed off in 2008, the negotiations alone had taken nine years to complete, as was noted with 'significant concern' by the Public Accounts Committee (PAC) in 2010.[32] Far from the private sector being agile and flexible, the complex mix of accountants, manufacturers, financiers and lawyers involved in these projects leads to lengthy and expensive delays. Projects of this size and value simply aren't suited to private finance structures; the profit margins demanded are not appropriate for such inflexible and long term deals — the taxpayer is tied in for 27 years. Consequently, negotiations are rarely smooth. As the PAC report commented, the project was 'at the limits of PFI in terms of complexity and scale'.[33]

It should be noted the MoD's own project team advised replacing the deal with standard procurement in 2004, only to be ignored. Pressure to use PFI was clearly coming from central government; New Labour, in its Faustian pact with the City, was intent on using PFI by default. As Alan Milburn explained, 'it's PFI or bust'. On the decision to use PFI without even considering alternative procurement, the Department described the difficulties with

> [persuading] HM Treasury why it was not using PFI, given the strong expectation across government at that time that PFI should be used for capital projects.[34]

Competitive markets are the vital link between private provision and public interest within the neoclassical model, yet it is striking just how rarely reality fits the theory. In the case of the FSTA project competition consisted of just two bidders, in part due to the excessive costs of tendering for PFI contracts. Having selected AirTanker as the sole bidder in 2004 the MoD spent another four years negotiating the deal. Four years, that is, without any constraint of competition

---

[32] House of Commons Committee of Public Accounts, 'Delivering Multi-role tanker aircraft capability', 2011

[33] ibid

[34] ibid

whatsoever. It's little wonder such projects are known for spiralling costs.

It was 'simply astonishing', the report continued, that the need for armour and defensive capabilities was not recognised until 2006, seven years after negotiations began. This was a project for *military* fuelling tankers. To the untrained eye, the ability to operate in warzones would seem an important consideration. Having finally identified this oversight the MoD was still hamstrung due to the inflexibility of the PFI arrangement; late changes would have led to yet more costly delays. The PAC report confirms the Department was 'inhibited from changing the specification because of the implications to the cost of the PFI'.[35] Consequently, our existing Tristar tankers are being deployed for the role until 2016 at a cost of £23.5m.

Private sector expertise also played an important role in the FSTA fiasco. With civil servants deemed lacking in experience of PFI, external consultants were brought in at a cost of £27m. On the value for money, if measured by the success of the project against the fees levied for their advice, the picture is not flattering. Nor does it become any better when examining the role of Tim Stone, the MoD's advisor on the FSTA project. As well as advising the Department of the dubious merits of the tanker PFI, Stone was also head of the PFI unit at KPMG, one of the 'big four' accountancy firms. At the end of 2002, KPMG had advised on 118 PFI deals worth a combined value of £22.2bn.[36] By the end of Labour's first term the company had received around £300m in consultancy fees, much of which was from PFI. With the scheme providing the firm so much revenue, it's difficult to see how they could be judged disinterested parties for advising the MoD on the PFI decision.

Having failed on every front imaginable the project was rightly described by Liam Fox, then shadow Secretary for Defence, as 'one of the most absurd procurement decisions taken by this Labour government'.[37] But the reasons why it failed have much wider significance; the obsession with private before public led to the adoption of a critically flawed procurement model. The Conservative Edward Leigh, who chaired the PAC before being replaced by Margaret Hodge, said:

---

[35] ibid
[36] 'How the big 4 accountancy firms have PFI under their thumbs', Unison, 2003
[37] Richard Norton-Taylor, 'Audit office slams MoD's PFI nightmare', *The Guardian*, 30th March 2010

By introducing a private finance element to the deal, the MoD managed to turn what should have been a relatively straightforward procurement into a bureaucratic nightmare.[38]

Yet PFI, at the insistence of the New Labour regime, was the default model for capital projects throughout the public sector. And there is now substantial evidence, as finally recognised by Parliament itself, that figures would be routinely fudged and manipulated to deliver the right result—that is, to ensure PFI came out as the cheaper option when measured against the 'public sector comparator' (the figures estimated for the cost of conventional procurement). This needs some explaining by those who maintain this preference for the private sector to arise from honestly held intellectual doctrines. The impression given is that whatever numerical fiddling was needed was unquestioningly done. If even the bloated estimates for the public sector comparator proved hard for PFI to compete with, last minute negotiations would ensure PFI scraped through, as happened in the case of a PFI contract for the MoD's main building in Whitehall.

Requiring the redevelopment and maintenance of the building, Modus was designated preferred bidder in January 1999 with a bid of £647m—around £25m cheaper than the public sector comparator. Having made Modus the preferred bidder and removed any competitive element from the process, in the 16 months it took the MoD to finalise the contract the price had risen by £99m. The total cost of the PFI came in at £746.1m. The estimated cost of the standardly procured alternative (publicly financed) came in at £746.2m, a difference of just £100,000. Considering the hazy guesswork of estimating the public sector comparators, the PAC report noted that trivial differences of £100,000 in a project of this size represented a 'spurious' justification for the use of the PFI.

Bungled PFI disasters are not, however, confined to the MoD's larger projects; what the smaller ventures lack in money wasted they more than make up for in farce. Earlier last year [2011], it emerged that the MoD's PFI project to provide kennels for military dogs had spiralled out of control. Signed off in 2000, the kennels were to be completed by 2002. In 2008 the kennels were still not complete: due to inadequate standards they were deemed unfit to house animals. A training school, also included in the project, had to be entirely rebuilt at a cost to the taxpayer of over £700,000. Realm, the PFI contractor, was eventually sacked leaving the MoD to procure new kennels from a standard provider.

---

[38] ibid

Showcasing the value for money for which it is renowned, for a building valued at £11m the PFi structure would see the taxpayer hand over £109m across 25 years. With each kennel accommodating only two to three dogs this equated to around £200 per night per kennel. As the *Telegraph* pointed out, 'double rooms [are] available at the five-star London Hilton, on Park Lane, for £40 less than that'.[39]

Driving much of the MoD's failures have been the new darlings of the political class — management consultants. In return for substantial sums of public money the likes of McKinsey, KPMG and PwC have ushered in a brave new era of chaos and waste. Their track record of actually delivering results raises serious questions about the expertise of the private sector in managing public institutions and services. Having paid hundreds of millions of pounds to PwC and at least £53m to KPMG for their services,[40] including substantial contracts for procurement work, it beggars belief that soldiers were dying in Middle Eastern deserts due to a lack of such basic gear as bullet-proof vests. Indeed, the *Smart Acquisition* procurement programme implemented by McKinsey in 1999 would later be described by the PAC as being 'at risk of becoming the latest in a long line of failed attempts to improve defence procurement'.[41]

On sound book-keeping — something the big accountancy firms used to take quite seriously — the picture is equally mystifying. From 1996, with a brief to 'design and implement the systems, redesign the financial processes and train staff', PwC led a consortium to modernise the Department's accounting systems.[42] Yet in 2003–2004, for instance, when questioned by the PAC the MoD were unsure whether they had overspent by £6bn or merely £4bn. Having blown £178m on consultants that same year it's the sort of confusion one would hope could have been avoided. The departure from reality appeared complete when under questioning from the PAC, the Chief of Defence Procurement, Sir Peter Spencer, insisted that the overspend 'is not money we have overspent on this'. Considering the inaccuracies of the initial projections in question — the projections of his own department, that is — the £5.9bn overspend should instead be considered as simply 'a level of disappointment'. As David Craig commented,

> One suspects that soldiers in places like Afghanistan and Iraq, who cannot get sufficient body armour or properly armour-plated vehicles due to MoD budget constraints, and families of soldiers killed due to

---

[39] 'Army kennels cost more than hotels', *The Telegraph*, 27th Jan 2011
[40] David Craig, 'Plundering the public sector', *Constable*, London, 2006
[41] ibid
[42] ibid

this lack of equipment, might feel more than 'a level of disappointment'.[43]

Alongside PFI the use of consultancy services has been a staple feature of the MoD's troubles. Quite what the fees are paid for is unclear; the end result has been a litany of blunders that have pioneered whole new realms of incompetence and profligacy. It was the very same *Smart Acquisition* procurement programme of McKinsey's that lay the foundations for what the PAC would describe as 'a new benchmark in poor corporate decision making':[44] the construction of two new aircraft carriers. With the order finally signed in 2008 at a price of £3.8bn, costs had ballooned to £5.2bn by the time the Strategic Defence and Security Review (SDSR) took place in 2010. Once that review was completed the costs had risen further to £6.2bn. By April 2011 the contractors involved were reported as quoting £7bn as a more realistic figure. Yet, according to Robert Peston, 'one defence industry veteran said the final bill was bound to be nearer £10bn'.[45]

As for the end result, one of the two carriers, The Prince of Wales, is to be mothballed as soon as it's built—a floating monument to ineptitude. The remaining Queen Elizabeth is not expected to enter service until 2019—at which point it's unlikely we'll even have any planes to fly from her. On top of the delays and enormous overspend involved Britain will be without a functioning carrier for the best part of a decade. One of the last words you would use to describe this abortive *Acquisition* would be 'smart'.

The myth of private efficiency is crucial to what Liam Fox, then Defence Secretary, described as the Department's susceptibility to 'fantasy projects'.[46] It is a myth that has led to both the widespread, and disastrous, use of PFI as a procurement model and the repeated use of management consultants who have failed to deliver. But this catalogue of fiascos has not been without its winners—for the accountants, banks, consultants and construction firms involved, many of whom are deeply enmeshed within the political class, it has delivered a profits bonanza.

---

[43] ibid

[44] House of Commons Public Accounts Committee, 'The Major Projects report 2010', 2011

[45] Robert Peston, 'Aircraft carrier costs to rise by at least a billion (again)', BBC, 28th April 2011

[46] 'Fox says "fantasy" defence equipment spending must end', BBC, 22nd February 2011

Consultants: The Rise of the Shadow State

A reliance on consultants was not, sadly, confined to the MoD. Under New Labour they would come to parasitize almost all State departments leaving the familiar trail of the good, the bad and the farcical—all of which seem to be charged at the standard industry rate: exorbitant. But they would come to play a major role in managing the Blairite assault on public provision at ground level. In doing so, they became pivotal actors in many of the worst disasters the public sector has witnessed in recent times.

The amount spent on consultants 'more than quadrupled under the Blair government, reaching a high water mark of £1.8bn spent by central government in 2005-6, and a further £1bn by other public bodies'.[47] Attributable partly to a misguided faith in private efficiency, the use of consultants was also the tool by which Tony Blair bypassed a reluctant civil service in his quest to 'modernise'—that is, *marketise*—public services. McKinsey, the American consultancy giant who became spiritual gurus to New Labour, saw their motto come to dominate the Blairite revolution in public service: 'everything can be measured, and what gets measured gets managed'. Target culture had arrived. On top of a private ethos Blair's real goal was private *delivery*. In his cancelled 2001 speech to the TUC he was to set out his aims in language which is now eerily familiar:

> The system needs fundamental reform ... A national framework of standards ... devolution of power to the local level ... New services in the hands of local leaders ... More choice for the pupil, patient or customer and the ability, if provision is poor, to have an alternative provider.[48]

This, as parroted today by both David Cameron and Andrew Lansley, is the unmistakable argot of privatisation. Blair's speech continued, quite correctly, 'Nobody is talking about privatising the NHS or schools. Nobody.' Indeed, the political class take great care never to *talk* about 'privatisation'. But what Blair began, and the Coalition is now finishing, is exactly that. And consultants, not civil servants, were to be the driving force of the revolution.

The explosion in the use of consultants was apparent across the entire machinery of state, though the most extraordinary largesse was reserved for the Department of Trade and Industry, the MoD and the Department of Health (DoH). It was here, at the DoH, that one project

---

47 David Beetham, 'Unelected Oligarchy', *Democratic Audit*, 2011
48 Extracts from Blair's undelivered TUC speech, *The Guardian*, 12 September 2001

would set a new gold standard in consultancy disasters: the *National Programme for IT*.

Begun in October 2002 on the recommendation of McKinsey, the NHS *Connecting for Health* (CfH) project is the pinnacle of procurement catastrophes, weaving together foul-ups from its full range of ill-conceived units. That the overall aim would be beneficial is not in question; a unified, comprehensive IT system for patient records and bookings across the country would be a serious improvement to the functioning of the health service. Initially called the *National Programme for IT*, Richard Granger, formerly a consultant with Deloitte, was installed to lead the project with a deadline for completion of 2010. By 2006, a hefty £6.5bn had already been awarded to a handful of consultancies. Many of their contracts, however, remained secret, shrouded by 'commercial confidentiality'; that the taxpayer forms one end of the contractual relationship is apparently not adequate grounds for access. One element of CfH, *Choose and Book*, was supposed to improve the process by which GPs booked hospital appointments. Budgeted at £65m, the total cost came in at over £200m. So dismal was the take up by frontline staff that in 2005 the DoH made available £95m worth of sweeteners for GPs to use the system. Sadly, for the taxpayer at least, *Choose and Book* still only managed to deliver a pitiful 0.7% of hospital bookings.[49]

By 2008, the early rollout of CfH was causing serious failures. In one hospital trust alone, problems included 63 patients having their operations delayed, a breakdown in the system of monitoring child-abuse victims, 272 elective operations cancelled for 'non-clinical reasons' and a near three-fold increase in customer concerns over their treatment.[50] By early 2011 the NAO filed its report, noting that,

> ... progress against plans has fallen far below expectations and the Department has not delivered care records systems across the NHS, or with anywhere near the completeness of functionality that will enable it to achieve the original aspirations of the Programme.[51]

The project lurched from one implosion to another before reaching its tragic climax in September 2011, when the Coalition finally announced the dismantling of the project. It had already run up costs of

---

49 David Craig, 'Plundering the Public Sector', *Constable*, London, 2006
50 Jamie Doward, 'Chaos as the £13bn NHS computer system falters', *The Observer*, 10 August 2008
51 The National Programme for IT in the NHS: an update of the delivery of detailed care records systems', *National Audit Office*, 2011

at least £12.7bn.[52] Designed, managed and implemented in no small part by the cream of the business world—consultants—it has been a failure on a scale previously unimagined.

For consultants, the DoH has proved a bottomless goldmine. Spending on management consultants had reached £470m for the years 2005–2008, whilst in 2009 a total of £114m was spent in London alone for the services of McKinsey et al. In terms of value for money, McKinsey's recommendations for the year included cutting 6,000 beds, 1,200 nurses, 600 GPs and 6,000 administrative staff.[53] That their own astronomical fees might be a more suitable area for cut backs presumably lacked the *blue-sky thinking* and cerebral élan required to make it off the McKinsey drawing board. As to why consultants have been so heavily used in health the answer is most clearly illuminated in the Coalition's Health and Social Care bill. Beneath a veneer of 'choice' and 'modernisation' the Blair government had worked hand in hand with consultants to move the NHS towards a commercial model, a project the Coalition is now finishing. Andrew Lansley's claim that the bill is merely a 'continuation' of Labour policy was a rare moment of candour from the Health Secretary.

Elsewhere, at the Child Support Agency, consultants were brought in to implement a new IT system which was finally launched in 2003. What they delivered was a system so woeful that, like *Connecting for Health*, it had to be abandoned wholesale; in 2006 it was announced that the CSA would be closed down. The Agency was reported as spending £1 on administration for every £1.85 it received in child support. It now appears it will be rolled into the new Child Maintenance and Enforcement Commission (CMEC). The CSA is in fact still spending £40m a year to process cases manually because of failures in its IT systems, something the CMEC will attempt to rectify by spending an additional £50m on a replacement system.[54] With the CSA having spent over £450m on management and IT consultants for the project, it's difficult to see exactly what benefit they bestowed. Though the value of consultants can be notoriously hard to measure, to produce a system so poor that the entire agency is closed down must rank as a fairly damning indictment.

In the 90s, Lord Birt brought McKinsey in to help get a grip on administration costs at the BBC. After endless morale-sapping

52 Daniel Martin, '£12bn NHS computer system is scrapped... and it's all YOUR money that Labour poured down the drain', *The Daily Mail*, 22 September 2011

53 Joe Murphy, 'NHS London splashes out £114m on advisers', *The Evening Standard*, 20 August 2010

54 Gill Hitchcock, 'CSA IT problems prove costly', *The Guardian*, 9 March 2011

reorganisations and initiatives, it was announced that a mere £6m spent on consultants had netted the Corporation £255m in savings on administration. When the reality finally emerged it was a little less flattering: consultants fees had actually amounted to over £20m a year, and the administration costs had not fallen at all. In fact, they had risen—by £140m.[55]

In 2003, the system developed by EDS for the Inland Revenue's Tax Credit launch was, yet again, shockingly poor, triggering another wave of faults, complaints and a general operational meltdown. 400,000 people received their credits late including 220,000 who faced major delays in receiving their child tax credit, resulting in nearly 200,000 emergency payments being made at a cost that ran into the tens of millions of pounds.[56] Of those successful payments, 'About one-third of all awards paid—nearly 1.9 million awards—were overpaid, at a cost of nearly £2 billion'.[57] The NAO report into the situation found that 'the Government has written off some £95m of overpayments and has made provision for a further £961m to eventually be written off'. By 2006, the government acknowledged that the system was leaking around £1bn a year and £3bn had been written off for overpayments in the preceding three years.[58] Against billions lost by the taxpayer, the penalty levied on EDS for delivering this useless system was a mere £71m in compensation; so much for the private sector taking on the 'risk'.

In 2004, New Labour launched a project to coordinate fire services, a standardised system that would operate from nine regional HQs, branded FiReControl. This puerile amalgamation of Fire and Resilience —FiRe—was probably the high point in fist-thumping exuberance at PA Consulting, the firm that led the project management. The project itself was an abomination. Costs at outset had been budgeted at £120m, yet the final result was a programme five years behind schedule and a product so poor that it too was formally aborted in 2010—at a cost of £469m. A total of £68.6m was lavished on consultants for this episode, a sum representing 76% of the cost of the project team, with £42m going to PA Consulting.[59] Over half the management team running the project were external consultants. There is no question that the civil servants in charge must shoulder much of the blame but for nearly

55 David Craig, 'Plundering the Public Sector', *Constable*, London, 2006
56 'Revenue chiefs in the firing line, *BBC*, 23 July 2003
57 Treasury Select Committee report on Overpayment of Tax Credits, 2006
58 Kirsty Walker, 'MPs to criticise tax credits fiasco', *The Daily Mail*, 6 June 2006
59 House of Commons Public Accounts Committee report on 'The Failure of the FiReControl project', 2011

£70m worth of private expertise the results were dismal beyond words. The Public Accounts Committee concluded:

> This is one of the worst cases of project failure that the Committee has seen in many years ... with none of the original objectives achieved and a minimum of £469 million being wasted.[60]

Though they have clearly had their hands full managing systems meltdowns and calamitous restructurings, the consultancy firms still found time for the greatest swindle of all: PFI. Indeed, they were leading figures. As Unison's 2003 report noted:

> They help devise and develop government policy by providing secondees and sitting on government working groups. They recommend which tender to accept on individual contracts. They advise bidders. In their own names they tender for and win contracts. They sponsor projects pushing for more use of PFI and PPPs (Public Private Partnerships) ... And they produce supposedly independent reports claiming that the PFI reduces public sector costs.[61]

And little wonder. The 'big four' accountancy firms have advised on around £50bn worth of PFI deals. Their exact fees are, of course, unknown but are likely to be substantial. Andersen, formerly the 'big fifth', produced a helpful report showing PFI deals to achieve savings of 17% against standard procurement models (the report was subsequently debunked). Coincidentally, what reduced the 'big five' to four was Andersen's collapse in the Enron scandal, where the auditor had signed off some highly questionable off-balance sheet wheezes — much like PFI in fact. Another glowing commendation for PFI was provided by PwC who, rather than nitpick over actual *data*, compiled a list of anecdotal endorsements from the managers tasked with running the schemes. The whole racket is a little like asking PepsiCo to advise on 'healthy eating policy', or asking major alcohol producers to guide policy on alcohol control (which somehow seemed good ideas to Andrew Lansley, he introduced both as Coalition policy).

Following this trail of incompetence and humiliations you might expect relations between Westminster and the consultancy firms to be a little strained, however the reality is an altogether more *collegial* affair. Over time the consultants and political class began to merge into a more unified entity, smoothed immeasurably by the 'revolving door' of staff moving between the private sector and government, often with glaring conflicts of interest. In 2005, Sir Michael Barber, head of Blair's Downing Street Delivery Unit, joined McKinsey to advise on public

---

60   ibid
61   'How the big 4 accountancy firms have PFI under their thumbs', Unison, 2003

sector reform, a role in which, five years later, he would be paid £5,505 a day to advise the government on overseas aid.[62] At Downing Street, he was replaced by Ian Whitmore, a former consultant with Accenture, while a former McKinsey partner, David Bennett, took over Blair's Policy Unit.[63] In health, McKinsey secured the services of Penny Dash who joined the firm as a partner; her previous roles included Director of Strategy at the Department of Health (DoH) as well as being the non-executive Director of Monitor,[64] the regulator which is to oversee the Coalition's marketisation of the NHS. Another destined for the consultancy giant was Lord Birt who, fresh from the BBC fiasco, went on to work as an unpaid adviser to Blair from 2001–2005. At the same time, he was also on the payroll of McKinsey, pocketing an estimated £100,000 a year. During Birt's years with Blair, McKinsey won around £40m worth of public contracts.[65]

KPMG have proved another central partner in the running of UK Plc. Sheila Masters (now Baroness Noakes), a former KPMG grandee, would go on to assist in the breaking up of the NHS with the creation of the internal market, as well as leading a large sell-off of NHS property under the NHS Estate review.[66] Tim Stone, another KPMG consultant, became an adviser to the DoH's Commercial Directorate on top of his illustrious work at the MoD (see above). Mark Britnell, who in 2009 joined KPMG as Global Head of Health, was from 2007 the first Director General for Commissioning and System Management at the DoH. His name may be familiar: it was Britnell's speech to the health industry that laid bare the intention of the Coalition's health bill:

> In future, the NHS will be a state insurance provider, not a state deliverer ... The NHS will be shown no mercy and the best time to take advantage of this will be in the next couple of years.[67]

Even before the mass exodus of New Labour's 'cabs for hire' into the private sector after the 2010 election, the door had been spinning furiously for years: from 2006–2009, forty-two former ministers sought advice from the Advisory Committee on Business Appointments

---

[62] Jason Groves, 'Ex-Blair mandarin earning £4,400 A DAY in austerity Britain to advise on foreign aid', *The Daily Mail*, 30 July 2011

[63] Lucy Ward, 'Blair reform monitor moves to McKinsey', *The Guardian*, 16 June 2005

[64] https://solutions.mckinsey.com/HealthTracker/Default/en-us/aboutus/our_experts.aspx

[65] Rachel Stevenson, 'Birt quits McKinsey over conflict of interest fears', *The Independent on Sunday*, 13 July 2005

[66] Allyson Pollock, 'NHS Plc', *Verso*, London, 2004

[67] Daniel Boffey and Tony Helm, 'David Cameron's adviser says health reform is a chance to make big profits', *The Observer*, 14 May 2011

(ACOBA) for approval on 109 appointments.[68] The 'big four' accountancy firms, PwC, Deloittes, Ernst & Young and KPMG, along with McKinsey have been some of the prime destinations for MPs and Ministers looking to cash in.

The relationship that has developed between the political class and business, particularly the large finance, outsourcing and consultancy firms now appears systemically corrupt. In a 2010 survey for Transparency International,

> Political parties ranked as the most corrupt sector, with Parliament and the legislature ranking third most corrupt after sport. The same survey also revealed that the revolving door comes a close second in the public's ranking of potentially corrupt activities.[69]

The pervasive impropriety of British public life might be excused if the results it fostered were a little more promising. What may seem a harmless, if expensive, dose of boardroom buzzwords and fatuous gimmickry has in fact taken tens of billions of pounds away from the nation's frontline services. But what a consultancy will deliver that a Civil Servant won't is enthusiasm for even the most inane government initiative—not an enthusiasm based on their superior efficiency or flexibility, but one based on financial gain. Consultants, being amongst the prime beneficiaries of the revolution, were natural allies and were only too keen to deliver reports on the efficiencies of the private sector: not only do they advise the government on tendering out services but they advise the firms bidding to run them. The safeguards against conflicts of interest are, let's say, less than robust. In 2003, for instance, the Wessex Regional Health Authority hired Andersen Consulting to evaluate the tenders for an IT project. After careful thought, Andersen announced the winning bidder: it was Andersen Consulting.[70]

Beyond nodding heads and tickets through the revolving door, there is a wider democratic crisis at play. And here a distinction must be made between IT and management consultancy. While the former have delivered some undoubtedly worthless systems the latter have played a much more ideological role, pulling the levers of government policy from a position of unelected privilege. Throughout the neoliberal realm there has been a slow process of removing policy from the accountable world of the democratic sphere to the unaccountable, opaque world of the private. At a domestic level, the consultants and

---

[68] 'Cabs for hire? Fixing the Revolving Door between Government and Business', Transparency International UK, 2011

[69] ibid

[70] 'How the big 4 accountancy firms have PFI under their thumbs', Unison, 2003

outsourcing giants now operate like a shadow state, their contracts shrouded in secrecy, their remuneration unknown and their members never subjected to parliamentary scrutiny. The situation is mirrored globally where critical economic decisions are now taken by supranational bodies, such as the IMF and the WTO, far from the meddling concerns of the *demos*. The transfer of policy making and implementation from a public Civil Service to a private consultancy cartel marks an important step towards the privatisation of governance itself. As an executive elite glide back and forth between boardroom and Cabinet room, the rise of the consultant is another clear warning sign that the public-private boundaries are in danger of collapsing.

PART III

Health and Education

Jonathan C.W. Edwards

The NHS: Health as Wealth

Almost everyone who has worked within the English sector of the National Health Service since the 1980s is agreed that something has gone terribly wrong with a once well-functioning machine. Despite a persistent and touching faith in the quality of the NHS amongst large sectors of the public, on counts such as survival with cancer, chances of being resuscitated during a heart attack or availability of new drugs for arthritis, Britain, amongst Western countries, comes somewhere near the bottom of the pile, struggling even to compare with Eastern Europe. Poles who need an MRI scan fly home for one rather than try to get one here. We do not have the worst system — Africa and the USA do worse in various ways — but we seem to making more of a mess of what we have than anyone.

Talking to anyone from electricians to bankers, one realises that part of the problem in the last ten years has been a general bureaucratisation affecting public and private sectors alike. Nevertheless, there seems a uniquely crazy destructiveness in the evolution of public bodies such as the NHS that goes back further. Repeated reorganisation is both a major part of the problem and, presumably, an indicator of its own futility. The pseudo-commercialisation of the internal market is another key factor. The imposition of false outcome targets is a third.

The puzzle is to understand why *we* are making such a mess of things. Why do we go backwards when others move forwards? The more one looks, the more complex the problem seems and yet there is a sense that the motive force must be something simple and powerful. To see the real nature of the problem I think one needs some practical examples and I have chosen three. Others, like Alyson Pollock, have commented in statistical, political and financial terms but I am more concerned with problems at the personal level that do not need statistics to be understood. The complexities become apparent here. I shall then pick out certain threads in terms of the patterns of behaviour that seem to underlie the practical difficulties. Finally, I shall make a stab at analysing wider causes for our predicament. These seem to have little to do with traditional left-right political dichotomies. Thatcher and Tony Zelig-Thatcher were equally part of the trend. In some ways the problem appears to be incompetence as much as misplaced motive. However, I suspect that the shared incompetence is symptomatic of a deeper problem: a failure to understand the relation between health and wealth, as part of a more general failure to understand the strange social interaction we call money.

Together with some other contributors to this volume I might be accused of age-jaded moaning, but this does not withstand inspection. I suspect most of us have had full and productive lives: the concern being not so much for us as for our children. Following my recent venting of frustration in a circulated email I was interested to receive the response from a junior colleague 'thank you for saying that, we would like to but are not in a position to', more of which anon. Something *has* gone wrong.

The Scope of the Problem

This year I resigned from my position as a Professor of Medicine at University College London (and Hospital). To be fair, there was a plus side. The medical puzzle I set out to explore thirty years ago had largely been resolved, at least to my satisfaction—and people's investment in my pension should get a decent return in terms of medical progress. Moreover, I have found another puzzle to play with. Nevertheless, I would probably have continued to look after people with arthritis for another five years if I had not felt that my job had become virtually impossible to do.

The sort of research that I had had success with in the 1990s was by 2010 no longer feasible for reasons of bureaucracy and commercial politics. Most research going on around me consisted of giving mice arthritis for reasons I found incomprehensible. But more immediately distressing was the problem of looking after people—making use of just the sort of treatments I had helped to devise. Increasingly, two thirds of the way through a four-hour clinic (the old three hours suited doctors and patients better) I would pick up a new patient's file and feel that I simply did not have the strength to make a makeshift job yet again with someone's health. The brand new PFI windowless clinic room seemed to symbolise a more pernicious claustrophobia—that of being in a job where nothing made sense.

I could start with that little lightless clinic room. Talking to people about life-long illness and the disappointments it brings does not go best when you both feel you are in a prison cell. We were told it was efficient building design. But this design included a vast sunlit corridor nobody has reason to walk down and a private ward that closed for lack of customers! The desk was so full of computer and printer that it was a struggle to set the casenotes on a corner to write in. The casenotes might contain sticky labels so badly printed that the lab refused to issue blood results on safety grounds. The computer would crash on a regular basis. I could go on, but these frustrations do not make one want to stop doing the job. They illustrate the incompetence that goes with muddled motivation but what matters is how bad for *patients* things have become. I have picked three illustrations.

No Room at the Inn

Perhaps the most frightening problem is that we no longer have a sensible approach to the acutely ill. Imagine the following, only modified for anonymity. A young adult is in casualty with what is judged by the junior doctor to be life-threatening sepsis. Antibiotics are needed and quickly: for every minute saved the chances of irreversible and potentially fatal complications such as kidney failure or brain abscess are reduced a little bit more. The problem is that the patient has been in casualty three and three quarter hours and if she is there for four hours she will cost the hospital managers Brownie points. So the nursing staff decide that antibiotics cannot be given until the patient gets to the ward because it would take too long. Getting to a ward and receiving treatment can take an hour and if someone is not on the ball, longer. The junior doctor offers to make up the antibiotic and give it personally but is told that this is not acceptable. Targets must be met.

Behaviour such as this could reasonably be considered criminally negligent, yet junior doctors have come to accept it as commonplace. Most conscientious trainees get out of emergency medicine as soon as they can.

The rationale behind the four-hour rule is that it may take four hours to identify the seriously ill and what is wrong with them, but longer is an indication that the hospital has not got enough beds. Yet at least until the arrival of the 2010 coalition government policymakers had decided that there were too many hospital beds in London. How this was calculated is a mystery; my understanding is that other European countries have larger numbers of beds per capita. And from my perspective it is easy to tell if there are enough beds. If a patient under my care had a life threatening complication of their illness, or pain sufficiently severe to prevent them from looking after themselves, I needed to be able to bring them in to hospital within hours or days. For extended periods in winter at UCH we were told that we could not arrange such admissions because there were no beds. Clearly we needed more, not fewer.

Managers might argue that bringing patients in to hospital is often unnecessary; tests could be done as outpatients. Yet for a patient with a nerve tumour, whose care had already been delayed by months through a breakdown in the appointment system, I was told that he could not have an MRI scan for three more months, unless I admitted him to hospital. The word 'cannot' plays an important role here. Another argument we were given was that if patients are ill enough to come in as emergencies they can come in through casualty. However, there isn't anything that needs to be done there so it makes no sense.

The sensible way to deal with people who become acutely ill on the background of a chronic illness is to see them in the clinic and if need be, bring them straight in to the ward. However, management came to believe, perhaps rightly, that doctors were bringing patients up to clinic to dodge the ban on 'elective' admission. To discourage this there appears to have been a policy to make things difficult. Patients who needed admission from clinic could NOT go to casualty, since the priority was off the street cases. The patients could NOT go to the ward because there was a queue of people from casualty who might breach the four hour rule. So patients from clinic had to queue in clinic *behind* everyone in casualty but with the same four hour limit, more or less ensuring that they *always* waited three and a three quarter hours.

The craziness of this has several aspects. Firstly, once a doctor has decided a patient needs to be admitted from clinic there is no reason to wait at all. Nothing needs any more time — and there are no facilities in clinic for emergency tests or treatments. Secondly, the four hour rule means they may wait in clinic for hours after everyone has gone home. Who is to look after them? The doctors in clinic have another dozen patients to deal with. The ward doctors need to be on the ward. The nurses in clinic are mostly not trained to look after the seriously ill. On one occasion our specialist treatment unit nurses were told to come and look after a patient despite the fact that they had no appropriate training either. Everything is based on who you can pass the buck to, not who is best placed to look after someone: no commitment to good care, just following procedures, and mostly *cannot* procedures.

Following repeated episodes, distressing for both patients and staff, I wrote to the medical director pointing out that the policy was indefensible. I did not even receive a reply. I decided to contact the pensions department.

The 'Paperless' Mountain

A key aspect of good care is record keeping. This may seem dull but recording which knee needs replacing or whether someone has sickle cell disease is quite important. Much of medicine is now long-term management of health needs to which decisions taken today are relevant for decades. If you suffer a relapse of rheumatoid arthritis and fear that your consultant may not have much new to offer to prevent pain and disability continuing lifelong then it will be more heartening if he has on the desk a record of what you had before rather than having to ask you if *you* can remember, and whether *you* can remember any serious side effects.

Traditionally, casenotes came in folders that contained everything. The system was labour intensive in terms of filing, so not perfect. However, in 1990, if a patient rang with a problem I could walk twenty feet from my secretary's desk to a record store and within two minutes have in front of me all I needed, and somewhere to write down decisions made then and there. Now, half of the patients' records are in files that are kept several miles away and have to be ordered in advance. The other half are kept on a computer system, except that the software is so limited in capacity that you never know how long it may take to access material, with the likelihood for x-rays that you will not be able to. The imminent arrival of a totally 'paperless system' is trumpeted like the Second Coming, while in reality the bulk of paper notes gets ever larger such that even if you have them the chance of finding anything is remote.

The way things have changed illustrates general features of bureaucratic canker—the triumph of form over substance and an assumption that the people doing the job cannot be relied on to carry it out. Casenotes were originally intended as a source of information about the patient. However, by the 1980s there was creeping mistrust of staff diligence. Casenotes took on the role of surveillance. It became a misdemeanour to throw away any scrap of paper, even if it recorded that the patient arrived at the ward five years earlier with a pair of pyjamas and a radio. Paradoxically, this hoarding was to make the record system so unwieldy that by about 2000 it was decided that if a patient had not attended for two years their entire casenotes could be destroyed.

One snooping policy contributed more to the problem than everything else. It became obligatory for every dose of drug to be recorded. There is some sense in this but note that alongside were 'empowering initiatives' allowing patients to take their own drugs, with no record. The medical justification was empty. Presumably because such records were considered so important, they were on thick cards, in fold-out sets of four. The minimum addition to the notes for one act of prescribing was twenty sheets of paper thick. Soon, about a third of the notes were records of drug doses. Then others cottoned on. Cards for anaesthetics, for pre-operative assessments and so on became the norm. To prove that the nurses had read the guidelines for preventing sores every set of notes had a wad of instructions put in it that contained nothing about the individual patient.

Thus, in this 'paperless' era, notes are growing fatter by the month, and there is no sign of any reverse in trend. Absolutely everything must be recorded, but it can also be thrown away once an arbitrary time has expired. Images of a right hand and a left hand come to mind.

The management might say that none of this need be worried about because in a few months all notes will be electronic. Teething problems will soon be sorted. Unfortunately, electronic 'teething problems' grow with time. With every 'upgrade', problems emerge. 'Quicker' software ends up slower. The problem is well known to anyone using a PC. It works fine at first but as you add programmes and update, everything wades into treacle. I met with the people who set up the IT systems and they admitted that their problems were of this sort and that the system they created was so complex that none of them knew where the problems were.

Another fact came to light at this meeting, precipitated by a rather tart response I sent in an email to a suggestion made by IT. Doctors had been commenting that computers were crashing when using them with patients in clinic. The IT response was that the doctor could try a machine in a different room. This is a bit like saying to a Tesco checkout clerk that if their till is malfunctioning they can nip to Sainsbury's and add things up there. It indicated a complete lack of understanding of what their system was used for. And at our meeting this was freely admitted. IT had little or no specifications for performance requirements in clinic.

The whole thing gives an eerie sense that nobody is actually in charge. It is as if the system has become what is known by philosophers as a 'zombie', something that looks and behaves for all the world like a person but who in fact has no awareness of being anybody: 'no light on inside'.

Except that we *are* dealing with people. Maybe there are lights on but not in the right place. Over a period of five years or so I had made comments about the problems with the IT system. The message I repeatedly got back was that others had reservations but there was little point in trying to stop the computerisation juggernaut because it was the brainchild of a top executive that he felt of special importance to his CV and personal prospects. Whether or not this was *true* was immaterial, this was the perception and therefore drove what happened. At one point I was approached by a patient involved in advising on IT who was seriously concerned about the pushing through of a system so ill fit for purpose. He confirmed the view that at the highest level this was the perceived agenda: patient care could go to ruin as long as the executive's chances of personal advancement were not hindered.

There was a time when it seemed ironic that 1984 had passed by uneventfully and life still seemed reasonably sane. Now it seems more that the subtlety of Orwell's prophecy is becoming apparent.

The Treatment Lottery

In my speciality of rheumatology the progress in what we can offer people with chronic disabling disease has been remarkable in the last few years. We do not have an answer for everything, and unlike the situation for cancer, where cures are now the rule rather than the exception, we have few cures yet, but maybe we have half of the misery under our thumb. Many people who would have had too much pain to sleep or to work are now free of symptoms. And even if there is a way to go, the treatments we have suggest that we are on the right track. Two major developments in treatment of arthritis in the last decade came from the University of London. Britain remains unbeatable in terms of research productivity. But when it comes to making use of these new developments we are at the back of the queue.

One might give the government credit for at least trying. As far as I know it was the first to set up a body to assess the value of treatments, to ensure that money was well spent. The new treatments use biotechnology and are expensive. The National Institute for Clinical Excellence seemed a good idea at the time. However, it soon became clear that the prime function of NICE was to say NO and that objective evidence did not really come into things.

The easiest way to say no is to stipulate rigid 'guidelines'. Medical decision-making is a poorly understood business that makes use of a wide range of considerations, often difficult to identify and absorbed over five and often more than ten years of training. It is conceivable that guidelines could be devised that indicate how to make decisions in up to 70% of cases but not credible that they could deal with all. Yet increasingly doctors are encouraged to use guidelines — and required to show that they are doing so.

In the case of assessing needs in chronic arthritis, the reality is that treatment is justified if it is likely to make a significant difference to being able to lead a normal pain free life or if it is likely to protect joints so that a normal life can be led in the future. Nothing more needs to be said if the doctor is well trained in how to judge the patient's problems and the factors that predict trouble ahead. Guidelines are only necessary if doctors are *not* competent.

The current 'guidance' is to assess how many joints are swollen and how many tender, to do a blood test that indicates unreliably the level of inflammation and to ask the patient how bad they feel. All these are added up and a number is produced which is supposed to indicate 'disease activity'. Any properly trained doctor should know that there is no such measurable thing as disease activity, but increasingly they are being led to believe there is. Why should a score like this make sense? There is no good reason why someone with five swollen joints deserves treatment more than someone with two swollen joints. The hip, one of the most important joints, rarely swells visibly even when severely affected, whereas swelling is easy to see in the little finger. The pity is that the scoring system, designed for quite other purposes, was fed to the authorities by doctors who like to sit on committees and invent camels.

The scoring system has now become a means for NICE to justify a NO. Yet not based on any evidence. In fact it is very likely that people with milder disease get more benefit from treatments than people with severe disease. Moreover, other NICE guidelines say the disease needs to be completely under control however severe. None of it adds up. The proof of the uselessness of the system is that for almost every drug assessed NICE has initially said NO and then after a year or so changed its mind to yes.

An interesting aspect of NICE's justification for a NO is that the company making the drug did not make a good enough case for approval. This indicates just how far NICE is from working in the interests of patients. It seems to see itself as a defence of the treasury against industry and makes no attempt to discover *for itself* what is actually best for patients. Would one not buy any shoes for one's children just because the manufacturers had not given enough evidence of their healthiness?

During the process of developing new treatment I found myself faced with various Catch 22s. The drug I had put in to trials was at one point licensed but not approved by NICE. This had the bizarre effect that the people who had volunteered to be in the trials could no longer have the drug. It could be supplied free as long as it was not licensed but once licensed that was not allowed and NHS payment was refused. When it came to the crunch arguing with Camden PCT about the injustice involved, 'evidence' was quoted initially, but when it was pointed out that this did not add up it was admitted that they just did not have enough money.

Another absurdity is that although something like NICE is justified, it is in logical conflict with local GP budget holding, which the present government plans to extend. If a treatment should be available to all, any funding constraint must be central. Funding should not be dependent on what other things other people in a particular area are having money spent on. The whole business of local allocation of spending is suspect. 'Giving money to GPs' really means 'saddling the absence of enough money on to GPs'.

A system so incompetently designed must reflect muddled motivation. Some of the motives are not too hard to divine. One of my patients wrote to her MP about the fact that government policy on prescription of drugs for her arthritis was unfair. The MP, Jeremy Corbyn, took an interest and wrote to a number of people including the head of NICE and a member of the medical profession taken on by the government as a strategic advisor. The latter wrote back indicating that there really was no problem: (I quote) '... However, NICE guidance does not replace the knowledge and skills of individual health professionals who treat patients. If a clinician feels that a certain treatment would be particularly beneficial to a patient, he or she can recommend it even if it has not been approved by NICE, subject to the Primary Care Trust agreeing to fund the treatment.' The first sentence is a straightforward denial of reality, since the problem being discussed was that PCTs only funded what is approved by NICE. The second sentence, despite sounding reassuring, effectively admits the emptiness of the first. It is a great shame that doctors should dissemble in this way, helping management to pretend that a good service is being delivered when in fact we are bottom of the pile.

Teasing out the Tangle

Common threads woven into these three examples of current chaos certainly include incompetence, penny pinching and the muddle that computers have brought in their wake. There are a few more specific strands that I would like to tease out. The nursing profession has suffered badly in this mess and to an extent seems to have been used as a lever for political aims. The trend towards *cannot* policies is a major issue. Last and not least is the question of the extent to which front line staff have been happy to contribute to the conspiracy for the sake of personal gain.

Nurses, Nursing Managers, Nurse Consultants ...

I have often wondered about the significance of an episode about ten years ago when I had the chance to bend the ear of 'a member of the Labour government who dealt with Health' (I think I only saw him once; after that he failed to turn up to his NHS appointments or to have the courtesy to cancel.) I made the point that it was a shame that nurses had to stop nursing and become managers to get a decent salary. I suggested that what was needed was for nursing to be like the medical profession, in which the highest rank, the *consultant*, went on caring for patients until retirement. Shortly after the government announced plans to introduce 'nurse consultants'.

It seemed at least that this politician shared a sense that nurses should be valued for nursing. We now have nurse specialists who do have the opportunity of both a sense of pride in using high level nursing skills and reasonable rewards. Nevertheless, the idea that, to be respected, nurses need to have a title other than nurse is symptomatic of a negative mind-set. We have 'clinical specialists' and 'extended scope practitioners' where we had nurses and physiotherapists. The tacit implication is that just being a nurse is not good enough. It also implies that to be at the top you need to do more than what you are trained for—to 'extend' your scope. Motivating people to achieve their potential is no bad thing but one of Parkinson's laws looms large here. People rise to the level at which they are no longer competent. Here there is almost a deliberate pressure to make that occur because the real reason for 'extending scope' is not hard to find—it is cheaper to have a nurse or physiotherapist extending their scope and doing something a doctor would have done than employing a doctor. The cynicism is transparent.

What seems to be a basic misunderstanding of the public sector ethos is the idea that people are best motivated by status rather than the work itself. What is needed in the co-operative environment of the public sector is an enjoyment of being one of many, solving problems as they come along. Politicians do not seem to grasp that the really useful people in the public sector are those for whom, unlike politicians it seems, the greatest incentive is being able to do the job they want to do.

The flip side of asking people to do more than they are good at is the pervasive sense that nobody can be trusted to do the job. Here the false culture of protocols and procedures raises it ugly head. Time and again we hear someone with a straight face saying that a disaster will not be repeated because 'procedures have been put in place'. What they do not seem to have an inkling of is that if procedures need to be put in place it must be because the people involved do not know why they are doing what they are doing. People who know do not need procedures. Putting procedures in place is *the problem*, not the solution. Procedures are intended to deal with unknown eventualities but can never do so — in fact they make it less likely that such unforeseen eventualities will be dealt with intelligently.

Nursing seems to have suffered particularly badly from the procedure obsession. The reasons may go back a long way. Up until the 1960s most nurses were young women wanting something to do while looking for a partner, supervised by a small number of older women, many of whom may have remained single because of war. Their combined dedication and vulnerability were exploited with low pay and a lack of respect for their skills. Arguably the profession then lost faith in its own judgement. It was co-opted by the bureaucracy. Procedures took over. This may seem an unfair analysis. However, I was interested to hear a personal account of health care experiences on the radio in July 2010 in which the speaker singled out nurses as having lost touch with what they are there for. Only very recently has there been some sign that this might be reversed. Restoring self-respect to the nursing profession such that they can see their job not as following procedures but as solving people's problems is a key priority for English healthcare.

The 'Cannot' Culture

Protocols do sometimes have a place in a complex activity, at least in training and double-checking. The real problem arises when they dictate what *cannot* be done, without saying how else a problem can be solved. A patient calling an ambulance *cannot* be taken to the hospital they came out of a few days before if it is a hundred yards further away from their home than another hospital. Patients *cannot* have their treatment in casualty if to do so would mean they are still there at the four hour deadline. In my case, I was *not allowed* to take a member of my family fifty yards in my car from one part of a hospital to another, resulting in a six hour delay in emergency treatment for the relief of agonising pain. I know what it is like to be on the receiving end. Repeatedly my patients have said they have gone away empty handed from pharmacy with my prescription, because a pharmacist has found a reason for saying something *cannot* be prescribed. It does not seem to occur to people that the patient might come to harm from the imposition of a *cannot* regulation.

One might be tempted to put this down to a general weakness of human nature. However, it seems that at present this is a peculiarly English problem. A colleague on an extended visit from Spain commented shortly after arriving that she had never previously encountered the sort of obstructiveness she found everywhere around her in London. In Spain people make mistakes but if told they apologise and try to resolve them. In England problems are seen as just the way things are; finding a solution is not the agenda. The only agenda is sticking to procedure.

The cannot culture seems to run deep in the philosophy of NICE. We are more or less at the bottom of the league in Europe for recommended use of new drugs for rheumatoid arthritis. NICE guidelines even require the prescription of more expensive drugs when a cheaper drug is available, apparently just because once a NO is in place it cannot be shifted. Saying NO is more important than making sense. There was a time when such behaviour was considered a quaint quirk of colonial outposts. Now it seems to be on our doorstep.

Toadies and Hush-Money

However easy it may be to blame management for all our problems we also need to ask to what extent front line staff collude in the process. One of the recent fall-out stories of the Baby P disaster was the revelation that doctors are paid large sums to keep their mouths shut when tempted to make public statements about poor service provision. Even I was slightly surprised that colleagues were being offered over £100,000 to maintain silence, but only because I thought such *overt* bribery would be illegal, not because of the existence of bribery.

The entire salary system for doctors now draws on a hush-money principle. Dating back to the early NHS, hospital consultants have been eligible for 'merit awards' putatively intended to reward hard work. How the system worked at first, and what motivated it, I am not sure. Putting in extra hours and significant innovation did get recognised, although no doubt there was an old boy network. Whatever the original situation, the scheme now fulfils a very different function.

Whereas, initially, awards were judged by peers, climbing up the ladder is now largely a matter of pleasing local management. This may not be overtly apparent but the way things are structured that is how it works. We are paid to sing the praises of the new system and its managers. Awards cannot be given just for looking after patients. You can only qualify on the basis of work done 'in addition'. Nobody sees patients other than on a contracted basis so the 'additional work' is sitting on committees, mostly chaired by managers, or others with an agenda of 'good practice' that traces back to political expediency. (Meetings are often scheduled for times when one is contracted to see patients so generally awards are given for doing less doctoring.) Thus the reason for sitting on committees is to get a pay rise through toadying. People who join committees to say something useful are marginalised because they cause trouble.

Is this unwarranted paranoia? It might have been, but curiously, once raised, the notion is *self-fulfilling*. This is how junior colleagues believe the system works so they keep their mouths shut at all times. Hence my colleague's comment that I could be critical but they could not.

More sinister is the rise of a group of doctors who turn toadying into a full time job. Rather than toeing the line they aggressively promote support for management antics. They are the new apparatchik, eager to take every opportunity to show their ability to slash through the undergrowth of human hopes and fears and show how uncompromisingly they can champion the cause of progress (otherwise known as cost-cutting). Machismo becomes a more important quality than medical skill. I remember a consultant appointments committee at which the appointing hospital's medical director's main concern about a candidate was not his competence or commitment to patient care. It was whether he was too nice a person to fight his corner in casualty in the dog-eat-dog world of who can get their patient admitted instead of someone else's.

The Wider Reasons

Much of the above might be put down to the natural playing out of Parkinson's laws. However, the patterns of change here are different from elsewhere — this is a new 'English disease'. It might seem that to understand why public service is in such a mess in England in 2010, ought not to be so very difficult. Nonetheless, I am not sure that anyone has a clear grasp of it. I can only offer some thoughts, under two broad headings: social tides and the mysterious business of money and growth.

Social Tides

Maybe our current mess goes back a long way in personal history. To lay my own cards on the table I will summarise mine back to 1900. Both grandfathers, sons of a yeoman farmer and a village baker, won university scholarships. In the Great War one rose from the ranks to Lieutenant Colonel. On demob the only work available was teaching and they reached the top of the profession, one also becoming a priest. Neither was a socialist but my parents, who became public service professionals after another war, were. The grandchildren were less sure about politics but retained a public service work ethic. The next generation seems savvy but even more unsure.

My thought is that we have been through a century of major upward social mobility, giving rise to an education-centred ethos that together with war (and population displacement) emphasised communal values. I grew up in the culture of school, not the market. Some would say this was a naïve culture but as the economic growth spurt of the last two centuries evaporates I think maybe not. This social mobility has now largely ceased, and I suspect not because of prejudice but because most of the major shifting that was going to occur has done so.

Cessation of change itself brings change. I wonder if the English problem is that we enter social change first — industrial revolution, universal education, public broadcasting, public health insurance — and as a result suffer the effects of deceleration first. Once impetus is lost the moss of bureaucracy and incompetence gathers. Change becomes empty: new logos, reorganisations for short-term political gains. I do not think that the newer generations are in any way less morally equipped; it is just that the imperative and the atmosphere may no longer be there.

It might seem hard to relate our poor state to the loss of social strata to move up in, when continental Europe was supposed to have lost formal class structure long ago. However, in truth, continental Europe is still much more hierarchical in professional terms than the UK. That hierarchy may bring with it a continued sense of pride in civic structure that we lack. Ironically there may be a price to pay for a truly egalitarian society.

Thus, paradoxically, our early development of the NHS may have worked against us. When the NHS was set up Spain was still a military dictatorship and there was still racial segregation in the southern USA. Modern medical technology really only started in the 1970s. The British supply-led system was kept 'lean' while commercial demand-led systems expanded in continental Europe. Lean then became penny-pinching. When public health insurance became general to continental Europe it evolved in a context of growth, at a time when this was appropriate. That has not been without its costs in countries such as France and Spain, but has at least meant that facilities are adequate. At the time when investment in building was most needed in England, in the 1980s, the political landscape had changed.

We also seem to have the problem of hankering after the USA approach despite the fact that in terms of public services the USA seems either to have slid further down than we have or never actually got started. Our trains were the first, now they are less good than in Europe; in the USA they are non-existent. The USA never took on universal health care. 'Poor' in the USA is a codeword for black (or

Hispanic brown). Much of the USA has, in reality, never accepted the right of everyone to share health benefits, although ironically the very poor get access even to the most expensive drugs. To ape such a deeply divisive culture is insane.

The whole picture now is one of dither and muddle and I suspect that at root this has to do with a failure to understand that change itself changes. Predictions from previous patterns are no good, as Mr G Brown discovered, and particularly in the context of money.

Money and Growth

At the bottom of all our problems is money, and perhaps in particular the problem that people do not understand what money is. The woes of the NHS are in large part a matter of underfunding. Certainly during the 1980s and 1990s we were way behind in health expenditure. But what has been an even worse problem is the cost of trying to cut expenditure. Negative change is expensive. The fact that spending has increased is not the point. A cutting agenda wastes money.

The strategy for driving down costs, under both political parties, has been to introduce 'competition'. What does not appear to have been understood is that competition inevitably means a drive to do more and spend more. Healthcare is one of very few elements of a national economy with a potential for using up resources that, although not limitless, threatens to be greater than can possibly be afforded. The imperative is to minimise activity. A drug company wishes its drug to be taken as often as possible. The public want to use it as rarely as possible. A surgeon in the private sector wants to do as many operations as possible. The public wants as few operations as they actually need.

Commercial competition will drive cost per item down but only on the basis that total spending goes up. That is no use. Commerce also introduces investment, but again that is only of any use during periods of justified expansion. In continental Europe commercial providers were made use of in the early days to good effect. In the UK PFI was brought in at precisely the wrong time and on the wrong terms.

What has even less logic is competition within a single co-operative organisation, particularly when it involves hospitals, as there is always a need for hospitals in a certain number of places to deal with emergencies. The madness of the internal market is a well-aired topic that I need not expand on here. Nevertheless, people may be unaware just how much time it wastes. Thursday afternoons for the combined Middlesex/UCH rheumatology department used to consist of discussions of difficult clinical problems or new research findings, designed to keep everyone working at their best. Now much of the time has been taken up with discussions of how to make money out of primary care trusts or how to comply with regulations about auditing our activities. Ten per cent of the week is wasted on infighting.

PFI was also a sap on motivation, quite apart from being a disastrous failure on financial grounds. It is very easy to walk away from an institution when it is effectively a way of making money for someone else. It would have been much harder to walk away from a historic institution based on public pride in quality for its own sake—which is what UCH used to be.

In addition to a deceleration of growth inevitable in a world of finite resources there is another pattern of change that I think may be important. There is an obsession with squeezing more and more out of a smaller and smaller public budget, and I wonder whether this may in part have to do with the structure of politics. Over the last thirty years politics has become a more or less full time salaried occupation. That makes it difficult for any politician to suggest spending more on public services because the majority of the populous think of taxation as taking money away from them. The Liberal Democrats might have bucked the trend but now seem to have managed a volte-face worthy of Napoleon the pig.

Even when the amount of tax being collected is going up, it has been made to seem less by lowering the rate of tax on any one transaction—whether a pay packet or a payment for goods. The ultimate effect of lowering tax *rates* is to make it necessary for there to be *more money transactions* to achieve the same revenue. This is usually put the other way around—that growth and economic activity generate tax and thus allow rates to be cut. However, this does not actually mean paying less tax and moreover, the system is a hostage to good times. If activity falters the whole system collapses, as we have seen. Moreover, it is extremely difficult then to increase tax rates quickly because there is no margin in transactions to accommodate them.

People do not appear to understand what money and tax are about. Money is not stuff. It is, at least in modern times, a token of a complex agreement between all members of a society that assumes common interests. Wealth is not a matter of having bank notes, as we saw in Zimbabwe. It is a matter of having well-functioning social agreements that encourage productive activity without waste. The professional advisors of the financial world might smile knowingly, implying that my analysis is naïve. However, these seem to be the people who most misunderstand money (unless of course, as may be the case, they are disingenuous charlatans). They did not predict the credit crunch, yet I can well remember repeatedly discussing on the pavements of NW11 with all and sundry around 2005–6 how odd it was to us in the street that such a crash had not occurred yet. Moreover, my experience of the circles of highest level of intellectual activity, whether immunology or philosophy, is that 90% of people do not understand the dynamics of the questions they are asking. Human beings are not actually very good at complex dynamic analysis.

We hear now that only the private sector generates wealth and jobs, with the knock on benefit of servicing jobs. But hang on. The public sector also provides wealth to the people who work in it in the same way: and jobs, and service jobs. Everyone in the public sector pays their taxes by PAYE unlike many in the private sector who dodge or operate a black economy. There is not an iota of difference in 'wealth creation' if the railways are public or private. Nor is there a legitimate distinction in terms of wealth between 'goods' and services. Is making a car 'creating wealth' any more than making people healthy? One may help you get to where you want to be, the other may help you to get to where you want to be. The idea that only the private sector generates wealth is a complete con.

Quite amazingly, all expert opinion on economic policy, including the Bank of England, says that people should be spending more and not saving so much, because then we will have 'growth'. If so, there is an easy option: the public services need more spending. Surely, this cannot harm recovery because it will generate wealth for health care workers and knock on tax revenues to restore wealth to others.

Perhaps a key error is the confusion of growth with wealth. Growth may be part of the currently favoured mechanism of wealth generation but is not in itself wealth. Two percent growth does not show that 'the economy is healthy'. Activity is not wealth; wealth is having what one needs with the *least* activity. The argument that more growth allows tax reduction is false—the same proportion of the population needs to be involved in healthcare. More growth simply causes more work and more waste. Everyone has to spend more time engaging in more transactions so that the same amount of tax can be collected to pay for health. It feeds the rich and makes the poor work ever harder to stand still. We are at the mercy of people who want to turn UK into a large version of Hong Kong or New York—crowded and dashing around achieving nothing.

This relates back to the issue of tax rates and I suspect that these are at the core of our current problem. I strongly suspect that the basic rate of income tax should be 25–28% starting with the *first penny earned*. Low tax rates on low earnings not only disenfranchise the poor by divorcing their financial transactions from communal benefit; I suspect they deny the low paid a sense of being active contributors to a shared ethic. The low paid would not themselves suffer from higher tax rates because the market would readjust. And if that changes the position within the global market that must readjust with exchange rates too. (There may be free lunches but there are no free lunches for everyone.) If the financial interactions of the low paid contribute more to public finances the only people to suffer are the rich entrepreneurs who depend on people spending money on consumer junk generated with cheap labour. The only problem is transition. Brown's error was to back us into a corner that will take years to get out of. The recent coalition appear not to understand the first thing about the situation, strangely combining the vested interests of the private sector with the misguided economics of the Liberal left that merely plays into the hands of their bedfellows.

Maybe a silver lining to all this is that once the deceleration has caused its pain, there must naturally be a tendency back to stability. It would, nevertheless, be nice to think that next time round the new people might get things more nearly right!

POSTSCRIPT

Plus ça change! The confusion in Lansley's idea seems well illustrated by a comment on Today this morning (September 2011) about GPs rationing care. I read the Bill last week and it includes the contradiction I thought it did. All decisions should comply with nationally laid down NICE rules yet somehow they are to be taken individually by GPs. (Note that this has nothing to do with patients choosing anything – that would have to be the patient's decision, with which the GP's 'business case' should not interfere.) The only thing a GP can decide on is whether or not to DELAY implementing the central rules. Delay is probably the single most important factor in the bad UK figures for cancer survival (and chronic arthritis care etc etc). It is the single most distressing feature of being a patient in the NHS. It is the one thing we want most to get rid of. As I understand it, the French have none of it because they do not have a general primary care middleman in the same way.

I have only just realised that the central absurdity of Lansley is that, arguably, there is no longer any clear function for GPs in this country other than as bottlenecks in provision – i.e. in delaying. The GP used to have the function of providing continuity of overview of a person's health. With group working practices that has gone. There is no function for 'primary care'. Why is one health problem 'primary' and another 'secondary'? It would be cheaper to provide general care in the same place as specialist care – in fact in what is called a polyclinic. The irony is that it has already been proposed that we should have a polyclinic (run by some independent commercial bidder of course) on the UCH site itself. Everything goes round and round in circles. Moreover for providers to be commissioners creates a clear conflict of interest. If indeed we do need a commissioning system to oversee fair distribution of care, as we may well do, surely it should be done by someone without a vested interest in provision (like a minister of health)?

Why is there such an eerie silence from the GPs? Perhaps they sense that by refusing to be left holding the baby they will render themselves as dispensable as everyone else.

Libby Goldby

Secondary Education

What happened?

When I graduated from university in 1958 I had no clearly articulated view on the nature of public service but had absorbed the general atmosphere in academic circles where activities directed towards making money — business and industry — were a bit of a mystery and slightly looked down upon. The ablest students went on to higher degrees and academia, others headed for the professions, law, medicine, teaching, the civil service, perhaps the BBC or journalism. The change in social attitudes since then has been great and mostly for the better; in the 50s, snobbery was rife and the small university educated elite (no more than 5% of the age group) felt a sense of unjustified entitlement. On the other hand, we were idealistic rather than materialistic and had faith in the public sector as a force for good.

Since then, the pendulum has swung; the public sector can now be abused as a wasteful drain on resources and the whole structure of the public services is being dismantled, fragmenting institutions and allowing competition and commercial interests to take over. There was a moment when this could have been avoided, when the weaknesses of the old approach could have been, and in fact were being, addressed without there being a need for a complete change of direction (the 'creative chaos' we are now experiencing). Unfortunately this moment passed and a confusion of special interests has taken the place of a desire for the common good. The attack on the old public service ethos has led to a politicisation of approach, and a willingness to twist and select evidence to suit populist policies in a way that the old style ethos would not have allowed. What follows is an account of how, in my experience, this affected secondary education, what happened and how I felt about it and finally why, in my view, we have arrived where we are today.

I chose to go into teaching. I knew very little about the maintained education system but was imbued with the post war vision of a fairer and more equal society. I had myself attended a very small independent girls' day school and spent four years at Oxford reading

Classics. I did no training, not a requirement for a graduate at the time, as I was keen to start work and be independent. All I knew was that if I settled for teaching, I wanted to teach in the state system, being aware that my own education had been a specialised one that had done nothing to integrate me with the majority of society. As it turned out, I taught for thirty-five years, including fifteen years as a secondary head teacher and, in retirement, have served for nine years as a school governor.

When I started out, it was assumed that my own education had sufficiently prepared me for the classroom. The school system in place was that set up by the 1944 Education Act where roughly a quarter of the age group, those who had passed the 11+ exam, went to grammar schools and the rest to secondary moderns (or in a very few areas, technical schools) and Local Education Authorities had considerable freedom in organising schools in their areas. I applied to a number of grammar schools and it was almost by chance that the first post I was offered was in a school, a Leicestershire Upper School, where this system was being challenged. Leicestershire Education Authority was led by a visionary Director of Education, Stewart Mason, who devised a plan to deal with what were already serious concerns about the selective system. Mason's plan involved using High Schools for the first three years of secondary schooling and large Upper Schools for 14–19 year olds. There was no selection except that, since the school leaving age was then 15, only those pupils willing to engage to stay on for at least two years moved to the Upper School, otherwise they stayed on for one more year at the High School. Although quite unqualified to do so, I taught English and Maths to 14 and 15 year olds. There were ten forms of entry, classes were strictly streamed and we set half termly tests when those with highest or lowest scores moved up or down a class: I taught mainly in the lower streams. I don't remember then there being any in-service training provided or suggested—I was given a textbook and expected to get on with it. I found I loved teaching, the interaction with the young and the collegiate atmosphere of the staff room, and was not initially troubled by the lack of oversight or accountability. I 'passed' my so-called probationary year without anyone ever watching me teach.

However, much though I enjoyed the work, I did quite soon become aware of my abysmal lack of expertise. The gulf between the teaching I had received in small classes of middle class girls in south London and what was required to teach pupils from a much wider variety of backgrounds and experience was obvious. I decided I ought at least to teach my own subject so after two years I found a post in a highly selective north London grammar school, taking charge of Latin. Here too the intake, three forms of entry, was streamed with a top stream expected to go on to sixth form and university and (as it seems in retrospect in any case) not very much expected of the rest. By now, the wastefulness of the selective system, as well as its social divisiveness, was being recognised and more LEAs were setting up comprehensive schools; there was an exciting climate of experimentation and idealism among teachers. This focus on universal education, rather than using schools to sift out the most able, led to the realisation that curricula and teaching methods needed drastic revision.

The traditional academic path, O Level, A level and university (as noted above, only some 5% of the age group actually went to university), could hardly be appropriate for a mass education system and yet it was the entry requirements for university that determined the bulk of the curriculum. My colleagues and I eagerly engaged in the ferment of discussion taking place, both within our specialist subjects and about the general purpose of education. We attended courses and seminars in our own time and at our own expense; I began to acquire some professional knowledge and greater skills. We felt we were part of an important drive to improve the lives of all young people through education.

In 1965 the government issued Circular 10/65 asking all LEAs to submit schemes for comprehensive reorganisation and by the end of the 70s the majority of secondary schools had been reorganised although a few LEAs dragged their feet and retained selection and still do (the Conservative government withdrew Circular 10/65 in 1970). By the end of the 60s, after a spell in the USA, I was teaching in a Derbyshire grammar school which reorganised in 1970 by amalgamation with the neighbouring secondary modern. Reorganisation had created an obvious need for more structured opportunities for retraining and staff development which was met by teachers and academics working together. Teacher training in colleges and universities was much improved, Teachers' Centres had been established by the LEAs, and the Schools Council, a national body working on curriculum and spreading best practice had been set up. There was plenty of encouragement to visit schools where interesting work was taking place. At the same time, academics and educationalists were publishing books about the organisation and purpose of education for all.

Shortly after this, the school leaving age was raised from 15 to 16 and the need for some sort of national school leaving qualification instead of or along side the O and A level became the major preoccupation. Enormous effort was put by teachers and academics into devising new syllabuses and new methods of assessment and a variety of national examinations emerged until eventually the GCSE was introduced with a wide range of grades, intended to provide a school leaving qualification for all at 16+. Through this period, I was a Deputy Head in a North Oxford Secondary Modern, due to reorganise as a comprehensive Upper School. I went on to a headship in a London Girls' Grammar that was gradually reorganising by admitting a comprehensive intake year by year. In both schools the development of the curriculum to serve the full ability range was our main interest.

In the eighties there was a major change of direction. In 1985 I was back in Leicestershire as Principal of an Upper School and Community College. The Leicester Upper Schools had been hot beds of curriculum innovation, good and bad, the teaching staff saw themselves as leading professionals. The Principal was very much a first among equals. The shock administered by the 1988 Education Reform Act cannot be exaggerated. The imposition of a national curriculum, the definition of working time based on a management/workers model, the abolition of the Burnham Committee (which had previously negotiated national pay scales with the teacher unions), the encouragement to schools to opt out of LEA control and receive funding direct from central government, the introduction of formula funding and local management of schools, the downgrading of the role of LEAs—all these developments led to a seismic shift in the way teachers (and heads) related to their work.

At the same time, comprehensive reorganisation stalled. Central government was no longer prepared to leave it to educationists or Local Authorities to set the way ahead. Politicians began to talk up the importance of competition between schools as a means to improve quality and highlighted the right of parents to have a choice of school. An attempt was made to find alternative education providers to finance City Technology Colleges. Rising unemployment led to extreme anxiety about educational standards and distrust of 'progressive' methods of teaching, all of which culminated in an overwhelming emphasis on testing and assessment of both pupils and schools to see how they were matching up to the demands of the national curriculum. OFSTED was established in 1992 as a more systematic way of inspecting schools and ensuring accountability. All of this was against a background of severe restrictions in public spending which LEAs could do little about since their ability to raise money locally had been curtailed by rate-capping.

Under the New Labour government, elected in 1997, there was a welcome injection of funds but no change of direction. The suspicion that public servants were 'vested interests' and somehow just in it for themselves was still there. A storm of initiatives followed to formalise schools' responsibilities for all aspects of pupil development, personal, social and health education, sex education, citizenship and so on. Most of the assumptions that lay behind the changes since 1988 were accepted; national politicians now felt that they, not professional educationists, should determine what was to be taught and even methods of teaching. National testing became even more important. The drive to reduce still further the role of LEAs (or rather Local Authorities — education committees were eventually abolished) continued with the creation of more schools funded directly by central government and the promotion of 'diversity' — as between types of schools, certainly not in relation to what was taught. The original national curriculum had proved far too detailed and burdensome and was gradually pared down, but despite the commissioning of a number of reports, little encouragement was given to innovative curriculum development; politicians were satisfied with lists of traditional subjects familiar to them from their own schooling. What they were interested in was measures designed to show whether and how much improvement was being made in schools, and they were anxious not to offend the middle classes whose interests had been well served by conventional approaches.

The coalition government (May 2010) finally abandoned the idea of a 'national system locally administered' opting for a push towards complete fragmentation, strongly encouraging all schools to cut their links to LAs and to become state funded independent schools. The belief that competition between schools was the best way to raise standards overall was unshaken; choice was what mattered, parents would choose successful schools, less successful ones would close, and with diversity of provision would come innovation and progress. Accountability would be achieved by the regime of tests, public examinations and league tables. At the same time, it was hoped that the influence of teacher unions on salaries and conditions of service (still agreed nationally) would be weakened as these 'independent' schools negotiated individual contracts with their staff.

How did it feel?

For most of my career I felt well able to concentrate on the purpose of my profession, the provision of the best possible education for the pupils in the schools where I worked. My colleagues and I enjoyed contributing to all aspects of school life beyond the teaching of a particular subject. We took part in school plays and choirs, ran sporting activities, took groups of students on educational trips, supported each other when there were problems, helped with duties in lunch hours and breaks, saw ourselves as part of a collegiate organisation. We valued our independence as educators but the other side of that independence was that we were tolerant of weakness amongst colleagues, accepting too easily that every school would have some teachers who were 'passengers'.

Most of us had ambitions and wanted promotion, not only or even mainly for the money but in order to have more opportunities to influence the teaching and learning of the pupils for the better. The work was deeply satisfying. My first ten years as a headteacher were equally rewarding. As a 'first among equals' my most important duty was to involve all the staff in planning for continual improvement. I am well aware (especially in retrospect) of the failings as well as the virtues of our approach, but to me that is how public service felt: work where you were confident you were contributing to a public good and the pay was a secondary consideration.

The 1988 Act changed all this, and it followed a long and bitter teachers' strike that did involve pay. The government, intent on reducing public spending, had offered a below inflation pay rise. Keith Joseph (Secretary of State for Education) took up an inflexible position and was intent on linking salary negotiations with changes in terms and conditions. In the dispute that resulted, the unions did not remain united and the tactics used in some places lost the teachers support. In the end, teachers won a reasonable settlement on pay but had to accept a very different approach to their profession.

Heads' salaries were raised sharply, they received instruction from central government on what to teach, or rather what curriculum we should 'deliver', teachers' hours of work and conditions were precisely defined (no more relying on good will), the head became a senior manager giving instructions to staff and looking after the budget (formula funding was introduced) and dealing with contracts for caterers, cleaners etc., Governors were given powers to reward successful heads with pay above the national scale. On this last point, it is clear how the world has changed: I remember that when talking to colleague heads at the time we all dismissed this idea, of course we would not dream of accepting above scale payments which would reduce the school budget and not be acceptable to our staff. How quaint. Such attitudes could not last long. A few years after this I retired early, not relishing the role I now had to play and believing that someone younger would deal better with the change.

I am not saying that all aspects of the new dispensation were bad, local management of schools in particular had big advantages, but if we are talking about the public service ethos, this is where the threat originated. Crudely put, from now on, the drive was to follow a business model with heads cast as ambitious CEOs out-performing their competitors. Although the rhetoric of collaboration and partnership was used more and more, the pressure was not in that direction: the weakening of LEAs, the setting up of independently funded Academies, performance management structures backed by pay, relentless emphasis on examination results and parental choice, all said something quite different. All implied that unless continuously monitored and assessed nationally, teachers would be slackers and not try to improve.

The public service ethos does survive, excellent young teachers are still joining the profession, many keen to work in difficult schools for idealistic reasons. The stress on accountability has led to better run schools, rapidly rising examination success and vastly increased numbers in higher education. It has, however, also led to a more rigid approach to teaching, too much 'teaching to the test' and a neglect of the wider purposes of education. The approach from the centre has become a strange mixture of Gradgrind-style instrumentalism (schooling is only about creating a disciplined and skilled workforce) and a libertarian free for all (allowing small groups to use public money to set up 'free schools'). Far from raising standards for all, such diversity is likely to lead to greater inequality between schools and a more divided society. When choice is the god, it is not the poorest or most disadvantaged who benefit.

Why did it happen?

There are many reasons why the professional educators ceded control of the agenda to politicians, starting with the shift in the political climate since the 80s and the major social changes which followed the decline in manufacturing industry.

The political weather changed after the election of the Thatcher government and the collapse of communism in Eastern Europe. It appeared that capitalism had triumphed, market forces alone and the individual pursuit of material gain would of themselves bring progress and a better society. The ideal of a more equal society and the state's role in supporting equality faded. Growing prosperity had led to a decline in deference; professionals and public servants no longer received the unquestioning respect they expected. As unemployment rose, it was easy to blame schools and teachers for having failed to make pupils employable. There was a reluctance to admit that social conditions, in particular the still high levels of deprivation in some areas, especially the inner cities, were a real barrier to learning and needed to be addressed. Teachers were no longer trusted to be partners in raising standards for all pupils. Why not? What were the failings of the educational professionals?

Looking back, I can see why there was so much concern. In the excitement of the period of comprehensive reorganisation, it was those teachers at the top of the hierarchy, i.e. grammar school teachers, who mainly had control of developments in the new comprehensive schools. They had experienced success with the easier to teach pupils and the encounter with the 75% of the pupil population who would have failed the 11+ was quite a shock. The aspirations of these pupils did not necessarily involve success in the traditional academic route via sixth form and higher education and their parents in many cases had themselves had very negative experiences of education. It was a stimulating shock and also one that called into question many unexamined assumptions about the purpose of education and priorities.

Some of us were perhaps initially too ready to value social harmony over learning, too complacent about the success achieved in most comprehensive schools and uninterested in the 'sink' schools that existed especially in deprived areas. Meanwhile in the more successful schools new curricula were enthusiastically invented and the diversity of provision among different schools became a headache, especially when a pupil had to move from one school to another mid-career.

More damaging was the failure to take parents and the community with us on our search for more varied and appropriate approaches to education. It is indeed surprising to remember how self confident teachers had been in the 50s and 60s and how little attention was paid to parents. Parents were supposed to hand their children over to the school and leave the professionals to do their work. If pupils did badly, it was because they hadn't worked hard enough. As for involving parents — my headteacher in the 70s strongly resisted even setting up a PTA (it was the progressive teachers on the staff who in the end persuaded him).

Those not in the profession were puzzled by all the changes; schools no longer conformed to what they expected. Conventional expectations were based on the old grammar school and the independent sector. Uniform, discipline and competition were salient features. In catering for a whole new population, in many schools discipline appeared more relaxed, uniform was abandoned, good personal relationships between staff and pupils were emphasised, individual learning and independent thought encouraged, internal exams and competition were replaced by cooperation and group work. These were largely positive developments but there were a few highly publicised cases where schools appeared to have descended into chaos as teachers withdrew from their more authoritarian role. The fact that overall academic standards actually rose after comprehensive reorganisation, that many more students gained examination qualifications and a happier educational experience with far greater opportunities available to them, was lost sight of in an excess of anxiety about the consequences of change, and the fear that the privileges taken for granted by many middle class parents were under threat.

English society was still divided along class lines. Those who had been educated in independent schools (perhaps 7% of the population) and selective schools controlled the levers of power. They believed that competition was the main route to success. Much lip service was paid to improving life chances for all but the attitudes of those in power were conditioned by the traditional, elitist approach that had worked for them. Grammar schools had been largely the preserve of the middle classes; the number of working class children who rose through that route was small. Some parents were nervous about all this social mixing and feared that their children would be held back by less well supported classmates. There was a suspicion that abler pupils were being neglected as teachers concentrated on helping the underprivileged. Politicians appealed to this constituency by giving great importance to parental choice of school, painting an unrealistic but appealing picture of a school system where parents could choose any school they liked.

Teachers must then accept some responsibility for the erosion of trust in the professional. However, when government stepped in to address these issues, teachers were very ready to recognise them and to cooperate. The Education Acts 1980 and 1981 were welcomed on the whole. These required governing bodies to have elected parent members and schools to publish information about their policies and results in public examinations. Parents' right to express a preference for a particular school was enshrined in law and procedures were set up to support children with special educational needs. Michael Rutter's *Fifteen Thousand Hours* (published in 1979) had considerable impact, showing the difference schools can make and challenging the assumption that home influences were all important. Sadly, the chance to build on the willingness of the profession to work collaboratively on school improvement was lost with the teachers' strike and the right wing ideology espoused ever more enthusiastically by the Thatcher government.

There is a great deal of evidence to show that the most successful education systems are those where all children attend comprehensive schools inside which there is plenty of room for innovative and exciting teaching. In individual schools, the most successful are those where there is a good social mix of pupils, with a reasonable proportion of those who are well supported at home and easier to teach. If results achieved by pupils from poor backgrounds are statistically disappointing, it is not because individually they are less able but because they tend to be concentrated in schools in neighbourhoods with a high level of social deprivation. This is the problem that should have been addressed by, for example, adjusting catchment areas, differential funding and local control of admissions. However, one result of the politicising of education has been an unwillingness to look at evidence objectively. Politicians rely on examples that suit their policies and ideology. The chosen route, diversity of provision, reduced administrative control by Local Authorities, encouragement to schools to administer their own admissions, support for the creation of more faith schools or so-called free schools, started by parents with their own view of whom they want their children to be educated with, can only lead to greater inequality between schools and more social division.

Curiously the rhetoric is all about setting schools free and localism, but funding and assessment are ever more rigorously controlled from the centre. There seems to be a constant fear that brighter pupils (who have always done well whatever the type of school) will somehow suffer and a total lack of imagination about what education should be offering the less academic. The real freedom schools and Local Authorities enjoyed in the 60s and 70s to innovate and experiment was exactly what frightened the powers that be and led to the clamp down in the 80s. Teachers will always find ways to subvert the more absurd demands of politicians and do their best to provide good and stimulating education for all their pupils, but for the moment we have lost the opportunity to create a genuinely fair and equitable system that would have given equal value to all pupils.

POSTSCRIPT

It was the role of Local Authorities to plan provision for the benefit of all, which could mean the loss of special advantages to some. This does not fit with the current view of education as something to be sought for individual advantage only. The aim of the Coalition is apparently to remove all schools from LA control (although in truth, since the introduction of local management of schools in the 1980s, Local Authorities have not *controlled* schools in any meaningful sense). The instrument used is the new academies programme and the encouragement of so-called 'free' schools. They may prove expensive.

The original academies programme was introduced by the Labour government as a speedy way to replace failing community schools in deprived areas with new ones, often with lavish new buildings; they would be independent of the LA and funded directly by central government. Of the 200 or so set up, some were very successful, most did well enough, a few did badly (similar proportions as could be found in the regular maintained sector).

Under the coalition, in order to ensure the creation of many more such 'independent' schools, academy status (i.e. funding direct from central government) has been urged upon schools that have already been judged 'outstanding' or 'good with outstanding features', the majority of which are in more prosperous areas. Since there is no obvious reason for such schools to change status, a bribe is offered: they would receive the share of funding that had previously gone to the LA to cover various authority-wide services. In the case of the secondary school where I am a governor the budget is about £9,000,000; the extra offered was a sum of at least £300,000, difficult to refuse at a time when severe cuts to Local Government funding have meant reductions in budgets for all local schools (and in our case probable redundancies). In addition, we were given £25,000 to pay for lawyers to help administer the change. Unsurprisingly, there has been a rapid increase in the number of academies: there are now some 800, out of a total school stock of about 20,300 (secondary and primary).

Public funding is also available for groups wishing to set up their own independent 'free' schools. The excuse is offering more choice to the few. So far some 24 such schools have opened, half based on different faiths, others on demand from various interest groups, parents and others. Like academies, these schools depend on funding agreements drawn up by the Department for Education: perhaps 'government schools' would be a more accurate description than 'free' or 'independent' schools.

Local Authorities, already reeling under cuts, now have an unspecified amount top sliced from their funding to fulfil the promises made to academies and 'free' schools — whether or not there actually are any such institutions in their area. For many this means that education departments are barely viable.

Exactly how much money is being siphoned off in this way is difficult to discover. 'Free' schools have been approved where there is already a surplus of places. Academies are encouraged to increase their intake without LA permission: rational planning for school places will become impossible. The inevitable result will be a squeeze on the majority of ordinary community schools and in the end, presumably, a chaotic system of individual schools struggling to survive as government largesse runs out. The cheerful assumption that the least effective schools should simply close shows a brutal disregard for the fate of the pupils in them.

It takes a truly Orwellian skill in new speak to describe this as a method of reducing inequality in educational opportunity. Confusion results for parents as different types of schools proliferate whose virtues are much hyped but which may well not be accessible in any particular area. What is likely to emerge is a hierarchy of schools with parents feeling obliged to go to any lengths to find places in the 'best' ones. DfE pronouncements on the curriculum also seem to be harking back to the past, to something very like the pattern of the old pre-1950 School Certificate: secondary schools are to be judged on the number of pupils who succeed in passing five specified academic subjects at GCSE O level. Can this is really be an appropriate system for the 21st century?

David Wiggins

From a Humanities Perspective
New Public Management and the Universities

At the suggestion of the Editor, I begin by reprinting a text from which, on the occasion of receiving an honorary degree, I drew an address to graduands at the 2005 degree ceremony at the University of York. Then I attach some further reflections intended to update my sentiments of 2005 and place them within a larger and would-be explanatory framework.

I. Homily to Graduands at the University of York (2005)

1. It is sometimes complained that lecturers and professors no longer care about teaching their students; that they think only of what they themselves will publish next; that, always to the detriment of their students, they narrow their efforts and interests to a smaller and smaller compass. What has happened to their sense of service to their proper constituency (it is asked)? Have they forgotten why, in any larger scheme of things, their own subject even matters?

Such accusations levelled at thousands and thousands of persons are unjust and absurd. But lurking behind the accusation there is something that needs to be understood and assigned to its place on a scene that is much larger than the university.

On the eve of your departure as graduates of the University of York to play whatever part you will play as the citizens of a wider polity, I want to describe for you the external forces which have come to threaten the ethos that is or was traditional to the university — threaten it even as a larger variety of causes has begun to confound the ethos and sense of service which once animated other professions, metiers, or walks of life. Dwelling on the particularity of that which I know about from first hand within the university, I shall try to explain how subversive these external forces are of the purposes one might fondly attribute to a democracy that was concerned for the intellectual capacities, the breadth and independence of mind, and the mental flexibility of its citizen body at large.

2. Once upon a time, it was not difficult for one with the vocation of a scholar-teacher to pursue both parts of that vocation in a university. In the humanities at least—I shall not try to pronounce upon very much else—one was paid to know and to teach one's subject, first and foremost to BA students. That was the first thing, the *sine qua non*. After that, in the time that was left, came what we called 'one's own work'—a pleasure and privilege that was made possible by fulfilling the first duty. In my own case (this was not universal but it wasn't atypical either), a large proportion of what I wrote arose directly or indirectly from fulfilling the first duty. Most directly of all, it arose from feeling sadly discontent with some of the responses I heard myself draw from the state of my subject as it then was (or as it still is) to the questions that students asked me. For, now as ever, some of the simple profound things we still search for in humanities subjects lie only one or two steps from the place where a beginner begins. If one cares about the subject, then one's passion for it is inseparable from a concern for the elementary.[1]

3. A decade or two ago it would have been a commonplace to say that in subjects such as philosophy we have always to renew our understanding of the interplay between the elementary and the speculative or contestable. But why does so little prestige attach now to the introductory (or even to the intermediate) that, as often as not, instruction on this level is delegated to the most junior or inexperienced members of the faculty, or even to hired labour?

One part of the explanation is as follows. Under a new and unprecedented system of rewards and penalties ('performance management') maintained by the Higher Education Funding Council (HEFCE, which took the place of the UGC, the University Grants Committee, in 1988), there is teaching on the one hand—well recompensed only to the extent that there are very large economies of scale—and, artificially disjoined from teaching, there is the business of 'research', For this, wherever its products are highly rated in the so-called Research Assessment Exercise (RAE), a university or its relevant

---

[1]   Compare Leibniz to de Volder: 'We despise obvious things, but unobvious things often follow from obvious things.'

department is handsomely rewarded. As a result (and because research sometimes leads to other rewards, highly approved, in the shape of grants from outside, especially grants that the central administration can 'topslice'), a university teacher's prospects of appointment or promotion have come to depend upon publication in prime or designated journals. A further and consequential result is the accumulation of a mass of force-fed material, produced under conditions ill-suited to patience or wisdom, much of it disproportionate in its bulk to the thought that produces it or to its prospect of being read. Lying uppermost, this mountain of new publications obscures from view all sorts of other work which might bear more interestingly, even if more indirectly, upon the questions treated there. Meanwhile the new duty of the academic workforce to contribute to that mountain has diminished the demands which can be made on behalf of teaching. As a result, the accounted cost of undergraduate teaching has risen constantly. Its costs begin to appear almost prohibitive. Not everyone is displeased by that.

4. Is this not a paradox—a paradox of democracy? We have more universities and more students, and more money goes into universities.[2] For, ever since the Robbins recommendations (1963),[3] that has been the general will. But, in effect, the administrators within the universities and without (i.e. in Whitehall) now place so much emphasis on the money and prestige attaching to other considerations that they are less and less concerned for our newly numerous first degree students, many of whom have barely survived their previous educational experience. Good universities such as the one where I am standing[4] to address you still do what they believe they can. But HMG, preoccupied though you might think it and its ancillaries ought to be with wise investment, is not moved to see the presence here of such students as its investment in anything so simple or important as the mental attainments of the population at large. For when they say 'investment', our statesmen and their advisers think only of bricks and mortar, of glass, concrete and IT, of 'spin-off', of performance indicators, international league tables and the status of UK universities ranked as 'World-Class'. They think only of simulacra. Nobody seems to care what a poor measure these things are of the efforts universities ought to be making to encourage students to find their own intelligence

---

[2]   These words were spoken in 2005.

[3]   On which the reader may wish to peruse Lord Robbins, *Autobiography of an Economist* (Macmillan, 1971), chapter XII.

[4]   That is the University of York.

or advance their own understanding of the subjects (the aspects of reality dare one say?) that they have chosen to study.

Such is the direction. In almost every British university, there are departments and subjects where it is seen now as a weird and subversive act and a threat to the interests of one's colleagues to insist that more attention to individual students is necessary or desirable. If students are not impassioned by the subject they are studying, if they will not learn to work at it over long hours, then whose fault is it but their own? Nothing must be accorded to any individual student that will not be accorded to every similar student everywhere. Anyone who proposes such a thing is branded as a reactionary or an elitist (in which meaning?). I leave it to you to consider what such denunciations show about their authors and to wonder at their shameful abuse of the discourse of equality.

5. Back now to the elementary. Here is a description of one of the greatest mathematical logicians of all time, one who was no stranger to elementary instruction:

> ... he explained everything with such passion and, at the same time, with such amazing precision and clarity, spelling out the details with obvious pleasure and excitement as if they were as new to him as they were to us. He wrote on the blackboard with so much force that the chalk literally exploded in his hand ... Methodically yet magically he conveyed a feeling of suspense.

There are few scholars who are quite like that (like Alfred Tarski, that is). But there are hundreds who have attained a full command of their field and could aspire to something similar. Those of us who were undergraduates in the three or four post-war decades encountered some of them. Where are they now? Such people are now boffins, back-room types, whose efforts (usually in some delimited area which they can make their own) are expected to bring both advancement to themselves and funds to the university from the next Research Assessment Exercise (RAE). The trouble is that, in the humanities at least, this Assessment, like so many of the deliberations of those who now run the universities, engages with little or nothing that gives the public a reason to befriend the universities. Nor yet can it be relied upon to promote the true interests of scholarship, scholarly understanding, or 'research'.[5]

---

5   Some scientists say the same, but such an assertion coming from me would be simple hearsay.

6. In so far as you recognize any of the things I am describing, what will you who are going out from this place do or say? Outside the university, whose every complaint is heard in Whitehall as suspect or self-serving, will you say loudly and clearly, in your own voices and your own way, that no good or great university ever became good or great—or served its constituency worthily—by aiming to be what HEFCE calls a 'world-class university', by brooding on the definition of 'centre of excellence', by day-dreaming in false images of Harvard or Stanford in the USA, or by having its most celebrated scholars delegate to others their duty to hand down their branch of knowledge to further generations? The good or great universities became what they are by recruiting and protecting scholars whose calling told them, in words I borrow from the eighteenth century, that:

> We live in the world to compel ourselves industriously to enlighten one another by means of reasoning and to apply ourselves always to carrying forward the sciences and the arts.

It's no simpler or easier than that. If statesmen will not listen to what you say on this matter, what will you do in order to see them replaced by others who are prepared to break the stranglehold that those who work the system I am describing have put upon the good will and the creativity of the academic workforce?

7. Up to now almost everything that I have said I have said on the basis of personal experience of the condition and scholarly prospects of one particular subject in the humanities and its near neighbours. I have to leave it to those of you who are graduating in a science subject to discern anything here that applies equally well to your own case. But I cannot break off without reminding you of a remarkable utterance in a famous work of science. In the preface to his *Lectures in Physics*, Richard Feynman wrote:

> There isn't any solution to this problem of education other than to realize that the best teaching can be done only when there is a direct individual relation between a student and a good teacher—a situation in which the student discusses the ideas, thinks about the things, and talks about the things. It's impossible to learn very much by simply sitting in a lecture, or even by simply doing problems that are assigned.

It would be hard to find a better statement of what is involved in the formation of good enquirers into anything. How could there be a wiser investment than in the process Feynman describes or in extending it to any who are ready and eager to receive it?[6] Feynman goes on to say that, in our modern times, we have so many students to teach that sometimes we must be ready to compromise. But he could be depended upon to insist that not just any substitute will do. And, if we have more students, why can we not have proportionately more teachers?

Well, there are other ends to be pursued of course and other claims on public resources. But, when money is said to be the problem, let it be insisted that the universities and their paymasters should explain what priority now attaches to that which Feynman calls 'education' — to its perpetuation and its propagation in our whole polity at large. Let the paymaster reckon up and declare what it now costs government and university to have HEFCE, RAE, QAA (Quality Assurance Agency) and the rest enforce a conception of the university that bears almost no relation to the very first reason for universities existing at all, or even to the second ('research') reason. Let the paymaster calculate what moneys could be diverted (within the university and in Whitehall) from maintaining this huge apparatus and assigned to ordinary, first order, better purposes.

II. Further Reflections

The words reprinted were uttered as long ago as 2005[7] and arose only from my own limited experience. But other contributors to this book

---

[6]   More explicitly, for the sake of Scrooge, sceptics and new Professors of the Dismal Science, the question I ask is this: if there are *any* purposes which it is in the interest of citizens qua citizens to promote (either for the sake of the purposes themselves or else for the sake of that which they contribute to the purposes deemed worthwhile in themselves), how can the process Feynman describes not qualify? Before Scrooge and the others answer, I urge them (more generally) to consider the economy of Germany and the status and standing there of higher education.

[7]   Since 2005 three important things have happened. Universities will no longer receive a teaching grant in respect of humanities students. At a moment of financial crisis partly induced by an ethos of debt, students will borrow money to pay full tuition fees.

Secondly, the RAE, on which the university has depended in order to support teaching, has been reorganized (2010–11) not in order to recognize the longstanding absurdity of dividing teaching from 'research' but to reward the promise of immediate utility or applications. That will be yet another distraction — for my subject at least — from that which is elementary, formative and foundational.

Thirdly, there is a new recognition that teaching is important, but no recognition at all either of the damage that the RAE has already done to it or of the indivisibility into separable components of the business of pursuing a worthwhile subject.

will surely describe a wealth of very different examples of the same processes by which practical reason is parted from its proper object and replaced by a rationality of abstractions which is incapable of registering or preserving within it any trace of the deliberated reasons why an end was proposed or adopted in the first place, or of the context for which it was endorsed.[8]

The question all such examples will provoke is how these processes can ever have started in the first place. Perhaps the explanation runs as follows. At some critical point in the history of a country's economic or political fortunes (a balance of payments crisis, say, such as the UK suffered in 1957 and thereafter), at some twist or turn in the evolution of political attitudes (towards the economistic or the utopian, or both), or at a difficult moment in the workings of some autonomous institution or institutions, it has appeared at Westminster, in Whitehall or further down the chain of command, that in the names of efficiency, justice, 'transparency', 'openness', answerability to the public ..., or else in the search for someone or something to blame ..., the moment had come to attend to the deficiencies, the fixed ways, the obsolescent methods ..., of the Civil Service, of local government, of the railways, of the legal professions, the school system, the health service, the fire service, the highways authority, the judiciary, the probation service, the universities, the charities ...

The nature of the reforms then projected has depended radically upon the character and extent of HMG's control or financial involvement in the thing to be reformed. But a pattern is discernible. Reform almost always goes beyond the simple enunciation of better or improved principles by which those who are under criticism are urged there and then to work, act and fulfil their functions. In past epochs that kind of moral or disciplinary exhortation might have been the most that was attempted, with or without changes in the law or the installation of new supervisory bodies. But in recent decades it has usually been held that that was insufficient or even irrelevant. In the age of management and IT, each reinforcing the other in costly fantasies of system, quasi-omniscience and quasi-omnipotence, it has seemed that, wherever possible, the sector in question should be reorganized to dispense entirely with any substantial reliance on the good sense or better motives of ordinary people, trusting rather to their self-interest. In other words, it should be reorganized on the principles of some contrived, imaginary or notional market, of competition

---

8 For the answer to this problem and the relations between ethos and ordinary practical reason, see section 3 of my 'Practical Knowledge: Knowing How To and Knowing That', forthcoming in *Mind*, 2012.

therein, of flexible salary scales, of the measurement of 'output' under 'key performance indicators',[9] and of constant reference (by performers and monitors alike) to the counterparts or equivalents of success in a real market.

All of a piece with this kind of reorganization as it affected higher education has been an offensive against 'the apparatus and ethos of the self-regarding academic producer'[10] — or in our case against the old world of scholar-teachers and the rest which I tried to describe or evoke in part I.

That world had its abuses, which were not always rooted out with the consistency or firmness provided for by the rules that existed.[11] Yet, well into the 1980s — and at the point when New Public Management (NPM) was being spread across the public sector and the Jarrett Report (1985) recommended that the universities be subjected to the practices and accounting methods of British Business (not itself at that time the object of world acclaim) — higher education in Britain was the object of widespread admiration abroad. Its methods of instruction (and some dedicated exponents of these) were eagerly sought out by ambitious young scholars from Northern Europe, especially from West Germany. Teaching loads were onerous, but there were few other claims and none at all of the kinds now constantly necessitated by each and every

---

[9]   In 'The Grim Threat to British Universities', *New York Review of Books*, (January 13th 2011, page 58), Simon Head describes the latest version of the management-by-objectives approach : 'The balanced score-card or BSC is the joint brainchild of Robert Kaplan, an academic accountant at Harvard Business School and the Boston consultant David Norton ... The methodologies of the BSC focus heavily on the setting up, targeting, and measurement of statistical Key Performance Indicators (KPIs). Kaplan and Norton's central insight has been that with the IT revolution and the coming of networked computer systems, it is now possible to expand the number and variety of KPIs well beyond the traditional corporate concern with quarterly financial indicators such as gross revenues, net profits and return on investment.'

[10] I owe the citation (and other things besides) to Keith Thomas, 'What are universities for?' *Times Literary Supplement*, 7 May 2010. Robert Jackson's invective against university teachers was prefigured by the terms in which, twenty years earlier, the Fulton Commission had assailed the Civil Service and presented the case for replacing the Service's methods of administration by 'management by objectives'. For a comment upon Fulton's sloppy, inaccurate and parti-pris characterization of the Civil Service as it then was, see Lord Robbins, *op. cit.*, page 184.

[11] It must have had other deficiencies too. Witness the apparent helplessness of the ruling elite who graduated from the universities of that period and have tolerated — scarcely even questioned — the very corruptions of reason which I have been commenting upon.

new 'benchmark', directive or ukase. In my subject, the work that was produced in that decade or the sixties and seventies is still read and referred to. Nor is that all. Without the bidding of any minister of education, the universities of the fifties and sixties and/or their constituent colleges had gone to remarkable lengths to find school leavers from the public education sector whom they could urge to seek college scholarships or Ministry of Education scholarships to study at the university.[12]

Am I trying to make the reader believe that by some wondrous transformation of human nature, the university under the UGC and before HEFCE was mysteriously exempt from all 'producer interest'? Of course not. I am inviting the reader to compare the avowed producer-interest of a university lecturer or professor who has an ordinary degree of self-interest, or a reasonable self-love as Hume might prefer that one say, but is also possessed of a real attachment to his or her subject and a passion for teaching or writing about it, with the unavowed but no less real producer-interest of the 'man of system',[13] the manager him/herself. I am also inviting the reader to compare the ordinary responsibleness and vigilance of an intellectual community of practitioners whose conduct is determined by their understanding of why their subject is worth doing and worth teaching with the innovated ways of the marketplace maintained by NPM and regulated, not by cherishing the benevolence, the esprit de corps or what Anatol Rapaport calls 'the sense of ought' of the workforce (these things are left to wither on the vine), but by finding more and more ways to steer things through the self-interest of the workforce. This is the set-up whose present trend/tendency/direction I sketched in section 3 of part I.

---

12 By 1938, 437 out of the 798 open scholarships won at Oxford or Cambridge were won by pupils from state or grand-aided secondary schools. Two thirds of these pupils gained exemption from payment of fees because of low parental income. By the mid 1960s, a point was reached where, among school leavers admitted to study at Oxford or Cambridge, the proportion who were state educated exceeded absolutely the number educated at fee-paying schools. In the later decades of the 20th century that level of achievement was never repeated. (Source: Richard Aldrich.) But that was not the fault of the universities. It must be traced to a miscalculation of Mr Crosland's or of Mr Wilson's cabinet, their failure that is to heed the Norwood Commission's 1944 recommendation for a huge increase in grammar school places; and then to the fault of subsequent administrations which decided not to tamper with the comprehensive schooling system which was Mr Crosland's legacy.

13 For an early portrait of the 'man of system' see Adam Smith, *The Theory of Moral Sentiments* (1759), vi.ii.2.15-18.

In the light of experience to date, which of these producer-interests do you prefer?

III. A Comment and a Response

Comment

'But all this has been heard a thousand times before—the loud but predictable complaints of university teachers from a bygone age—most of them coming from the humanities, which now account for a bare 18% of the present academic work force—who are unable to understand the demands either of the modern economy or of the democracy of the second decade of the twenty-first century.'

My response

(1) If all this has been heard a thousand times before, then what was the answer to the complaint? So far all we have is a countercomplaint against the complainant.

(2) If humanities represent only 18% of the university sector, so be it. Does that make it all right for a form of management to distort and corrupt, at mounting expense, the motivations of even as much as 18% of the academic work force? What reason is there to think, leaving aside the 18%, that NPM is more sensitive to the needs of the other sectors of the university?

(3) Everything under the sun is imperfect—not least the humanities sector. But only in the eyes of a crazed utopian could it have seemed that the existence of ordinary imperfection sufficed to demonstrate the superiority of a totally new way of running things which was to be developed from a remote and utterly abstract analogy between a well-functioning university and such admirable but different things as a factory or a business enterprise. The imperfection of the one way cannot suffice to prove the superiority of the other.

(4) I note the democratic pretensions of my critic. But NPM is democratic only in this bare sense: ministers of the Crown who find themselves working on a scene where everything is done already by the methods of NPM are members of a party that is democratically elected. But the real foundation of democracy is the human ideal of the consent of the governed; there is no trace of that ideal in the theory or the practice of NPM.

(5) Suppose we judge NPM and its antecedents by the same criteria that NPM or its antecedents applied to the spheres of human activity which it undertook to reorganize. The first thing we then notice is the staggering increase it has occasioned in administrative costs both at the

centre and in the universities themselves. From a mass of evidence collected by Iain Pears, let me quote one fragment:

> The expansion of management and its increasing separation from the institutions it commands can be tracked in the explosion of administrative costs, of which vice-chancellors' salaries are only the most visible part.

> At the university of Bristol, which in 2006 saw protests by students over what they saw as inadequate teaching due to financial pressures, between the financial years 2000 and 2009 spending on departments rose by 85%, but administrative costs increased by 261% and the vice-chancellors' reward … was up 113%. At University College London, while spending on academic departments rose 79%, administrative costs climbed by 120% and the vice-chancellor's salary jumped by 168%.

> At Kings College London, administrative costs rose to £33.5 million in the financial year 2008–09, from £28.5 million the year before—a rise of 17.5% and more than twice that of the rise in the costs of academic departments. In 2002–03, administration costs were £16.5 million— meaning there has been a 103% rise over six years.

Times Higher Education Supplement, 1 April 2010, page 42.

IV. Producer-interest versus the Public Interest; and the Sense of Public Service

The theorists of management who pioneered NPM and its antecedents began the campaign for the reshaping of the British universities with the idea (we said) of defeating 'the apparatus and ethos of the self-regarding academic producer'. But the arrangements the theorists hit upon have failed signally to protect the university from the producer-interest of administrators-turned-NP managers, an interest no less real for being unself-conscious. If their dedication and persistence has some saving grace, I do not know what it is.

The saving grace of the academic producer-interest was that a scholar-teacher's conception of his or her own interest has often embraced the interests of the subject s/he taught and worked in—and embraced (unless the scholar/teacher was dissuaded) the interests of its students. These concerns furnished a that-for-sake-of-which—an internalized purpose, an attachment to that purpose and a sense of service to the cause of learning and its recipients—which cannot be replicated by any market mechanism. In a world replete with imperfection, is not the agent with such a purpose—provided that this agent have a care also for how the fulfilment of that purpose contributes to the larger set of purposes which the citizens of a country have in common qua citizens[14] – the least imperfect instrument one could find of the public interest in education?

In truth though the public interest – here the public interest in education – should not and cannot be entrusted to any one person or group of persons. It should be entrusted neither to the minister of the Crown, nor to his or her civil servants, nor to the managers at the highest echelon in the array of 'line managers' which holds sway over the marketplace which controls the academic workforce, nor yet to the workforce itself.[15] Besides a university's own internal defences against the incompetences, laziness, false objectives, follies and irresponsibilities of academic or administrative members, there has to be some sort of oversight. Nothing that I have said has been intended to go against that. Indeed, given the damage already inflicted upon the ethos of the university, the matter of oversight is at least as urgent as it is difficult.

So much is clear. But let it also be clear what it implies to say that, for every institution of the kind we are concerned with, there has to be some overseeing body or guardian of the public interest. The thing that is not implied is that there must be one overarching body or guardian – still less some large agency of government such as HEFCE with its supporting apparatus of committees and sub-committees – to oversee all institutions of higher education and translate its conception of the public interest in education into a single set of criteria, universal prescriptions or best practices. If anything at all has been learned over the last twenty years, it is how easily and inevitably such criteria and prescriptions result in perversions and frustrations of the real end in view, namely true education and understanding.[16]

By prescribing very little in advance, the old UGC was in a position to interpret the idea of the public interest in a way that permitted each

---

[14] Compare Jane Green, *Education, Professionalism and the Quest for Accountability* (Routledge, New York and London 2011), pages 108–9. That larger set of purposes needs to be distinguished (as she points out at page 210, note 20) from the 'utility sum of individual preferences' – an inscrutable and internally incoherent totality ill-suited to serve as a signpost for the direct attention of HMG.

[15] Nor even to the students, who frequently complain about absolutely the wrong things, as well as the right ones.

[16] Once these criteria, prescriptions and inducements are in place, there is a constant temptation for agents to stop asking whether they are doing their job properly, concentrating instead on being able to show that what they are doing satisfies some criterion or conforms to some directive. See John Lucas, *Responsibility* (Oxford 1993), page 186. See also M. Griffiths and J. Lucas *Ethical Economics* (Macmillan 1976), page 197: 'The more we limit discretion, the less we can look for in the way of actual achievement or new initiatives'. See also Jane Green, *op. cit.*, page 89 foll.

institution, each subject and each department of that subject to be judged by criteria appropriate to it, to be encouraged to contribute in its own way and explain in its own way what its contribution was to the creation and perpetuation of knowledge and understanding. But, rather than revive the UGC in a bloated and expanded new form to cover a mass of new responsibilities, let us hold out for a policy of fragmentation and a plurality of smaller bodies on which public-spirited persons, persons of learning and persons of common sense, can regard it as an honour, not as a source of emolument, to scrutinize the universities and their works at once sympathetically, frugally and critically. In that way let the public interest in higher education be determined incrementally, collectively and at large.

POSTSCRIPT

The Conservative/Liberal Democrat Coalition has proved more eager than enterprising in its efforts to reduce the National Debt or to look for places where the reduction of management would lead, as in the cases I have been concerned with, to large positive improvement in the thing itself that is managed. Indeed, as a result of the developments described in note 7, there has been a very significant increase in bureaucracy—in the closer and closer supervision of universities' admissions policies, for instance. In response, the universities have had no alternative but to expand their own bureaucracy—at the expense no doubt (and as usual) of academic budgets.

On the level of detail—and saving money is always a matter of understanding relevant detail—the Coalition depends on its advisors. Among these advisors will be officials, invaluable but not, alas, temperamentally disposed to reduce management. From elsewhere and from central party research departments, there will be (or will recently have been) further advisors, some of them subject to special (e.g. commercial) interests or even representative of them. But can the Coalition not look for advisors prepared to venture forth from the closed world of file, White Paper, tick-box survey and party dogma to attend to what happens on the ground, where Feynman's wise words might yet inspire university teachers and their students.

PART IV

Facing the Problem of
Public Service

Rebekah Carrier

Legal Aid
A Welfare Service?

Research commissioned by the Legal Action Group in 2011 found that 84% of respondents believed that advice on civil law should be free to everyone or to those who earn less than the national average income (£25,000). Only ten per cent believed that such advice should be available only to people on benefits. Summarising these findings LAG reported that 'support for legal services paid for by the state was remarkably consistent across the social classes … (indicating) that there exists a strong culture of fair play in respect of legal rights.'

Earlier this year I spoke to a group of students at South Bank University and asked them to predict the findings of the survey and to guess at what the current levels of entitlement to legal aid are. Overwhelmingly the students predicted even higher levels of support for legal aid and (in common presumably with the respondents to the survey) were shocked to discover that levels of eligibility fall far short of universal eligibility for those earning less than the national average income.

Currently few people are eligible (financially) for legal aid and fewer are lucky enough to find a competent legal aid lawyer accessible to them and willing and able to take the case.

It is very hard to even attempt to write anything about legal aid without considering the deficiencies of the current system but even harder to ignore the cataclysmic changes proposed by the current government.

It is also hard to see legal aid practitioners as anything other than firmly in denial: it is likely that few of us will have jobs in five years time and even fewer of us will have jobs that resemble anything like our current jobs. I often joke that my only future is managing a call centre but this has come to seem less and less like a joke, particularly given the proposals for a 'telephone gateway' for all legally aided advice and the preference for even those cases identified as eligible for specialist advice (and allowed through the gateway) to receive that specialist advice on the telephone. One of the reasons that we may be in denial is the decline of legal aid which governments both Tory and Labour have presided over in recent years. This government confronts a system for providing legal advice to the poorest that is so weakened and so used to feeling beleaguered that the lawyers in the system have been arguably slow to appreciate the enormity of changes ahead.

What do I do?

'I am a lawyer.' That does not tell you much about what I do. Most of us have an idea what a doctor, nurse, teacher or social worker does. We all need health care sometimes, and have been to school. Some services may be different in quality, quantity or form, depending on whether they are provided by the public sector (free or subsidised) or paid for directly (private education, health or social care). This is largely not the case with legal services, because if you are poor, you are likely to need advice or representation about different things from your richer neighbour. This is not always true, and was perhaps less true before the demise of the high street lawyer who provided advice about a range of different areas of law, charging some clients privately and sending the bill for legal aid work to the state. It is also of course not true of advice and representation in criminal cases.

We all have an idea about what a criminal lawyer does, largely informed by film, television and literature. Of course those most affected by crime, as 'victims' or 'criminals', are far more likely to be poor, and paying clients will always be a minority of those needing representation in the criminal justice system. I am not a criminal lawyer, and know little about criminal legal aid. So much of what I say may not be true of the criminal legal aid system.

But if I say I am a lawyer many people will imagine a criminal lawyer: the criminal lawyer is an image we can understand and the criminal legal aid system forms a distinct and necessary part of the welfare state. Few would disagree with the proposition that anyone accused of a crime, particularly where their liberty may be at stake, should be represented whether or not they can pay. In fact means testing for criminal legal aid means that this is not necessarily the case.

But if I am a lawyer, and I don't deal with cases in the criminal courts, what do I do? What do other lawyers do? A lawyer may be an academic or a teacher; may be an 'in house lawyer' employed to advise a private or public organisation: a local authority, a hospital, a multi-national business, a newspaper … may be partner or employee of a firm that advises 'corporate' or 'private' (individual) clients about anything from tax to divorce; from planning to 'intellectual property' to 'slips and trips' (personal injury).

It is almost impossible to identify common skills and knowledge across the very diverse groups of lawyers but it may be true to say that as well as some very basic common academic legal training, good lawyers should be able to apply their legal knowledge to factual situations, using problem solving techniques (sometimes identifying and therefore avoiding future problems) and providing information. I usually describe my role to clients as threefold: identifying and explaining to them the relevant law; advocating for them by presenting their case to an external body as best I can; and making sure that they have up to date information about their case.

A lawyer may have one client, or thousands; may go to court every day, or never. A lawyer may earn £15,000 a year or may get bonuses of £150,000 on top of their salaries or earnings. There are so many different types of lawyer that it is no surprise that telling people that I am a lawyer leaves them none the wiser. There is of course a general perception that lawyers are probably wealthy, so the fact that a legal aid lawyer is quite likely to earn less, work longer hours, have less holiday and worse or non-existent pension provision than, say, a teacher does surprise many. Legal aid lawyers also have little or no job security and limited career choices. (By contrast, it's also true that there are many who have made a lot of money out of legal aid, and many who continue to do so).

Perhaps because I am a lawyer and am used to ensuring that there is nothing personal in what I write, I find it hard to write from a personal point of view, and therefore hard to describe what my experiences as a legal aid lawyer have been. This is made harder by a feeling that I first need to explain what my work involves, and by awareness that there are many different ways of providing legal aid advice and representation and that no experiences will be typical. It is also of course hard to consider how attitudes to the provision of legal aid have changed without looking at the future and at how the way we work is already being affected by spending cuts (in advance of specific cuts to legal aid).

Perhaps the easiest way to explain what I do now, to facilitate consideration of what the role of legal aid is, has been, might or should be, is to tell a story about just one of the things I did last week at work.

Anna's case

The Law Centre I work in provides advice and representation funded by the legal aid scheme. We also have funding from the local authority and use some of that funding to provide a telephone advice service to local agencies that do not provide specialist advice, are not lawyers, but work with clients who may need our services. Sometimes (ideally) we can provide workers in these other agencies with advice which enables them to help their clients resolve disputes or access services without legal representation. Often the clients will need face to face advice and representation: in those cases ideally we should see the clients and take on their cases. All too often we are unable to do so, usually but not always because of lack of resources. The demand for our service in common with probably all other legal aid providers far exceeds supply (and probably always has done).

On Thursday I received a telephone call from Debbie, a support worker in an agency which provides counselling and other services to victims of violence. She had spoken to one of my colleagues earlier in the week. She was assisting a young woman, let's call her Anna, who had fled her family's home because she had been seriously assaulted by an older male relative. There was a history of sexual assault, followed by violent but non-sexual assault as reprisal for Anna disclosing the sexual assault. The abuser had been away from the home but had just returned.

Anna had been told to leave the family home but in any event did not feel safe there because of the risk of violence. Whether or not remaining in the family home would result in actual violence, and whether or not she could remain there (and she could not lawfully as she had been asked to leave by the owner of the property) she did not wish to remain there because she was receiving counselling to enable her to recover from the effects of the assaults and believed that she would not be able to recover if she had to remain under the same roof as her abuser. Debbie also told me that Anna had a complex mixture of disabling medical conditions.

My colleague had explained to Debbie that in these circumstances (and, in this case, given that there was no issue about on her immigration status) Anna had an immediate right to temporary shelter: she simply needed to approach any housing authority and they would have to provide temporary accommodation whilst they considered what longer term duties were owed to Anna. Debbie had therefore passed this advice on to Anna and had arranged to attend the homeless persons unit in a neighbouring local authority with her. She had been at the homeless persons unit all morning and her client had been repeatedly refused assistance, with a variety of different excuses being given for the refusal to accommodate her that night.

Debbie wanted some ideas about what to do next as she had understood that the law required the council to help Anna, who had as far as she knew literally nowhere else to sleep that night. She and I discussed whether Anna could find a friend or relative who might put her up that night, or whether she could borrow any money to fund accommodation for one night. Debbie told me that her charity had an emergency fund earmarked for those 'without recourse to public funds' (that is, those prevented from accessing any services at all because of their immigration status) but that Anna did not qualify for that fund and in any event the fund was empty.

I had a number of telephone conversations over the course of the afternoon: encouraging the support worker and Anna to stand their ground and to explain that Anna needed somewhere to sleep that night and that they wanted the council to comply with their legal duty to provide emergency shelter. Anna was financially eligible for legal aid. The case was clear cut. She had a right to somewhere to stay that night and that right (in theory at least!) was enforceable.

It was difficult however to decide how to approach the case practically and effectively. Anna was in the homeless persons unit, but it had been shut to callers since 3pm. If she left, she would not be able to get back in. She had not been given a definitive 'no' yet and told to leave. If she left and came to my offices (so that I could take on the case) there was the risk that the council would later say 'oh well we were going to house her but she left before we could'. On the other hand, if she did not leave and come to see me I would not have legal aid forms signed, I would not be able to get started and carry out the steps necessary to force the council to house her. At one point she had been told to 'call the out of hours team'. This is an emergency service: and not accessible until 'after hours'. We were not sure if the out of hours service would open at 5.30 or 6.00 pm. As she had been in the council's offices since shortly after they opened that morning, she was understandably confused and distressed by the suggestion that she might get housed if she went away and phoned a telephone number that night, by which time she would not be able to access assistance from her support worker or a lawyer.

Because English was her first language, because she had a mobile phone which was fully charged (although she had no credit), because she had good phone reception, because she was able to communicate well on the phone, because she had a confident and articulate support worker with her, I was able to take instructions from Anna and give some basic advice over the telephone. I was able to agree that I would take her case although I was taking a financial risk on behalf of the Law Centre in doing so because if she, for whatever reason, decided not to travel from the council's offices to the Law Centre that evening after leaving the council's offices (or if for any reason she was prevented from doing so) I would not be able to process the grant of legal aid and the Law Centre would not get paid. I was able to decide to take that risk and by luck was able to put off other tasks and prioritise taking on her case.

I took details on the telephone and wrote a letter to the council's housing and legal departments, summarising the relevant facts and explaining that it was clear that there was an immediate duty to assist and indicating that if Anna was not housed we would ask a duty judge at the High Court to order the council to house her. In practical terms my worry was that an order from the High Court would not assist that night if I could not find anyone from the council to serve it on. I arranged for a colleague to see one of my other clients who had come to see me that afternoon about an ongoing case and I apologised to another and rearranged her appointment for the following day.

Because the case was entirely straightforward at this stage I hoped that my correspondence would resolve the question of where Anna would sleep that night but I was not confident that it would. I telephoned the council's legal department: I knew that there was no point trying to telephone the homeless persons unit as I would be unlikely to get through and the officers who had seen Anna had refused to give their names. I had no named contact to ask for and given the way that services are organised I had little chance of getting to speak to anyone who knew about the case and would be able to influence the way it was dealt with that afternoon.

Eventually at the end of the afternoon, many telephone calls later, we came to the conclusion that there was no point in Anna waiting in the homeless persons unit any longer and we arranged for her to travel to my offices. Fortunately she had a bus pass to facilitate this, and I was able to make an assessment about whether I would feel comfortable staying with her in my offices after they had closed so that we could try together to reach the 'out of hours' service.

I received a fax from the legal department confirming that the council would house Anna that night: although it went without saying that this would only be through the out of hours service. Anna was asked to attend the homeless persons unit again the next morning whereupon the council would decide whether to house her further.

When Anna arrived at my offices she was tired and unsettled. She did not know where she would sleep that night and both she and Debbie were surprised by the treatment she had received. (A client with greater experience of attempting to access public services might have been less surprised but more angry). Debbie was particularly distressed by the lack of courtesy shown to both her and Anna, and by the changing goalposts throughout the day as the client was given entirely different reasons for a refusal to help her. When Debbie had expressed the (correct) view that the council had a legal duty to house

Anna that night, housing officers had been very angry and aggressive and suggested that she should not tell them how to do their jobs; why would she question their actions when they had twenty years experience?

In the event this young woman eventually found a bed for the night at just before 11pm, having started out with her support worker first thing that morning. I won't set out the further practical steps that she and I went through to obtain that accommodation. What she obtained was, literally, only a bed for the night as the next morning she left the bed and breakfast hotel to make sure that she was back at the homeless persons unit again when it opened. The next day was little better: she was sent from one office to another and back again. Fortunately I happened to phone her when she was with one officer who was telling her that she could not obtain accommodation without an appointment for an interview and the first appointment was a week away. If she wanted accommodation in the meantime she would have to use the out of hours service each night.

Several letters and phone calls later and with much persistence on Anna's part, she was eventually booked into a hostel initially for six weeks at about 6pm on Friday evening.

This story is unremarkable. Indeed, Anna's case was particularly straightforward as there was a clear breach of statutory duty, relatively easy to enforce. As I tell it I am struck by the fact that Anna should not have needed a lawyer at all. A properly run housing department staffed by appropriately trained officers should not turn away those to whom they quite obviously have a legal duty to give assistance. But every housing lawyer will recognise this scenario and everyone who works with those trying to access social housing and/or homelessness assistance will know that the last Labour government's culture of targets encouraged what many councils often call 'homelessness prevention' and those working with the homeless are more likely to call 'gatekeeping'.

Local authorities have for some time been under great pressure to decrease the number of homelessness applications and many report huge successes in reducing the numbers of homeless people occupying temporary accommodation. These successes were achieved in many different ways but one way of increasing the number of 'homelessness preventions' and decreasing the number of homeless 'applications' is to make the process of accessing homelessness assistance so difficult that only the most persistent and well supported (and perhaps those with simple good luck) will make it through.

It's worrying to think about the vast numbers of applicants like Anna, who are unlawfully denied homelessness assistance. It makes me angry to think about what would have happened to Anna if she had not had a support worker with her; if she had not had a telephone; if she had not been able to speak English; if she had not been able to stay calm and had lost her temper and therefore been ejected from the homeless persons unit and denied assistance because of 'aggressive' or 'threatening' behaviour (which 'will not be tolerated').

I know that if Anna's support worker hadn't happened to phone my office at a time when I or someone like me was available to answer the phone and if we hadn't been able to meet in my offices then she wouldn't have been able to charge her mobile phone so she wouldn't have been able to give the emergency service a number to phone her back on ... there are so many 'ifs'. It is certainly the case that 'if' the current plans for legal aid are implemented in anything like their current form, it is unlikely that Anna would have been housed that night.

It is clear that Anna should not have needed a lawyer at that stage in her housing application, whereas there are many people whose cases are less straightforward and will always need legal assistance. From the state's point of view if legislation gives certain classes of homeless people the right to accommodation, then those who have a duty to provide that accommodation should have the resources to provide it and staff able to work appropriately with those who need support. They should also arguably have proper procedures to ensure that those who are not entitled to assistance and whom for policy reasons they have decided not to prioritise, do not nonetheless obtain assistance through incompetence or fraud. There should be mechanisms for ensuring fair and transparent decision making and those mechanisms may well include access to legal representation at some stage.

Anna's case in the context of government policy

It may not necessarily be desirable for the state to legislate to provide housing rights; to develop a system where many (possibly the majority? — it is, logically, almost impossible to carry out any research to show how many people are turned away, but should not have been) are denied access to these rights. Whether or not a homeless person — certainly in London — accesses the assistance they are entitled to now depends on luck and for the very few, on finding a good legal aid lawyer. It would probably be more sensible for the state to remove from the statute rights which it considers it cannot afford to deliver; or to resource and monitor local authorities in a way that facilitates consistent and lawful delivery. It is probably not logical or cost effective to focus resources on lawyers who are able to identify and enforce those rights. However it is certainly the case that litigation can in many areas including the delivery of public services be a very effective tool for encouraging better practice. That can include practice which is more cost effective in both the short and the long term.

Anna's case is neither a good nor a bad example of the sort of work that legal aid lawyers do. It's certainly not untypical, and there are myriad examples of extremely poor decision making by public authorities where good quality representation makes the difference between a roof over the head and long term homelessness; between deportation and the right to stay in this country; between the provision of many different services and a total failure of service; in some cases literally between food and hunger, safety and danger. In some of those cases a lawyer's intervention will work quickly and effectively; in other cases there will be long and costly litigation and that may result in a good outcome for one individual at the expense of others, or may result in an organisational change of practice for the better.

It's not really possible to describe all the different ways that lawyers funded by legal aid work for individuals and groups, or to identify common themes easily. There are plenty of instances where persistent and creative lawyers have been able to protect the rights of groups of individuals or to effect change, for example when the then government sought to restrict the rights of asylum seekers who did not claim asylum immediately on entry to this country, leaving many of those managing to reach the UK having fled torture and persecution literally starving on the streets. Lawyers were able to work very effectively to challenge the way that individual after individual was treated, eventually forcing the government to change its position.

Is the provision of free advice and representation to all, or to those who cannot afford to pay for it, necessary or desirable? Will there be any legal aid, or any lawyers skilled and willing to provide it, in ten years time?

One of the things that I think typifies the responses of legal aid lawyers to questions about legal aid is a consideration firstly about whether or not there will be any legal aid in the future, and what the loss of our service will mean for our clients who are likely in the future to be unrepresented. It's harder to get lawyers to provide a personal response save for an expression of flippant concern about whether or not there will be any jobs for us in the future (unfortunately there may be stiff competition for that job as a call centre manager). Nonetheless it is no longer scaremongering to say that many if not most legal aid lawyers are unlikely to survive the current proposals for change, and that the clients that we would have represented will have lost access to good quality advice about their rights, at a time when many of those rights are also being eroded.

Today, in many parts of the country, it is not possible to find a lawyer who will advise and represent someone who cannot pay. In other areas there may be lawyers, but few competent ones. Even in inner London, where supposedly legal aid coverage is at its best and one might assume that it would be easy to find a good lawyer working under the legal aid scheme, good advice can be inaccessible. (Anna was 'lucky' to find a lawyer at all.)

For the few however, free state funded advice is available about housing rights, immigration, employment disputes, entitlement to welfare benefits, education, community care and family law including disputes about property and children. The government's current proposals will remove entirely from the scope of legal aid many family law disputes, almost all employment and education law, welfare benefits, many housing and immigration cases. When the Labour government took personal injury cases out of the scope of legal aid, parts of the profession simply changed working practices, adapting to run cases which had previously been funded by legal aid under a 'no win no fee system' instead. This was not without its difficulties. But there are more fundamental problems that are likely to face both the legal profession and our clients when/if the current reforms are introduced. It is hard to see how anything resembling the current system will survive. Changes to the legal aid system are justified entirely on the basis of cost: legal aid is too expensive, savings must be made. This is the rationale given for all of the proposed changes.

There is little explicit recognition that to understand the government's agenda we need to understand who uses legal aid services and what they are used for. Many of the changes proposed appear likely to increase rather than reduce overall costs to the state. For example, the government proposes removing funding for advice about housing benefit, whilst retaining funding to defend possession proceedings brought on the grounds of rent arrears.

History

Summaries of the history of the establishment of the welfare state tend to describe the four pillars of the welfare state as the National Health Service, universal housing, social security (welfare benefits) and universal education. Reference to access to legal assistance in mediating either disputes between citizens or disputes between citizens and the state is notably absent. Lawyers are rarely perceived as public servants: indeed the public image of lawyers is as 'fat cats'. Steve Hynes, Director of the Legal Action Group, said recently at a debate about the future of legal aid hosted by the College of law for their students who are still intent on pursuing a career in this sector that legal aid was not properly seen as an arm of the post war welfare state but should instead be seen as something that had evolved in the decades since the establishment of the welfare state.

There remains a residual view however that legal aid should be seen as fundamentally important in the maintenance of an effective welfare state, perhaps not least because more recently legal aid has been used to fund litigation protecting access to welfare state services.

The Rushcliffe Committee reported to parliament in May 1945, three years after the Beveridge Report:

> ... it would be impossible to expect any extension of gratuitous professional services, particularly as there appears to be a consensus of opinion that the great increase in legislation and the growing complexity of modern life have created a situation in which increasing numbers of people must have recourse to professional legal assistance ... It follows that a service which was at best somewhat patchy has become totally inadequate and that this condition will become worse. If all members of the community are to secure the legal assistance they require, barristers and solicitors cannot be expected in future to provide that assistance to a considerable section as a voluntary service.

The committee recommended that: (1) Legal aid should be available in all courts and in such manner as will enable persons in need to have access to the professional help they require; (2) This provision should not be limited to those who are normally classed as poor but should include a wider income group; (3) Those who cannot afford to pay anything for legal aid should receive this free of costs. There should be a scale of contributions for those who can pay something towards costs; (4) The cost of the scheme should be borne by the state but the scheme should not be administered either as a department of state or by local authorities; (5) The legal profession should be responsible for the administration of the scheme; (6) Barristers and Solicitors should receive adequate remuneration for their services; (7) The Law Society should be requested to frame a scheme ... providing for the establishment of Legal Aid Centres ... throughout the country; (8) The term 'poor person' should be discarded and the term 'assisted person' adopted.

The term 'assisted person' has survived; most 'assisted persons' however would now perhaps properly be described as 'poor'. Legal aid has survived only as a service of last resort for the poor and the trend in recent years has been to look more and more towards assistance once again as a voluntary service (with the growth of 'pro bono' work).

It was clear that the Rushcliffe Report envisaged a change of culture, including a transformation of legal aid from a charity into a right. Discarding references to poor persons and paupers was necessary to change the focus from philanthropy to the protection of rights – that protection facilitated by the state (even where, as in recent years, legal aid was required to protect the rights of individuals from encroachment by the very state that was funding the lawyers).

The cost of legal aid was likewise to be transferred from individuals or businesses to the state. The lawyer/client relationship was to be retained (and the methodology for doing so). An often artificial connection was therefore retained between the lawyer and the legally aided and therefore non-paying client and the funding of the case. This has at times been problematic. Legal aid was not to be restricted to the poorest, but was to be widely extended, so that no one should be prevented by lack of means from access to the courts.

Those of us born long after the establishment of the welfare state are used to the idea that education and health should be available to all and free at the point of delivery. Indeed, many if not most of us are shocked to learn that the 1997–2010 Labour government legislated to restrict access to health care, so that failed asylum seekers can no longer expect to receive treatment and those working in the health service now often ask questions about immigration status. The erosion of the principle of free education to all is perhaps one of the reasons that changes to the funding of higher education have seen such widespread opposition.

Most people at some time or other will access health and education services, and simply assume that these are made available by the state without charge. Rights to social care have been eroded, with some significant opposition, but the care that we may or may not receive when elderly or unexpectedly injured or sick is not something that the young or the healthy choose to think about too much. Some benefits to those unable to work of course have always been means tested, but the majority who do not need to claim means tested benefits may make false assumptions about what would happen to them if they were unable to work.

By contrast legal aid, also means tested, and largely unavailable to any other than the very poorest for many years, is a service which many people will never need. It has become increasingly a service only needed by the very poor. This is not only because access to the service is restricted to those on a low income (and for many years restricted to those living on state benefits or an equivalent income only) but because the nature of the disputes which are funded by legal aid means that these disputes often involve the very poorest.

When the 'green form' scheme was introduced in the 1970s, any lawyer could provide a legal aid service. In many ways, this was 'legal aid for all' in its simplest form. A potential client could walk into any solicitors firm (whatever its usual client group or expertise) and receive advice and assistance just as a privately paying client would. The bill for services would simply be sent to the state rather than to the client. The most familiar model of the delivery of legal aid was a 'high street' firm providing a range of services including conveyancing, wills and probate, landlord and tenant disputes, and matrimonial/family law.

The 1970s also saw the development of an alternative model for providing legal advice specifically about the sort of issues which most affected the poor, by lawyers who perhaps for the first time were making a positive choice to use their legal expertise for a particular client group. Law Centres saw themselves as providing a very different service from the High Street lawyer with, in many cases, an emphasis on local campaigns or representing groups of litigants — for example groups of tenants affected by the practices of particular landlords.

The idea of a 'legal aid lawyer' as a different sort of lawyer, choosing to specialise not only in work funded by the state but in particular areas of law, perhaps grew both out of increasing specialisation in private practice as well as a change which saw an expansion of legal aid services in what came to be known as the 'not for profit' sector (encompassing law centres and community advice agencies as well as many citizens advice bureaux and specialist agencies for example agencies specialising in advice in one or other area such as immigration).

Legal aid was indeed administered by the profession for the first forty years. The Law Society, from the forties to the end of the eighties, had a triple role: as the regulatory body for solicitors, responsible for training, admission to the profession, and discipline; as the voice of solicitors; and as the administrator of the legal aid scheme. The Legal Aid Board (LAB), the predecessor of the Legal Services Commission, was established in 1989. The Law Society is no longer responsible for the regulation of the profession.

The eighties saw an increased pressure from the LAB for solicitors to specialise. The introduction of 'franchising' was the beginning of the end of the generalist solicitor expected to know enough about any legal issue that might walk through the door. The Legal Aid Board introduced a voluntary 'franchising' scheme in the early nineties, becoming compulsory by 2000. Firms which had been successfully providing good quality legal aid services for many years were no longer able to do so unless they could obtain a 'franchise'. The language of 'franchising' was perhaps deliberately misleading with the suggestion of 'branding', a desire to sell services.

Franchising undoubtedly had many benefits initially for the consumer as the franchising process involved some quality controls, despite the problems inherent in the processes. Any firm desiring a franchise had to first prepare and present for inspection an 'office manual', the contents of which were largely prescribed. The extent to which this prescription was necessary is questionable given that the professional obligations imposed by the Law Society if enforced to a large extent covered common ground, for example the provision of costs information at the beginning of a case. Many of the changes either imposed by or consequent from the franchising process would probably have come anyway given that the imposition of franchising coincided with widespread computerisation.

Some firms may have dropped out of legal aid with the imposition of franchising but it is unlikely that drop out would have been entirely due to franchising. Legal aid rates which had been regularly increased ceased to do so; in 1989 the hourly rate for work carried out under the green form scheme in London was £37.50. In 2011 that rate is hardly relevant as much 'green form' work is paid at a fixed amount per case but the nominal hourly rate is £53.15. Adjusting for inflation would give an hourly rate of £71. During the same period deregulation and cut price conveyancing coupled with a slump in house sales had seen the end of conveyancing as a reliable source of income to 'cross subsidise' legal aid work.

Any firm wanting to continue to carry out legal aid work had no choice but to go through the franchising process. Practitioners seemed to have varying approaches to the process. Some embraced it as a way of ensuring that the quality of their service was recognised. Some had organised their businesses in a way that meant that minimal further investment was necessary. Other practitioners experienced inconsistent decision making by 'auditors' who were neither legally qualified nor appropriately experienced in the provision of legal aid services.

The goalposts were constantly moving as the LAB devised ever shifting auditing processes. We were constantly devising different methods of satisfying their latest whims; often trying at the same time to improve efficiency. 'Improvements' in the service for clients were incidental or coincidental only. For example, at one time the LAB announced 'transaction criteria'. Any file could be selected for auditing 'against' these criteria. Each area of work had its own set of transaction criteria. There was an immediate market in transaction criteria checklists. But the transaction criteria were designed to do the impossible: reduce the skilled process of extracting the relevant factual information, organising it and assessing and applying the relevant law to a tick box exercise. Auditing 'against' the transaction criteria was carried out by inadequately equipped (and again not legally qualified) auditors. At some point the transaction criteria were abandoned and replaced by a series of different assessment processes.

Lawyers are if anything uniquely aware of the importance of doing their jobs properly and of recording that they have done so. They know that they can be held to account if they fail to do so. Our training means that we are always mindful of the consequences of mistakes. The franchising process was not objectionable because of the added scrutiny of our work that resulted (indeed scrutiny if anything became more randomised because of the changes in the way that decisions were made and that fees were paid) but rather because of the concept of 'franchising' itself. A legal aid 'franchise' was not, truly, a franchise but rather a prerequisite for the provision of legal services which would ultimately usually (not always) be paid for by the state.

The real difficulty with the changes in the way that legal aid is provided that started with the franchising process is more fundamental and arises from the way that the provision of legal aid was organised in the first place. Whilst retaining the independence of lawyers and the lawyer client relationship (independent of literal payment: the 'legal aid certificate' being the payment) the key difference between the provision of legal aid and health services was the retention of legal aid firmly rooted in the private sector. Hospital doctors moved to direct employment by the health service; GPs whilst retaining self employed status enjoyed all of the advantages of public sector procurement and employment, including investment in premises and infrastructure. By contrast solicitors firms remain independent businesses.

This had numerous consequences: not least for the way that the businesses themselves were run, so that recruitment practices were variable, with a lack of transparency not only about recruitment but also about pay, terms and conditions and little career structure for both qualified and unqualified staff even within medium to larger sized firms. The traditional practice of expecting solicitors to 'bring in' three times their salary (one for them; one for their secretarial and overhead costs; one for the partners' profits) continues today.

Legal aid is also provided by the 'not for profit' sector: Law Centres, advice and specialist interest agencies, citizens advice bureaux. Within both the 'private' sector and the not for profit sector cultures, methods of 'delivery', the quality and type of service provided varies enormously. The client described at the beginning of this piece might have received advice from a lawyer working in very different environments. Within legal aid, the difference between a private and a not for profit provider bears no relationship to the difference between a private education and health care provider. Many Law Centres like to think that the service provided in the not for profit sector is unique and qualitatively better *because* the service is not being provided by a business which seeks to make a profit. But the increasingly difficult climate for legal aid providers has revived interesting debates about the very way in which legal aid has developed.

The recent past and the future

Certainly despite the stark reality of the proposals to remove whole swathes of legal aid 'from scope' (so that you simply won't be able to get legally aided advice about particular areas of law at all) and the proposal for a 'telephone gateway' to services (which is likely to destroy much of what is left of the legal aid sector and fundamentally change the way that any 'survivors' operate) it's easy for us to have little sense of how huge impending changes may be. Perhaps that is because legal aid is used to feeling like a sector under attack, and because there have been so many fundamental changes in funding that those of us still here can be lulled into thinking that what's ahead is just more of the same.

For the past twenty years it has been hard to predict a 'future' for legal aid. The reorganisation of legal aid started by the franchising process was consolidated in 2009/2010 with the requirement that all 'suppliers' wishing to continue to carry out civil legal aid work should apply to do so in a computerised competitive tendering process. The way for this process and a fundamental change in the volume of provision had been prepared so skilfully that with hindsight it almost looks like it must have been stealthy design.

Before the introduction of a new contract with suppliers in 2007, suppliers (as solicitors who contract with the LSC to provide legally aided services are now called) were not limited to a fixed number of clients or cases. Although expansion of the sector had been controlled by the introduction of franchising (because under the post franchise regime setting up a new legal aid firm became infinitely more difficult: previously any solicitor could open doors as a new firm and carry out legal aid work) there was no limit on how many clients or cases any existing firm could take. This meant that existing firms with a franchise in any one area of work could expand as much as they liked: so that if a firm wished to employ more staff to take on more cases, it could do so. Presumably the 'market' could be relied upon to limit the expansion of the sector as a whole.

But there perhaps lay the problem. Whilst successive governments have seemed to believe that legal aid providers will compete for clients, in most areas there are more clients than lawyers willing and competent to take their cases. Neither the Legal Services Commission nor policy makers seem to have understood this either in the language used or in planning for change. Of course as much legal aid was provided by firms whose primary source of work was not legal aid work, and as presumably partners in those firms had expectations of levels of fee income commensurate with historical standards of living for lawyers, restricting or abolishing hourly rates of payment and imposing ever more costly bureaucratic requirements did the job that an increasing rather than diminishing supply of clients did not.

The real change which was not even really noticed let alone effectively opposed was the introduction of the concept of 'matter starts' in 2007, and the move to geographical distribution of matter starts. A 'matter start' is a new case for a client. This change came at the same time as fixed fees, which attracted far more opposition, ultimately unsuccessful for many reasons. The Legal Services Commission hid the significance of the idea of matter starts (perhaps unintentionally) because when fixed fees were introduced suppliers received an 'allocation' of matter starts tailored to keep their income from this sort of work at the same level as it had been when cases were paid for based on work actually carried out. This resulted in many suppliers being 'allocated' unrealistically high numbers of matter starts, and was followed by a lack of clarity and transparency about the significance of numbers of matter starts or of starting or completing them. But the concept of matter starts was then adopted as the key concept for the competitive tendering process.

This process was fraught with difficulties and has still not been completed in part due to numerous legal challenges, many by suppliers who had previously had contracts to carry out legal aid work but whose tenders were unsuccessful. As tendering loomed practitioners should have been alert to the future when the Legal Services Commission started to exercise a control over the allocation of matter starts in a way not previously seen. Practitioners would have had no reason to think that they would ever be in a position where they had the capacity (available staff time) to take on cases and clients asking to instruct them, but were unable to do so because there were no available matter starts.

It was certainly a shock to immigration lawyers in London as the financial year 2009/2010 drew to a close and requests for additional matter starts were refused. In other words, lawyers had started their allocated number of cases, and were therefore told that never mind that there were clients who needed lawyers and were unable to find them, never mind that they were willing to take on these clients who were financially eligible for legal aid, they could not do so: they did not have the matter starts. As legal aid had never previously been rationed in this way, few if any suppliers would have thought to monitor or restrict the numbers of cases they took on.

Meanwhile, the much heralded tendering process stuttered on with frequent changes to the timetable and delay after delay in the release of the tendering documentation. Eventually a tendering process was completed for immigration and for 'low volume' categories of law (including for example employment education and community care) as well as for what had been rebranded 'social welfare law'. (The family law tender process has still not been completed, following legal challenge.) Social welfare law included debt housing and welfare benefits law and no supplier was able to tender for one of the social law categories unless they could also 'deliver' the other two categories either on their own or through a consortium with other suppliers (although family law providers would also be able to bid for housing matter starts).

The process was yet another costly one for legal aid providers. Those who wanted to continue say to practise housing law could not do so without also providing debt and benefits advice. The tendering process worked using fixed yet often arbitrary points scores and fixed number of matter starts per category of law for each geographical area. In London this produced particularly anomalous patterns of available matter starts, as starts were allocated by borough, but most 'providers' advised (and continue to advise) clients across borough boundaries and the pattern of provision owed more to chance, where one or other firm which was successful, expanded and happened to be based, than to where need was the greatest. Suppliers were forced to make unfamiliar calculations about whether to 'over' bid; about whether to bid alone or in a consortium; about how their business would survive if they were allocated more matter starts than they really wanted, or less then they really needed. 'Matter starts' remain the most financially unattractive way of providing advice but remain a prerequisite for a contract allowing suppliers to do any legal aid work at all.

When after many post tender delays the Legal Services Commission announced the results of the tender round, many long established legal aid providers had failed to obtain the contracts they needed. Others had been unable to bid for the number of matter starts that they wanted, because there were insufficient numbers available in their areas. Others were awarded more than they could properly manage to 'deliver', but remain contractually bound to do so. There has been little clarity about procedures should one supplier shut down or withdraw from the contract. One thing is clear, however, despite impending wholesale change which requires us to reconsider how if at all we can continue to work, expansion (as opposed to merger) is not a realistic option, because numbers of cases are now quite explicitly limited. The post tender contract for social welfare law only commenced in November 2010: it will be some time before we start to see clients being unable to find advice not because there are no lawyers but because the lawyers who would like to represent the clients have 'run out' of matter starts, as happened in immigration law in 2009/10.

Of course there has been a change of government and huge policy changes are planned: but it appears that the sector is now — as a result of the changes of the last twenty years — organised in a way that makes it very hard to see how there can be any coherent and effective cross sector response to the proposed changes.

Change will mean different things to the private sector and the not for profit sector. Many private practices will simply, finally give up on legal aid altogether. Those who practice in areas of law which are being removed from scope (and there are few of them left) will have no option. If employment law cannot be funded by legal aid then a private supplier cannot advise a non paying client about employment law. If many family law disputes are removed from legal aid scope, then only a client who can pay will receive advice. It's quite simple. Private businesses, even those who have spent decades building up the expertise of their legal aid lawyers, will not be able to continue. Those who do little other work, either legal aid work which remains, or non legal aid work, will have to close.

Parts of the not for profit sector by contrast are not solely dependent on legal aid (but the alternative funding is also at risk). Many Law Centres already (despite many difficulties) provide services to those who are not eligible for legal aid, or provide services which legal aid does not cover at all. For example many not for profit providers provide representation at tribunals: this is not paid for by legal aid. Citizens Advice Bureaux will wish to and probably need to continue to provide free advice about debt and benefits. Most Law Centres would be loath to cease providing advice about employment rights or entitlement to benefits, and will be looking for alternative ways of raising funding for that work.

The proposals for overhaul of the civil legal aid system do not only involve removing areas of work from the scheme altogether but what amount to reductions in rates of pay and an expansion of telephone advice both as an initial gateway to advice and as a substitute for face to face advice and proper representation. One problem facing Law Centres and others is that they must confront not only major changes (cuts) to legal aid but also the likely loss of many other sources of funding (many receive local authority funding which is also at risk) at a time when demand for legal advice and in particular advice about entitlement to services is likely to be greatly increased.

For as the benefits system experiences large scale reforms, more people will need advice about reductions in benefit. The bureaucracy involved in administering change is likely to mean that mistakes are made, and advice and representation will be sought by those affected. As local authorities cut spending on housing and social care, the pressure on staff who control the distribution of resources will increase, and there are likely to be longer and longer delays in decision making and in the provision of services themselves. The quality of services and of decision making is likely to decrease. Again these are the circumstances in which lawyers working in Law Centres are likely to experience hugely increased demand not only for individual services but for participation in local campaigns which as explained has traditionally been part of the function of local community based Law Centres.

The Law Centres Federation (LCF, the umbrella organisation for Law Centres) has facilitated debate amongst Law Centres about how to prepare for and adapt to change and in particular the likely future pressures on funding including legal aid cuts. This debate has raised old arguments and divisions about the philosophy of the Law Centres movement and the difference between working in private practice and working 'not for profit'. The current regulatory position appears to prevent Law Centres from charging clients for legal services and some argue strongly that this needs to be changed to allow the many Law Centres at risk of closure to diversify to survive.

The debate has exposed wide ideological differences. It's clear that some see the movement of Law Centres towards carrying out legal aid work at all as a mistake which has led them to lose sight of their rightful place rooted in communities, focusing on collective action. Some see the mere idea of charging clients as the 'line which must not be crossed'. It seems to me however that the debate in many ways is a false one. It's not realistic to think that the poor who seek legal advice to enforce their rights to housing, benefits, the right to stay in this country or not to be victimised at work, are ever going to be able to pay what it costs to fund a legal practice. Law Centres who argue that the prohibition on charging should be lifted often talk unrealistically about charging different sorts of clients for other legal services (which Law Centres don't specialise in) as a way of raising funds. This is a distraction from a real debate about whether legal advice and representation is best provided charitably, or whether it is something that those who need it should be entitled to.

I think that how legal services are funded and delivered can have a real impact on the quality of those services. Too often, legal aid clients have received and still receive a poor service. Sometimes this is from unscrupulous or incompetent private sector lawyers whose only motive appears to be profit (although its hard to guess where that profit might come from). Sometimes this is from not for profit agencies who have either failed to maintain sufficient independence from funders, or have become too focused on a charitable model where their role is seen as 'helping' unfortunate clients, providing tea and sympathy, rather than informing them and where appropriate enforcing rights. There are incompetent as well as highly dedicated skilled and effective lawyers across both sectors.

It seems to me that what 'Anna' was entitled to expect was access to a clear, accurate and informed view about what rights if any she had to shelter that night. She did not have the means to pay for that advice. If 'legal aid' has any role as part of the welfare state it must be provided as of right to those who need it: but it cannot be effectively provided unless there is a relentless and continuing focus on quality. Poor quality legal advice is worse than no legal advice. It is just increasingly hard to imagine any system in the foreseeable future that will work.

As well as the passionate debate about not whether Law Centres *should* charge for services, there is discussion about whether a Law Centre which decides to charge for some services should be allowed to call itself a Law Centre. The whole discussion is fraught with complicated regulatory issues but interestingly much debate has also focused on comparisons with the provision of medical, dental and social care. This illustrates the way that some legal aid lawyers see themselves as part of the welfare state, or as aspiring to be so, without recognising the difficulties arising from a charitable role or the numerous issues relating to the need to retain independence and the primary duty of a lawyer to his or her individual client. There are unresolved issues arising from the ways that the traditional individual lawyer/client relationship can conflict with creative ways of using the law to act for the rights of groups rather than individuals, an aspiration of most Law Centres who see themselves as rooted in their local communities.

It is not yet clear whether LCF will vote to allow Law Centres to charge for their services; we do not know whether the government will pay attention to the huge volume of responses to the consultation paper on legal aid, some of which will mean the end for many providers of legal aid across both sectors. What is clear is that it is almost impossible to grapple with issues about the role of legal aid and the relationship between lawyers their clients and the state at a time when the very existence of any legal aid service at all is under threat.

Without some consideration of what our role is and why, we remain ill equipped to contemplate the future.

POSTSCRIPT

Since May 2011 (when this chapter was written) the government's response to the consultation exercise and the bill to implement the proposed reforms have both been published. With some minor changes, the bill largely incorporates the changes suggested in the green paper. It is currently on its way through parliament, and whether or not it passes in its original form, or with some amendments, the changes we feared seem likely to become law. Two large providers of legally aided advice, Immigration Advisory Services and Law for All, have closed because of financial difficulties. On the 3rd October 2011, legal aid rates were reduced by 10%: the legal aid sector has yet to feel the impact of this reduction to a rate which has not increased since 1997. But it will be felt soon, and we are already seeing increased numbers of potential clients who cannot find lawyers and increased numbers of people who need to seek advice because of the direct or indirect consequences of cuts in publicly funded services.

Chris Richardson

Britain's Railways

Introduction

I begin by setting out a potted history of the development of the British rail industry. This is not meant to be the definitive work (there are mighty tomes to be found elsewhere on the subject) but I believe some background information is necessary to enable the reader to comprehend, detect and indeed opine on similarities and differences, which may or may not be attributable to specific ownership.

'Britain's Railways'; 'England's Railways'; 'British Railways'; 'The Railways of Britain'. Where does it begin? Where did it begin? Whose are they? Of course, they have always belonged to people as speculators and shareholders but it was for less than 50 years that they were actually in public ownership.

And why, from the early part of the twentieth century through to the 1980s did the public complain and petition as many branch lines—and indeed some main lines—closed? As with the similarly emotive disappearance of local cinemas and corner shops it was usually lack of patronage that led to their demise! (Interestingly, the use of rail has grown significantly over the last ten years and I shall return to this later.)

Just some of the questions. What follows will not provide all the answers but it will attempt to put some of the issues into context. The narrative will address the circumstances relating to the railways of England, Wales and Scotland. Historically much of the Irish railway system (both north and south) was developed or acquired by the big English companies but nationalisation in 1948 excluded them from the new 'British Railways'.

The first truly publicly (open access) available railway opened in 1825 with the inauguration of the *Stockton and Darlington* route. Prior to this the advantage of 'guided' vehicles (away from potholed and mud-ridden tracks) had been recognised in many an industrial/agricultural application. This led to 'plateways' (where the track rather than the wheel was flanged) but the inflexibility and fragility of this system quickly gave birth to the conventional method seen today. Before steam power became practical, power was provided by man or horse. 'Standard' gauge of 4 feet 8 and a half inches was generally adopted – anything more or less than this being known today as 'broad' or 'narrow' gauge. It is said that George Stephenson arrived at the standard gauge after measuring the rutted tracks of farm carts. It is also said that Roman chariots had the same distance between their wheels! Both may be true.

Static steam engines in primitive form were in use in the eighteenth century, mostly employed for pumping out water from coal mines. Despite the ready availability of coal and water – the natural ingredients of steam power – the early machines were wasteful in that heavy fuel consumption was required to produce relatively low power. There was no pressurisation of the steam generated. Every schoolchild has heard of James Watt (1736-1819) and his 'eureka' moment as he watched his mother's kettle boil. Watt, an instinctive scientist and engineer, used his childhood observation to good effect in later life when he produced equipment able to place generated steam under pressure and thereby produce more power. As his machines became more sophisticated their use was extended to spinning and manufacturing applications.

Continuing development of the steam engine extended to other manufacturers and eventually a viable 'locomotive' was produced and thus the nineteenth century saw a massive spread of railways – boosted both by the ever expanding industrial revolution and by what became known as 'Railway Mania'. Numerous schemes were developed with the promise of riches for investors, rapid transit (compared with canal/waterways and horse drawn road transport) and more distant markets for perishable and consumable traffic. Fish, agricultural produce and coal featured heavily as strong selling points to potential investors but many hopes and aspirations for healthy returns on investment failed to materialise. Indeed, even at this wildly optimistic time, some schemes were recognised as non-runners by Parliament who refused to grant the necessary powers for development. Many unlikely schemes nonetheless did secure an authorising Act (some sponsored by one railway company to prevent another gaining access to what was deemed as 'their' territory) and some were built – destined never to make a profit.

Amalgamations and takeovers were a feature of the second half of the nineteenth century but bitter rivalry continued. During the First World War (1914-1918) the government of the day recognised the crucial logistical role railways had to play in the prosecution of hostilities and that there was an absolute requirement for the railways to be focused on the task in hand. For the duration a Railway Executive was created and this effectively controlled and managed the railway network as one. After the war the success of wartime centralised control was recognised as well as the part such a system could play in the peacetime recovery. In pursuit of this there was a considerable movement in favour of state ownership through nationalisation but at the time this was unthinkable for many (perhaps the Russian revolution was still fresh in the mind?) and the outcome was a compromise which led to the 'Grouping' which came into being in January 1924.

The Grouping

With some exceptions this saw the amalgamation of all the mainland railways into the 'big four', viz. the *London & North-Eastern (LNER)*, the *London, Midland & Scottish (LMS)*, the *Southern (SR)* and the *Great Western (GWR)*. Exceptions included one or two 'joint' lines, for example the *Midland & Great Northern (M&GN)* and some of the 'light' railways, including those under the ownership of Colonel Stephens.

'Joint' railways were those owned by two or more of the old pre-grouping companies and where the owning companies were absorbed within the same new group they tended to lose their individual identities. In the case of the *M&GN* quoted above administration continued to be shared, albeit now by the *LMS* and the *LNER*.

'Colonel' Stephens (1868–1931) is so known because of his army career from 1896 until 1916. In 1916 he was transferred from regular military duties to the Territorial Reserve to enable him to manage his 'light' railway network. His railway career had begun in 1890 and when the *Light Railways Act 1896* was passed he saw an opportunity. The 1896 Act provided for the construction of railways avoiding heavy engineering. Routes were able to follow the landscape and tended to be circuitous thereby avoiding the cost of building tunnels, cuttings, numerous bridges etc. wherever possible. Stephens built or acquired a number of such operations which were often found in rural areas.

Constrained by weight limitations and speed restrictions (and thereby perhaps reduced expectations from customers) Stephens was able to keep costs to a minimum. Safety was an issue for all railway operations but the challenges were less onerous than for the heavy, high speed main line companies. Many of his trains ran as mixed passenger and freight services and this often rendered precise time-tabling—and journey planning—difficult! It was not unknown for passengers to 'enjoy' the 'shunting experience' as their train moved freight wagons in and out of station yards. The remaining Stephens' railways retained their independence until nationalisation.

The grouping created challenges for management and staff alike. Different working methods, inconsistent conditions of service and benefits of employment, variations in signalling and locomotive practices to name just a few contrived to test the resilience of those former rivals in the new companies in striving to adopt common policies. The 'new' *Great Western* was fortunate in this respect in that it's former boundaries and territory were virtually unchanged. The new *Southern* had to address an inherited conflict in electrification systems and plan for the gradual transition to what was slowly developing into a 'passenger' railway, with conflicting demands of commuters and long distance travellers. Further electrification was seen as vital to providing the frequency and convenience of service commuters were demanding, particularly in the inner suburbs of London. The *London, Brighton and South Coast Railway* began electrification as early as 1909 but this was installed as an overhead line system. In 1915 the *London & South Western Railway*, another constituent of the new *Southern*, began electrification of its' suburban lines but by using a 'third-rail' to provide the current. It was this system that was adopted by the *Southern* as standard and a modernisation programme progressed quickly up to the late 1930s eventually including conversion of the Brighton route.

The *London & North Eastern (LNER)* and *London, Midland & Scottish (LMS)* needed to bury inherited rivalries amongst their new constituents quickly to allow them to concentrate on the new contest between the 'big two' on the east and west coast routes respectively.

More reliable and sophisticated road transport competition to traditional railway business (both freight and passenger), industrial recession, the general strike of 1926 and the need to modernise rolling stock all placed a significant strain on the new companies' resources and 'profitability' was at a premium. Various initiatives and campaigns (including 'The Square Deal' campaign) were launched in the 1930s to stimulate business and support for the railways but by the end of that decade receipts were in decline. Indeed, the 'Grouping' inevitably led to rationalisation, efficiency savings and the closure of branch lines.

The advent of the Second World War in 1939 brought about, just as during the first, the creation of a Railway Executive to co-ordinate rail activity and resources for the duration. During the war traffic carried grew to an extent that stretched men and machines to breaking point. With little opportunity for other than absolutely essential maintenance, by 1945 the infrastructure was all but worn out. The rail companies were desperately short of the funding needed to revitalise the network and again the future of the industry was being discussed. In 1945 the nation returned a Labour government to power and with that came the apparent solution, albeit driven by political conviction.

Nationalisation – the History

The Transport Act of 1947 gave birth to the *British Transport Commission (BTC),* an organisation designed to oversee the integration of all transport, including rail, road, waterways and docks. Within the *BTC* a Railway Executive was created and whilst the principle of geographically based rail businesses was retained, the previous 'Big Four' became six 'Railway Regions'. As in 1924, the *(Great) Western* and *Southern* Railways virtually retained their existing boundaries but new *Scottish* and *North Eastern* regions cut off both the *LNER* and *LMS* routes at the Scottish border (and further south in the case of the former *LNER*) leaving the *London Midland* and *Eastern* regions reduced in size when compared with their predecessors.

One can only speculate as to the creation of the *Scottish* region and why no similar proposal was made in regard to Wales! The 1945 General Election produced large numbers of members of parliament supporting the successful Labour Party in both countries, trades unionism was firmly established in both and nationalism existed in each. Neither Nationalist party was particularly influential at the time, unlike the present day where the Scottish and Welsh assemblies enjoy devolved powers from Westminster. (The current privatised railways include dedicated franchises in both Scotland and Wales and I shall return to this under 'Privatisation'.)

The new regional structure provided the opportunity to make one or two logical boundary changes but otherwise, apart from the imposition of the *BTC* and the *Railway Executive* into the hierarchy, day to day management was left to regional headquarters. The 'integrated' railway style of the old companies was perpetuated, with the Regional General Managers overseeing operating, commercial and engineering functions with their associated 'service' activities of Personnel, Finance etc.

After 1945 the need for British industry to revert to peace-time production (aimed specifically at the export market) was paramount and it was recognised that railways had a key part to play. Recovery from war-time deterioration and neglect demanded heavy investment in overdue maintenance and modernisation and to this end the first of what was meant to be a series of '5 year plans' for the rail industry was developed. Not only was much of the track and infrastructure in need of urgent replacement, much freight and passenger rolling stock was worn out and no longer appropriate for the new era.

Freight stock in particular was sourced not only from the previous 'Big Four' companies but also from many private owners (e.g. coal/fuel, steel, manufacturing businesses) and much of this was old, incompatible and unsuitable for the 'modern' railway which had to compete with growing road opposition. Ironically much of this competition came from the newly nationalised *British Road Services* (freight) and bus companies. Coaching rolling stock (passenger carriages plus non-passenger carrying vehicles designed to run at speed) was, with a few exceptions, similarly nearing the end of serviceable life or indeed incompatible across the old company boundaries. Locomotives were, almost without exception, steam and the future of motive power was to be a significant area for debate.

The former *Southern Railway* had standardised on 3rd rail electrification and had slowly expanded its network of electrified routes. Localised southern suburban electrification in the early twentieth century followed the principle established by the various underground and tube railways by laying a 3rd rail carrying electric current at 600v to 750v dc (in some cases a 4th rail too for technical reasons) alongside the running track. The *London, Brighton & South Coast Railway* had electrified its main line by erecting an overhead wire traction current collection system but this was replaced with the standard 3rd rail before the start of the Second World War. 3rd rail is certainly less intrusive on the landscape although the decision to adopt it was based more on cost (both in provision of infrastructure and current generation) than environmental concern. (Beyond *Southern* territory modern main line electrification is at 25,000 volts ac and is always provided by the overhead wire system.)

Non electrified branch lines were worked by steam and the cost of conversion to electric, set against costs and revenue, had led to some closures. Early trials were made with electric locomotives but normal passenger trains were exclusively 'multiple-unit' (i.e. powered coaches in 'sets') formations. The 'multiple unit' system continues to this day with non electrified branches and routes being diesel powered. The 'multiple-unit' is a train without a separate means of motive power, i.e. no locomotive is required for hauling as driver's cabs are provided at each end. Whether electric or diesel powered, motors are slung under the carriages or on motorised bogies. With driving cabs provided in the ends of each set the driver moves from one end to the other on completion of a journey. This facilitates the simplification of track layouts, reducing costly maintenance of complex signalling and point work etc. and speeds up turn round time of trains and staff.

The former *Great Western* and *LMS* companies were largely steam hauled but had a number of diesel powered railcars used mostly on lesser routes. The *LMS* also had electric multiple unit trains in localised areas and commissioned two mainline diesel locomotives after the Second World War (the second being delivered after nationalisation) and experimented with these on long distance trains. The *LNER* was entirely steam hauled for mainline trains on the East Coast but did have a number of electric locomotives for localised schemes as well as electric trains of the 'multiple unit' type in the Newcastle area. These latter were withdrawn by *British Railways* in the 1960s and replaced by diesel trains.

The variety of stock outlined before caused the *Railway Executive* to call for a plan to standardise both motive power and rolling stock. This produced the 'Mark 1' passenger coaches in the early 1950s and these endured for many years, running alongside later designs up to 'Mark 4', examples of all marks passing into privatisation. Similar developments were seen in the freight fleets.

What caused the greatest debate was motive power (i.e. traction) standardisation/replacement. Electrification as experienced on the Southern Region showed the associated advantages of cleanliness, attracting custom, speed, high utilisation and staff economies. No fireman was required on an electric multiple unit although the debate on the need for a second man on non steam locomotives was to be the subject of discussion and dispute for many years. Experimentation with mainline diesel locomotives showed they could be as efficient as, and certainly cleaner than steam. Diesel (and electric) power was also much less labour intensive in maintenance and availability for service was significantly greater. However, at the time of planning, the cost of imported oil was regarded as prohibitive as was wholesale electrification. The decision was taken to continue with steam for heavy and long distance haulage and this led to the development of the 'standard' *British Railways'* locomotive, across many classes, in an effort to cover all traffic and infrastructure demands. To what extent this decision was influenced by a perceived need to protect domestic industry and levels of employment, particularly within coal, steel and heavy engineering is not known. The post war economy was certainly in a parlous state and there is little doubt that weakness of the pound and Trades Union pressure had their parts to play. The probability of direct political influence, now of course facilitated by legislation, cannot be disregarded.

Modest trading profits were achieved in the early years of state ownership and this partly enabled the government, by the 1950s of a different political hue, to grasp an opportunity to curtail the 5 year planning programme, which of course included schemes for rolling modernisation. Nonetheless, efforts to restore profitability to increasingly costly branch lines did lead to the introduction of diesel multiple units (dmu's) to replace steam operation. But in many cases this was too little too late and the withdrawal of passenger services continued, in fact from the onset of nationalisation and through the 1950s and into the 1960s. Any hopes that a publicly owned railway would bring closures to a halt were dashed from day one!

In 1963 Dr. Beeching's famous 'Re-shaping of British Railways' report was published. 'Visionary' and 'infamous' were adjectives used by others to describe the impact the recommendations were to have on the railways. Some sound—and to be adopted—proposals were included within the report, particularly in regard to freight traffic, which by this time was suffering seriously from road competition. Increasingly customers were demanding fast, 'just-in-time' and door to door transits as well as competitive rates. Wagonload traffic, in many cases still carried in slow moving vehicles lacking continuous braking, did not lend itself to this. Observers, both within and without the rail industry, had long recognised that there was no level playing field in regard to the cost base of rail versus road. This was particularly so in regard to provision of the permanent way. (The 'permanent way' was so called because, particularly in early days, construction gangs very often worked from temporary access routes or tracks until the established route was laid.) Rail was obliged to provide and maintain at total cost its own track (i.e. the rail way) whereas road transport, both passenger and freight, paid only a contribution through *Road Fund* taxation for the national road system. This was a situation unlikely to be addressed (although in later years *road fund* tax has increased considerably) and proposals to rationalise the way freight traffic was managed were gradually introduced. This entailed a move away from wagonload business and the introduction of block and container trains carrying traffic in bulk. Railheads became focal points for freight business with many branch services being withdrawn and local terminals closed. The obligation on *British Railways*, as 'common carriers', to accept any traffic proffered (unlike road transport) was also to disappear in due course.

The *Beeching* proposals in regard to passenger services were seen by many as draconian and generated much comment, mostly critical, across the population. As mentioned earlier, as with the closure of local cinemas (and in later years the closure of local post offices) the most vociferous opponents to service withdrawals were often those who used them least. This is perhaps an indication that not all proposed closures were unjustified!

1964 was a General Election year and the Labour Party returned to power. To what extent the *Beeching* threats to the future of British Railways, and a hope for salvation, secured the Labour victory is for conjecture. Whatever the truth may be in this regard it was a hope without realisation. The greater part of the recommendations for closure was actively pursued and whilst professional railwaymen throughout the organisation regretted the network contraction most recognised there were some genuine lost causes. The Minister of Transport was charged with producing an 'integrated transport system' and this led to the 1968 Transport Act which created Passenger Transport Authorities (PTAs). Very few of these were in fact established but where they were, positive steps were taken to support and integrate local rail (and bus) services.

The *British Railways Board*, by now the ruling body created by a Conservative Transport Act of 1962, oversaw regional and divisional management initiatives which led to closure proposals beyond the *Beeching* recommendations. There was little withholding of Ministerial authority for these proposals and as a consequence what was seen by many within the industry as 'steps too far' were taken in regard to closures. There are a number of examples of these but to quote just one, the closure of the Cambridge to Oxford cross-country route is prime. Strangely, this route ran through three of the regional boards' territories, the Eastern, London Midland and Western regions, but the London Midland region declined to play ball and to this day the central section, from Bedford to Bletchley, remains! Every decade since the 1960s has heard expressed regrets at this closure.

During the 1990s and to this day schemes for (re-)establishing an east-west corridor, avoiding London have been on the drawing board — mainly with growing railborne freight traffic in mind. It is not only freight carryings which have grown, however, since privatisation. The passenger railway has also seen significantly increased patronage. In 2010 (the last full year for which figures are available) passenger numbers matched those last seen in the 1920s. Having in mind that ninety years ago car ownership was in its infancy, many of the branch lines closed in later decades were still open and that rail travel was relatively cheap, this is an interesting phenomenon. Certainly the Scottish and Welsh governments have funded the re-opening of some routes since devolution but these have not impacted to any great extent. The congestion charge in London may have had a part to play around the capital but I doubt pretty coloured trains and some of the highest fares in Western Europe are the attraction!

Staff and Organisation — the Nationalised Years

Railways had been extremely labour intensive from the very beginning. Unionisation was influential by the early twentieth century with the majority of membership centring on three main Trades Unions which today are recognised as ASLE&F (Associated Society of Locomotive Engineers and Firemen), RMT (Rail, Maritime Trades) and TSSA

(Transport Salaried Staffs Association). Apart from a period in the 1970s/1980s when a 'closed shop' applied, trades union membership was voluntary. Nonetheless strong support for Trades Unionism within the industry has always been evident.

Prior to 1948 the 'Big Four' had substantially similar conditions of service for their active staff but retirement and pensions conditions varied significantly. Schemes for salaried ('white-collar') staff were based on final salary/years service qualifications and as such produced a reasonably healthy income post retirement. Pensions for the other grades (essentially 'blue-collar' staff) were much less beneficial and in some cases income only came from schemes which had been established on what was in effect a charitable status (e.g. 'The Great Eastern Sick & Orphan Society').

Changes and improvements to working conditions were an expectation after 1945 — particularly so within the newly nationalised industries. Traditionally working practices had been determined by management imposition, efficiency, or negotiated settlements with workforces or trades unions. Until 1956, within rail, it was largely by inherited consultation and negotiation procedures that deals were struck. The 'unified' rail industry recognised the need for a more enlightened and disciplined approach to discussion with staff and one that was common to the whole network. In 1956 an industry wide 'Machinery of Negotiation' was published which clearly defined what topics were suitable for consultation or negotiation and crucially at what level of staff representation they should be discussed. Simply, this determined that key, industry wide issues such as pay, length of working week, holidays, pensions etc. should be settled at national level between Trades Unions and the *British Railways Board*. The application of such matters in the regional or local context was to be resolved via elected representative bodies at those levels.

In 1968/69 the British Railways Board put the negotiation process to good effect with proposals to overthrow generations of traditional methods of working. A system of staff grades and clear lines of demarcation had evolved with the railways. By the 1960s rationalisation of train services, de-staffing of stations, route closures, conductor guards etc. had brought about, almost by default, a 'fogging' of the demarcation lined 'who does what' culture. At the same time it was recognised that rail industry pay and grading structures were no longer relevant to the industry; nor were they particularly attractive to job-seekers. This led to prolonged discussions with the Trades Unions which eventually resulted in what became known as the 'Penzance' agreement and the introduction of *'Pay & Efficiency'*. 'Versatility' was the keyword of the process and made clear provision for a more relaxed approach to working practice but at the same time improving efficiency and economy by permitting some rationalisation of staffing. In return for the 'management gain' a new and simplified grading structure was agreed which also afforded a significant pay improvement for staff.

Whilst the *Pay & Efficiency* initiative essentially addressed those staff below the graded management structure attention was regularly directed to the administrative and management organisation during the nationalised years. The inherited 'one station, one station master' system of the 1940s, overseen by 'Districts' quickly became irrelevant with the ongoing contraction and closure of services. Merging of single station master stations into groups of stations under 'Station Managers' and then to larger groupings under 'Area Managers' were witnessed from the 1950s through to the 1970s. (The creation of Area Managers was the 'local' part of a very expensive masterplan known as the 'Field Organisation', never to be fully implemented beyond that level.) At the same time the old 'Districts' were assimilated into 'Traffic Manager' and subsequently larger 'Divisional Manager' geographical areas of control. The *North Eastern Region* was abolished and absorbed by the *Eastern Region* with the re-location of that office from London to York. So it can be seen that the impact of organisational change extended throughout the industry.

In the 1980s a new 'experimental' *Anglia Region* was created as a device to test how successfully a functionally integrated, 'pseudo' independently managed part of the system would/could perform. This was seen as a sort of 'trial run' and a test as to how a privatised operation might work and was at a time when the then Conservative government was considering (and then abandoned) an earlier privatisation exercise. This had the effect of reducing the sphere of control of the previously enlarged *Eastern Region*.

Major structural change followed the *Anglia Region* experiment in the 1980s with the creation of business sectors and functional organisations. The business sectors were, simply put, the 'public' face of railways, i.e. Passenger, Parcels and Freight and each ran their own completely self-contained operations which included staff, finance, property, rolling stock etc. Examples of the 'Functional' organisations were the various engineering activities, i.e. Mechanical Engineering, Signal & Telecommunications Engineering etc. It was in this format that the railways were to be privatised.

Nationalisation — the Gains

Inherited working methods, infrastructure, staff conditions of service and 'perks', application of 'Rules and Regulations', rolling stock and traction varied and differed from company to company. Nationalisation, co-inciding with the need to replace worn-out equipment, presented the opportunity to adopt a standardised approach where it was deemed to make sense.

The immediate challenge was to restore track and the associated infrastructure to peace-time status. This was easy in the sense that manpower was again readily available although financial constraints ensured a steady pace of recovery rather than an overnight return to universal pre-war standards. As far as rolling stock and motive power were concerned, once the steam versus diesel/electric debate had been resolved, the plan and progress towards standardisation were more measured.

Development of a fleet of standard steam locomotives, designed to fit all purposes; introduction of a common design of passenger coaches (the Mark 1), moves towards a common management structure were all able to take advantage of the economy of scale and the 'one' railway.

From the 1960s onwards particularly the publicly owned railway, despite the financial constraints placed upon it by government, was in the vanguard of adopting modern employment practices within the United Kingdom. Legislation in regard to equal opportunity was embraced, quickly outlawing prejudice in the recruitment and promotion of staff. Whilst racial, gender, age and religious bigotry *per se* did not feature highly within the workforce, there were nonetheless unofficially established practices whereby women, for example, were extremely unlikely to become guards, drivers or senior managers. Equal pay was adopted with the *Pay & Efficiency* initiative mentioned earlier, so finally jobs with 'female' in the title (and the inferred lower rate of pay) finally disappeared.

Prior to nationalisation promotional opportunity had essentially been confined to the individual companies. Internal advertising of vacancies was thus restricted to existing staff and offered no opportunity to change employer (despite still being within the industry) without sacrificing seniority and service credit. The terms and benefits of pension and sick pay schemes varied as did such fundamentals as retirement (pensionable) age, particularly so for salaried staff. The uniformed grades, by definition, received clothing appropriate to their tasks and company, clearly carrying the identity of their particular employer. Travel facilities—always a gift of management rather than a condition of service—varied and were largely confined to the company's geographic area although there was some concession to severely restricted 'foreign' travel, i.e. free or reduced rate fares for employee and dependant family on the other companies' territory.

The differences were, over time, swept away and by and large best practice was adopted. Promotional opportunity became, in stages, nationwide and with removal assistance offered by the *British Railways Board*, was available to most staff. Thus career opportunity for the mobile and ambitious was enhanced. Travel facilities were placed on a common, incremental basis and available across regional boundaries. Contributory pension/superannuation schemes available to all staff were implemented. A common standard and design of uniform clothing was introduced across the network thereby enabling ready identification of responsibility irrespective of location.

Introduction of standardised and improved holiday and sickness benefits and pay were introduced along with in-house welfare and counselling services. The hours of the working week were gradually reduced, and whilst railway pay was never high, and did not always compare well with outside industry, each shortening of the basic weekly hours served to increase earnings in an essentially 7 day 24 hour industry.

Regular organisational change is a feature of most large businesses and *British Rail* was no exception. As mentioned earlier this did occur, perhaps too frequently, but generally speaking the outcome was beneficial to staff and customer alike.

In terms of the 'hardware' a vigorous *Research and Development* department, largely based at the Railway Technical Centre at Derby alongside the *Mechanical and Electrical Engineering* and *British Rail Engineering* organisations grew into worldwide respected operations. The ubiquitous diesel *HST 125* train was developed here and introduced in the early 1970s as a 'stopgap' until electric versions and the tilting *Advanced Passenger Train (APT)* were ready to roll off the production line.

The *APT* tilting train was designed to use existing track formations — many still following the original meandering Victorian routes — as a means of ironing out speed limited bends and curves. Increasing competition from internal UK flights had triggered this response from the *British Railways Board* who were seeking a way of speeding up intercity services. Starved of investment funds and after some extensive trials the *APT* was abandoned. Some main line electrification, notably the East Coast route from London King's Cross to Edinburgh, still went ahead but with a severely constrained budget the total speed and frequency potential was not realised.

History and the railway of today, with imported, electric tilting trains and talk of new high speed lines show how plans can change!

Nationalisation – the Losses

It is easy to conclude from the previous section that by definition there were no losses. This is not the case. Whilst nationalisation was undoubtedly timely it did bring with it the aura — or stigma — of standardisation and state control. *The Transport Act 1947* sought to integrate all forms of transport and to bring them into public ownership. Apart from railways this entailed the nationalisation of large fleets of freight road vehicles (to become *British Road Services*), passenger road vehicles (buses), waterways (canals and navigable rivers), and air (to become *British Overseas Airways Corporation* and *British European Airways*).

Transport integration envisaged by the *Act* was intended to ensure the best use was made of the most suitable transport for particular traffic consignments. For example, rail freight destined for delivery to points beyond a railhead required onward road haulage. Where railway owned vehicles were not available the expectation was that *British Road Services* would be the preferred provider. In regard to passenger traffic the eventual aim anticipated booked connections between rail and road. Integration in practice was minimal and as far as passenger business was concerned was best realised in later years in areas served by *Passenger Transport Authorities*. (This latter is briefly mentioned also under Nationalisation — the History).

The very fact of state control meant that the railways — and indeed the other subjects of The *Transport Act 1947* — were sensitive to political dogma and financial interference in subsequent years. For example, whatever justification had been made to take road transport into state ownership in 1948 was quickly rejected by the Conservative government of the early 1950s when *British Road Services* began to lose its protected status and privately owned road haulage companies re-emerged. They, like their state-owned predecessor, continued to win business from rail.

Similarly, the contemporary state of the national purse rendered railway modernisation plans susceptible to variation and curtailment. The vast amount of investment and modernisation required post war had to be carefully managed and planned; unexpected National Budget driven interruptions to the programme served to delay modernisation thereby increasing the cost of maintaining life-expired equipment and consequently price increases to the customer. These inevitably led to customer loss and with rising private car ownership impacted particularly on the passenger railway.

It is of course a matter for speculation what continuing private railway ownership after 1947 would have done for the 'Big Four'. Profit for the latter depended partly on income from ancillary and complementary businesses and operations. To varying degrees the old companies had owned hotels, shipping, station and on train catering, entire and parts of omnibus companies as well as shares in leisure activities (for example golf courses and holiday camps). Under state ownership many of these activities were made into autonomous businesses (for example 'British Transport Hotels'; 'SeaLink' and 'Traveller's Fare') within the *British Rail* group and sold off — in other words privatised. This as a principle was later extended to property (British Rail Property Board), the cross Channel and cross Solent hovercraft services (Seaspeed), the 'sundries' (small goods) service (National Carriers Ltd.) and Channel Tunnel services (Eurostar).

Nationalisation — a Personal Perspective

As an 18 year old sixth-former I determined (as did poor 'A' level results) that a University life was not for me. Mature 18 year olds of course unwittingly cling to juvenile ways and a guaranteed trigger for reducing those of us in the common room to laughter was for someone to say 'British Railways'. I have no idea what started this habit and it was with considerable amazement to myself and my friends that I followed up a career opportunity in the local press with said organisation. It was July 1961 and the advertisement offered an enhanced salary of £410 (as opposed to £370) per annum to selected candidates with 6 or more GCE 'O' level passes. The job on offer was as a trainee booking office clerk and having satisfactorily passed the selection process, including medical examination, my railway career began in September 1961.

I was assigned to a small rural station with a Station Master, a clerk, two porters and a signal box which was open 24 hours a day and required three signalmen as well as relief cover. There were freight facilities in the yard and the Station Master was also responsible for a couple of level crossings down the line.

What struck me immediately was the camaraderie amongst railway-men. Old, young, experienced and 'green' (myself) alike seemed to be part of a bonded brotherhood irrespective of grade. From day one the sanctuary of the signal box was available to me as a place to eat my sandwiches and to have a cup of the signalman's tea at lunch-time! At the time I joined the majority of railway staff were former employees of the 'Big Four' — it being only thirteen years since nationalisation — and they had grown up in a fully integrated, self contained industry. Dependency on others was part of the culture, essential in such a safety orientated environment. There is no doubt that this dependency had been stretched, tested and proved during the difficult Second World

War period. As described elsewhere, the war had a devastating effect on infrastructure and manpower alike.

Relatively low pay and unsocial hours contributed to a degree of staff turnover throughout the ranks but in my experience it was amazing how many people who left returned after a few months! There was a genuine 'family' feeling and pride in the industry bringing with it friendly familiarity but at the same time a clear understanding of where responsibility and instruction giving and taking lay. I also believe that by the early 1960s there was a growing awareness that change had to come. Quaint and traditional as it may have been it was difficult to envisage the age of oil lamps, high labour intensivity, low passenger patronage and declining freight traffic being allowed to continue in an age when elsewhere in Britain the 1960s were regarded as 'swinging'.

The next thirty-five years afforded me job and promotional opportunities backed up by excellent training and development facilities supported by meaningful succession planning. I witnessed these aspects of people management as they developed through the 1960s, 1970s and 1980s to such a degree that the reputation of *British Rail* as enlightened employers was held high within British industry. At the same time, certainly during the 1970s, employment legislation, especially endorsement of the 'closed shop', gave the strong industrial trades unions' undue power and influence and this served to tarnish the reputation earned on the 'pastoral' side of employee relations.

Nonetheless, overall, the industrial relations challenges and government imposed financial constraints turned the *British Railways Board* into the most competent managers of adversity and the years leading to privatisation saw some remarkable business/financial achievements.

In terms of my own career the opportunities and mobility available through the excellent nation wide advertising of vacancy system enabled me to progress to a senior position at British Railways Board Headquarters. Having served all of my working life with the state-owned railway it was perhaps ironic that the last few years until retirement in 1996 were largely spent with the privatisation process.

Privatisation

Denationalisation, or privatisation, was mooted on more than one occasion from the 1970s onwards. This was seen as a logical extension of earlier governments' policies of disposing of state-owned assets – the steel industry, road transport and the airlines being prime examples of these. Always the intent of Conservative rather than Labour led administrations rail privatisation had continued to be filed in the 'too difficult' box but finally the process was ratified and passed into the statute books under the *Railways Act* of 1993.

During the 1980s considerable work had been done on an earlier privatisation proposal and at that time the vision had been of a possible return to the structure experienced under the 1924 grouping arrangements. In this way companies would have been geographically based and autonomous by providing and being responsible for their own infrastructure as well as rolling stock etc. By 1993 European Union (EU) legislation had intervened, in particular *EU Directive 91/440*. This required that all railways within the EU have ready access to all infrastructure (essentially the running lines) within the Union. To facilitate this *91/440* required member states privatising railway businesses to create separately accountable infrastructure companies.

In consequence, apart from the creation of geographically located passenger franchises (licences to be granted on lease), freight businesses (to be sold outright) and the various supply companies (rolling stock etc.), *Railtrack* was established. Initially entirely government owned, this was eventually sold off until the creation of the publicly owned 'not for profit' *Network Rail*. (*Railtrack*'s early privatised years were extremely profitable for the shareholder but a break with some traditional working methods, some serious rail accidents, a decline in share values and political intervention led to its demise.)

One of the drivers of the Privatisation process was undoubtedly political and there was a belief (mostly held outside the industry) that private ownership would reduce government interference, bring tighter financial management and eliminate the annual state subsidy. Many such claims were indeed echoed by those bidding for the passenger franchises.

Some lessons were learned very early on. Passenger peak time rail travel brings its own particular challenges. This often calls for maximum demand on rolling stock and fixed infrastructure with little by way of available diversionary routes. The 'knock-on' effect of staff stranded in the wrong place at times of disruption is one factor which determines the number of staff required to be employed at key locations. Commuting customers especially are schedule driven and are intolerant of interruption to their journey whether by delays or cancellations to the advertised service or even restricted ticket purchasing facilities.

Railway operational management and provision is a particular skill. The idea that the rostering of (expensive) 'spare' men is essential to cover staffing emergencies or that the absence of a key signalman ('signaller' today) can cause the closure of a key route are phenomena unique to the railway. Railways have always been labour intensive and whilst the concerted efforts of past management addressed this issue most competently there was no doubt amongst rail professionals that there is a limitation to staff reductions.

Because of this some airline and bus/coach practices of operation and service did not comfortably transfer to rail. Disposal of experienced and fully trained staff by franchisees in the early days worked against the credibility of the 'new' railway. It was soon understood that new train liveries and company names did nothing, on their own, to enhance performance. The rush to dispose of experienced professionals (who were deemed too traditional), the cutting, by the replacement management teams, of apparently excessive key graded jobs and a fundamental lack of comprehension of how 'to run a railway' impacted on train service provision. One major operator suffered significantly in the early days of their franchise by failing to understand the number of drivers required to run an intensive commuter railway.

Unlike the passenger businesses, freight operations were not put out to fixed term franchise but were direct 'one-off' total asset sales to successful bidders. From day one these had to be run on the basis of making profit—no franchises with government financial support here! The initial sales of freight businesses all went to experienced operators.

The preceding paragraphs in this section are not to be read as a criticism of rail privatisation *per se*. In principle I believe the time was right, but the method was wrong. The disposal of subsidiary and ancillary businesses recorded earlier had already removed net income, thereby affecting levels of achievable profit by the *British Railways Board*. The private sector suffers from no constraints as to ownership of related or un-related activities and is therefore free to diversify in the interests of overall financial performance to the ultimate benefit of the shareholder.

Under **Nationalisation—the Losses** I referred to the irony of the state-owned railway having to compete with the similarly state-owned British Road Services, the most organised and co-ordinated road haulage operation ever seen in this country. Now irony reared its head again. In the same way that the state-owned *British Rail* had been obliged to dispose of it's profit-making subsidiaries (they being deemed 'non-core') in the mid twentieth century, the newly privatised railways were saddled with 'buying-in' what had continued to be regarded as part of the 'core' railway. The creation of separate providers also striving to operate at a profit—infrastructure and rolling stock in particular—impacts directly on bottom line prospects of the new train companies. In addition, passenger rolling stock acquisition is still controlled by the Department for Transport (as successors to the *Strategic Rail Authority*)!

Conclusion

This short final section may be better headed 'to conclude' or 'summary' — it is not the product of a logical sequence which leads to a definitive answer. If there is a case to be made for keeping 'service industries' in the public sector then it is my belief that railways do not fall into this category. What has gone before has related chronologically the birth, growing pains, various mid-life crises, surgery and some rejuvenation of the railways. It has also shown that the 'living' experiences are common to both private and state ownership. Railways were created by necessity as commercial enterprises to support other businesses but also as undertakings in their own right. They are not the sole provider of transport any more than one steel works, one coal mine or one vegetable packing factory has a monopoly of their particular product.

The success of rail freight privatisation demonstrates that profit is achievable within the industry. It can of course be said that had privatisation been approached in a different way, based perhaps on the 1924 to 1947 companies, profit from freight could have continued to be used to give financial support to the needs of the passenger business. Similarly, infrastructure and rolling stock provision would have remained on the books on an 'at cost' basis. In this way, as the reader may care to reflect, the 2010 annual subsidy of approximately £6bn. would have been eliminated by now, or certainly be closer to the figure of £2bn. paid to the nationalised railway in its last year!

As to the future of Britain's rail industry? What has gone before relates the industry's susceptibility to outside influences. Its very success and structure has rarely been entirely in its own hands and I suspect that this will not change whilst the current legislative approach prevails. As a retired railwayman I take pride in much of the past and draw a deal of satisfaction from the present. I take comfort from the belief that railways will continue to have a vital part to play for generations to come.

Liz Kessler

Public Service

Why it is so difficult to ensure that places meet the needs of people, especially in areas of multi-deprivation

Key to transformation was stealth. We had to do things quickly because next week we might not be here any more. And you have to be quick to avoid your own bureaucracy. Bureaucracy is like a fungus that contaminates everything …

Jamie Lerner, former Mayor of Curitiba, Brazil

Why is it so difficult to ensure that places meet the needs of people, especially in areas of mult-deprivation? Changing existing places such as these and making them good and enjoyable places to live is a challenge and requires stealth: all too often much money is spent on them without significant difference.

For the last ten years I have been trying to bring about lasting change to three areas, all New Deal for Communities (NDC) areas. The first, in Southampton, I left after two years realising that I could knock my head against a brick wall and achieve nothing in ten years. I then worked in EC1 NDC, in Islington, London for six years during which time much positive change took place. I had a window of opportunity, it was open—I took my chance and much was achieved before the project closed. I am now trying to use what I learned in another area, Stepney in east London. Very late in the day, I have been invited to try to replicate what was done in EC1. Inappropriate contracts were signed before I arrived and the will to change tack is minimal.

In this chapter I explore why working in the public sector makes it so difficult, and indeed rare, to secure major improvements, and to see dysfunctional places — the estates, streets and parks of a neighbourhood — truly transformed for residents. It is not always due to lack of knowledge or an absence of concerned people in local authorities. Nor, in recent years, is it primarily due to inadequate investment in these areas. Within the context of public service my comments will refer to the experience of working for arms length organisations, the NDCs, as well as for local authorities that are typical of many, their Planning and Housing Departments, in particular. My reflections will also draw on previous experience of working for Shelter and local authority Housing Departments back in the 1970s.

I gave up working in housing in the late 1970s after working in Housing Action Areas, an early government initiative aimed at improving housing in deprived neighbourhoods, when it became obvious that the only way to progress was to go into management and administration, losing contact with those people whose situation I hoped to improve. I was also aware that too much of what was being done failed effectively to address the needs of people, or neighbourhoods as a whole. Too often I was left with a sense of tinkering but not really solving problems.

I returned to these issues in 2000, after completing an MA in urban design and having gained a more focused and informed understanding of what makes places work for people. I then wanted to use my skills and knowledge to help make existing places work better.

The NDC programme, which was launched in 1999, coincided with the Urban Summit of 2000 and provided an opportunity to do things differently, in a focused way at a neighbourhood level, with unprecedented funding. From 2004 to 2009, I had a wonderful chance to contribute to the transformation of a neighbourhood of multi-deprivation in south Islington, by working as an urban designer for EC1 NDC. The starting budget for this work was £6m, which sounds a lot but was small in comparison to the overall need.

Now, and in 50 years time, the vast majority of people live and will be living, in homes and neighbourhoods that already exist. Urban Design is about understanding what makes places work for people; it takes a holistic approach and is fundamental to what worked in the EC1 NDC area. It is not however a background that is shared by many people working in areas such as these.

Typical of many such districts the EC1 area felt bleak and colourless; there were few people out and about and residents complained that it felt unsafe. Over six years of concerted effort much of the area was transformed by a number of projects all of which aimed to increase the safety, attractiveness and use of the public spaces — the streets, external areas around blocks of social housing and the parks. The quality and quantity of planning throughout was fundamental to this, and the changes included the redesign and improvement of four parks, major improvements to two others and improvements to seventeen streets and public spaces making them feel safer, less dominated by vehicles,

CHANGING A NEIGHBOURHOOD
Examples of change from the EC1 NDC area

'It's like a cork bursting out of a bottle! I had no idea there
were so many children cooped up in these flats'
— Elderly Resident, 2009

Brunswick Estate Play 2009

Brunswick Estate Play 2007

Brunswick Estate 2007

Brunswick Estate 2009

CHANGING A NEIGHBOURHOOD
Examples of change from the EC1 NDC area

'It's created an instant community!'
— *Resident referring to Radnor Street Gardens, 2009*

Radnor Street Gardens 2008

'There's a real buzz of excitement in the air ...'
— *Resident commenting on the changes*

Spa Fields 2008

CHANGING A NEIGHBOURHOOD
Examples of change from the EC1 NDC area

'Before the revamp, I wouldn't have dreamed of walking through Spa Fields—it was quite threatening. But it's now a beautiful and peaceful place for everyone'—*Resident, 2009*

Spa Fields 2009

Spa Fields 2005

Spa Fields Play 2004

Spa Fields Play 2009

CHANGING A NEIGHBOURHOOD
Examples of change from the EC1 NDC area

'It no longer looks like a council estate'

— *Resident, 2009*

Wenlake Estate 2009

Wenlake Estate 2005

Whitecross Street
Market 2004

Whitecross Street Market 2009

more attractive and useable for pedestrians and social activity; this included the revival of an almost moribund street market. Five estates also underwent major change to their outside communal areas, creating attractive gardens and places for children to play, people of all ages to spend time, sit out or grow vegetables and flowers. The photographs on the preceding pages aim to give a flavour of some of these changes.

Each project made a vital contribution to its immediate area, but taken together they added up to more than the sum of their parts and contributed to transforming the neighbourhood as a whole. Much was achieved, but more could have been done. Resident satisfaction with the area has soared and people feel safer, as was documented in the MORI survey of 2008 and subsequent NDC evaluation. There are now many more people of all ages and backgrounds out and about, and people comment on the area feeling more neighbourly.

Many people from different departments of the local authority, independent designers, residents and local councillors contributed to the change, felt involved and took pride in what had been achieved. The experience indicates that such change is possible, but why is it so difficult and so seldom achieved?

Changing neighbourhoods:
the New Deal for Communities (NDC) programme

In 2000 and 2001 thirty-nine neighbourhoods of multiple deprivation throughout Britain, with average populations of around 12,000 people, were given government money of around £50m each, as part of the NDC programme which aimed to turn them around over a ten year period by concentrated and co-ordinated investment to tackle poor health, low educational attainment, unemployment, crime and community safety and the environment.

The programme was the latest of a number of area-based initiatives that were aimed at transforming areas of deprivation. It overlapped with, and superseded, the SRB (Single Regeneration Budget) programme which ran from 1994-2004 and had aimed to bring together funding from a number of sources, encourage partnership working and be more responsive to local need. The need for a longer period of time to bring about change was recognised and the NDCs were a ten year programme.

The NDCs responded to the recognition that large sums of public money were being spent in areas of multi-deprivation but that because the public services being delivered to residents were poor and disparate the problems remained and required more and more funds while there was always a perception by residents that they were being neglected and that their needs were not effectively addressed. In response to this the NDCs were established as separate organisations, with a Partnership Board made up of local residents and representatives from the different statutory organisations responsible for services in the area. The objective that they should be 'resident-led' was ill-defined. The local authority acted as the 'accountable body'.

Partnership working, joining up services and a co-ordinated, time-limited approach to transforming neighbourhoods that had been failed by public services over many years was both an opportunity and a challenge. There was an opportunity to do things differently, to understand why services had failed in the past and to develop radically different approaches with the longer term objective of influencing the way public services operate.

My particular role was to work on the environment theme, with the aim of transforming as much as possible of the bleak, vehicle dominated and poorly used public parts of the neighbourhood: these looked neglected and felt unsafe. This included all the areas that were not built on—the parks, streets and, most significantly in an area where 94% of the residents lived in local authority owned estates, and almost no-one had a private garden, the communal areas around the blocks of flats.

Improving people's day to day experience of living in such an environment was the focus of this work, which was affected by the organisation and management of a number of local authority departments and services, central government control and funding, the management of the NDC and by politics and political will. Securing worthwhile change also necessitates engaging with residents but also depends on the quality of professional expertise and design skills that can be used to implement change. So there are many factors to weigh up and hold in balance but all are essential if lasting improvements are to be made.

Unlike most of my colleagues I came to the work with specialist knowledge of the theme I was working on, and a clear vision of what needed to be done to improve residents' health and well-being through improving this environment. This was based on my training in urban design and experience. I also benefited from my post being well thought through from the outset by the Policy and Projects Manager in the Planning Department of Islington Council who had initiated the role. Although I was employed by the NDC I worked two days a week in the Planning Department of the local authority.

I was both an insider and an outsider. *I could access funds and I was not part of the local authority departmental and hierarchical structure.* But I was not immune to the myriad of barriers that together so often prevent effective and long term improvements to a neighbourhood.

With hindsight, and having eventually seen considerable change in the neighbourhood where I was working, I have understood more fully those barriers and frustrations preventing positive change and how they can be negotiated. I can also fully understand residents' frustrations and why so many people's working experience is so debilitating and far removed from the commitment to public service that frequently motivated them at the outset of their careers. It is easiest to merge into a dysfunctional organisation, to be busy and achieve very little, or spend much time gathering figures, information, writing and researching documents while not actually progressing the implementation of work.

The desire for more and better maintained green spaces as well as for a safer and cleaner environment has been highlighted by numerous surveys and consultations carried out by local authorities, housing associations and other organisations, including MORI. At the same time evidence from research carried out by health professionals and organisations, including the last government's Healthy Boroughs Programme, as well as CABE (the Commission for Architecture and the Built Environment, currently being merged with the Design Council) has increasingly highlighted the obvious connection between health and the quality of the environment. This link is particularly striking in areas of multi-deprivation where both of these tend to be poor and children in particular are more vulnerable to health problems and car accidents.

Increasingly there is also recognition that improving the quality of the public places fosters better mental health and encourages more active and healthier lifestyles. Health benefits follow from a focus on walking, exercise, outdoor play and growing vegetables and fruit, especially when addressing conditions such as obesity, heart problems, diabetes and poor diet. Yet despite the wealth of evidence, adequate resources and opportunities for effective change remain extremely limited while budgets for maintenance are constantly being cut, or are under threat, and the resources required for real change to the environment are all too often considered unaffordable. Compared with other expenditure, on redevelopment or a new community centre for instance, the expenditure required can be comparatively small but it is all too rarely prioritised. The focus of capital spending in areas of deprivation has tended to be on new buildings, a facility, or redevelopment which can leave poor and neglected areas untouched, or leads to long term upheaval and an increase in a short term sense of neglect. It could be otherwise as the work in EC1 has demonstrated.

The NDC programme offered the opportunity to do things differently, to demonstrate that change is possible and can be appreciated. The integrated work on estates, parks and streets carried out in EC1 also highlighted a wide range of issues that would seem to be comparatively straightforward but which are all too often so difficult to achieve. My experience illustrates why some aspects of working for public services, local authorities in particular, make effective work so difficult. The next section will consider some of the elements that worked well and also highlight some general issues that made the working experience so challenging despite the ultimate satisfaction of knowing that much that was positive was achieved in a comparatively short period of time.

What worked well

Partnership Working

All the work that was carried out to improve the environment was carried out 'in partnership' with the local authority. This worked well because I was able to work in both organisations at the same time to achieve the same outcome, something that was made easier once an overall 'Vision' for the area had been agreed by both the Council and the NDC. This Vision was supported by an agreed overall strategy that identified how the work would be planned and implemented, both practically and organisationally. Linked to this strategy was agreement for £6m of the overall budget of £52m to be allocated to the work to improve the parks, streets and environment around the buildings on housing estates. This funding was invaluable; it made effective planning possible, encouraged the local authority to put resources of staff time, as well as further funds, into the programme. It helped to kick start work on the ground and acted as match funding to attract further funds for implementation. By the end of 2011 around £17m had been spent on the public space programme as a whole.

Time Limitation

The fact that the NDC programme was time limited and that there was considerable pressure from central government to spend funds on an annual basis certainly quickened the pace of implementing work. This helped a great deal in galvanising local authority departments and far more was achieved in a shorter period of time than is usual. But it was not comfortable.

The NDCs were set up as ten year programmes in recognition of the fact that changing places takes time; unfortunately however this time was truncated. The programme of public space improvements in EC1 did not start until 3 years into the overall programme, in 2004. It was effectively halted towards the end of 2009 when most of the NDC posts were deleted, mine included, and the structures that had been put in place to develop and implement environmental projects were disbanded; outstanding work reverted back to the local authority.

My post, like other project posts in the NDC, was initially established with a two year contract. The benefits of having a reasonable period of time for the overall programme were immediately undermined by the short term project approach so typical of most initiatives aimed at improving public services. I was fortunate that I managed to extend this two year contract into almost six years, but the original ten year timescales would have allowed for a much more effective programme.

Short termism in project work of this kind, characteristic in my experience of much public sector work, is thoroughly unsatisfactory. It raises hopes that are then not seen through, leads to insecurity, wastes time and energy and does nothing to create a sense of commitment or achievement, let alone learning and embedding that learning in the relevant organisation. It was regrettable that despite hopes to the contrary the NDC programme remained locked into a short termist approach.

Changing places takes time, it requires consistency, attention to detail, much of it small, unglamorous and difficult to fund unless it forms part of a wider whole, as well as input from a wide variety of local authority departments, voluntary and community groups working together within the context of an overall objective. I was fortunate that for six years I was able to maintain consistency, carrying out a role that could be created by working in partnership with the local authority, with a clear focus on a specific neighbourhood – a role that does not generally exist.

Team working

The principle of working to improve different places within the neighbourhood as a whole was embedded in the strategy from the outset and supported the establishment of an interdepartmental team to work in the area for the best part of four of the six years. We established a team of Islington Council officers and myself that included someone from the Planning, Street Management and Parks Departments and, rather notionally, someone from Housing. We had a clear purpose, a shared vision, time to plan, co-ordinate across departments and sections, build up relationships with elected representatives as well as residents, and get to know the area in all its detail. Everything worthwhile is a struggle but everyone involved was able to see positive change, and to take pride in what was achieved by implementing a number of co-ordinated projects that together had an impact far in excess of the sum of their individual parts.

This outcome was important as was the impact on residents' lives; the job satisfaction for those involved was greater than their normal way of working, acknowledged by the members of the team and—when EC1 NDC was wound up—sadly lost.

Design and problem solving

Fundamental to the approach was an emphasis on design. This involved working with independent multi-disciplinary design teams and using their expertise, creativity and design skills to work on different parts of the area, analyse them, resolve problems and work with officers, residents and stakeholders to develop a shared vision for these areas and raise aspirations. Most importantly, they used their skills to introduce people to ideas and solutions that would not otherwise have been imagined or thought about; these were not necessarily complex, dramatic or even costly interventions but they made a huge impact on the area and made the difference between repair of what had functioned poorly and real overall improvement. The focus on design added quality and pleasure as well as solving problems.

These design teams were able to focus exclusively on the different parts of the area in a way that overstretched officers cannot. At the same time, the team approach referred to above was invaluable for managing the whole process. Most local authorities do not have 'in house' design teams that have the dedicated time, expertise and resources required to analyse an area, think out of the box and respond creatively while engaging effectively and building up trust and support with residents and officers. The design teams that worked in EC1 did just that. Their work led to transformational change (see photos above between pages 186 and 187); they produced area plans and then detailed designs for individual projects. They worked at all levels:

- completely re-designing parks;
- adding attractive planting to estates and streets;
- changing the feel of a street by removing parking;
- changing the flow of traffic while also redesigning the street to prioritise pedestrian movement;
- closing off redundant road space and creating an attractive new public space with plenty of planting;
- changing the materials used for estate roads and introducing planting so in effect changing the feel of buildings and their context, framing the blocks of flats so that instead of calling for them to be demolished residents commented on how attractive

they were and how the they no longer 'looked like a council estate'; and

- providing allotments on estates and designing attractive opportunities for play.

Working effectively with design teams is however time consuming and all too often officer time for this is not made available, dialogue is minimised and the benefits of using such teams substantially reduced.

What worked badly

'Resident led'

NDCs were established in the wake of failures by local authorities and other public service organisations to provide the services people required or needed. From the point of view of those who are at the receiving end of public services, especially those in areas of multi-deprivation, there is the sense that they have been failed by the public services and the professionals who implement them. Residents in areas such as these have recognised that as poor people they have become an industry and have given middle class professionals a plentiful supply of jobs. There was an expectation that this could be changed if programmes were 'resident-led', hence the focus on 'bottom up' and the intention behind the NDC programme that it should be managed by 'resident-led' partnerships. The hope was that this would provide the opportunity to do things differently, to understand why services had failed in the past, to develop different approaches and really respond to the needs of disadvantaged people.

Many residents in large social housing estates and areas of multi-deprivation have indeed been sorely let down by the system. The idea that, as resident-led organisations, the NDCs would effectively meet the needs of residents was beguiling, but the concept was woolly and ill defined. By establishing these partnerships as being 'resident led', and giving the impression that residents would be in control of budgets, expectations were raised that could never be fulfilled, especially since the pressures, and control, from central and local government were so stringent. The scope for residents to lead on financial decisions was limited indeed. Conflict was endemic between different residents as well as between resident groups and the local authorities; having been let down by service providers for many years, the trust of local resident groups was particularly hard to gain.

Governance issues and poor leadership in many of the NDCs seriously impeded the programme as a whole, and in EC1 in particular, from being as effective as it could have been. The 'resident led' element of the programme was largely abandoned quite early on although, to varying degrees, resident involvement continued. In terms of making successful places such involvement is essential, as it is in many other aspects of the work. It needs to be based on residents communicating a clear understanding of their lived experience as residents—what does and does not work for them—and responding to proposals for change with a clear understanding of their rationale.

This is crucially different from raising the expectation that by identifying problems the most effective solutions will be easily identified. As with a medical problem it is important to be able to describe the problem; it is then the task of the doctor to diagnose what is wrong and prescribe effective treatment. Similarly in areas that are not working well, professional knowledge and expertise are essential but need to be informed by local knowledge to make places work. What is required is effective communication between the two as well as trust, which takes time to develop.

Compartmentalised Approach

Despite the rhetoric effective partnership working was fiercely resisted, largely due to the on-going power of the service providers and to government control of the programme. Many of the issues that make some people's experience of working in the public sector problematic were replicated including the compartmentalised way of working, non-specialist management and an emphasis on processes and ticking boxes.

For all the implicit recognition that in areas of multi-deprivation there is a link between the core NDC themes, health, education, crime, unemployment and the environment, the connections were not made. The 'joining up' of services was always seen in the context of service providers working more closely together rather than developing strategies that would address a number of issues at once, such as highlighting the health benefits of improving the external environment to encourage more healthy lifestyles and thereby maximise the benefits of working together. As a resident Board member for the Southampton NDC graphically put it 'Don't ask me to give up smoking until I can get a bit of joy from my surroundings'.

This lack of linking up was reflected in the staffing structures of NDCs that followed existing public sector structures. Officers were appointed to lead on the different themes but not to plan, discuss and develop an overall strategy that recognised the relationship between themes and the benefits that could be gained from a holistic approach. The generalist NDC officers responded to applications for funding from the service providers and 'project managed' the expenditure of NDC funds rather than leading and engaging with the service providers in a dialogue to do things differently. This project management approach was largely dictated by the need to meet targets, convoluted, complicated and time consuming processes for releasing funds and endless monitoring and evaluation forms. This combined with the need to respond to thwarted expectations and disappointment of needy people added to problems of achieving really transformational change.

Management and process

The NDCs replicated and had to respond to many management problems prevalent in local authorities: restructuring, rigid hierarchies, cumbersome processes and lack of focus, added to which working with local authorities required responding to constant flux, both political and in terms of personnel. With a clear and agreed vision of what needed to be achieved to improve the parks, streets and around the estates, the first years of working in EC1 were challenging in trying to find a way through local authority procedures to effectively ensure that projects could be realised. A change in the political climate after elections in 2006 made this more complex, although by then a strategy for improving these public spaces had been agreed and much was underway supported by policy decisions. This meant that the public space programme was secure so long as there was someone in post dedicated to seeing it implemented.

The change of Director for the NDC in the same year was however more problematic; the new 'chief executive' was imposed by the local authority. He had been a senior departmental administrator who had been made redundant, and who, like many new heads, wanted to change things, wanted a clean sweep of staff and to establish the NDC hierarchically as a mini local authority despite the fact that it employed less than twenty five people. He made life extremely uncomfortable for those who remained. New so called 'strategic managers' were brought in, generalists again, recruited on the principle that anyone can manage anything and that specific skills and knowledge are not required to run a programme. They duplicated and were short lived but contributed to a high turnover of staff and increasingly low morale.

In the remaining years the EC1 NDC programme as a whole achieved little, but kept the lid on things and, through effective spin, was able to placate both central government and the local authority. As the chief executive of the NDC said to me 'it doesn't matter if none of your projects get implemented provided you follow the right processes'. The working environment was dispiriting, wasteful of energy and money, constantly undermining, characterised by petty harassment and frequent changes of procedure, controlling but with no clarity of direction. Staff came in and left within weeks, frustrated and realising that they could achieve nothing of value while the highly paid strategic managers remained, segregated, not communicating, doing little and achieving less.

I remained because I had an approved strategy and programme that was beginning to gain both results and recognition, within the neighbourhood, as well as at a London wide and national level. There was a unique opportunity within a short period of time to effect significant change to the neighbourhood as a whole. This could prove that it is indeed possible to change places for the better, without redeveloping them, and that by using good design it was possible significantly to improve how they feel, look and are used. It was an opportunity too good to abandon and the work would certainly not have been continued had I left; nor was there the likelihood of developing a similar approach elsewhere, at least until sufficient work had been completed to prove that the way of working was effective.

Restructuring

Throughout the period in which I was working for the EC1 NDC the council's planning department was being restructured. This was unsettling for staff, led to lack of clear leadership, to drift, and to decisions being avoided. There was little evidence that proposed changes were being considered from the point of view of solving problems, or indeed implementing a vision for creating a better environment; it appeared to be driven by economics and, as Richard Sennett has pointed out, by the public sector adopting the private sector model of managers reorganising, merging and restructuring as a means of demonstrating that they are doing something, but not basing this on effectively analysing what needs to be done and how it can be done better — and this was before the current focus on cuts. A Planner who has worked in local authorities for many years has recently said he has never experienced a working environment that was not being restructured, and it wasn't just Planning, it was endemic in most departments.

Hierarchical structures, accountability and the working environment

Local authorities have rigid hierarchies and this combined with constantly changing personnel and a focus on accountability, but not responsibility, makes it hard to be effective from within or indeed effect change from without. Issues are not discussed but 'accountable' trails, now usually email, are emphasised. There are systems to prove that things are effectively controlled but with no-one in reality taking responsibility for resolving problems and ensuring that an effective service that meets people's needs is in fact the reality.

Listening to Margaret Hodge MP (chair of the Public Accounts Committee) describing the processes for defence procurement—the extremely long time scales, frequent changes in personnel and buck passing in a long process where funds have already been committed—was reminiscent of many a situation I encountered whether as part of a major contract or a small improvement. Unsatisfactory though it is for defence spending it may be understandable given the scale of planning and expenditure required, but the same should not apply to getting a play area fixed, reusing and reintegrating derelict space or replacing failed bedding plants.

Work is planned departmentally but improving neighbourhoods and public places requires input from a number of people in different departments and sections and needs to be planned on a 'place' basis, with the different elements then being carefully co-ordinated. The team approach used in EC1 did just this but such a way of working is not the norm. More commonly those working on regeneration projects dip in and out and will have moved on long before projects are completed. Officers tend to work on one element, like a cog, and are not seen to be responsible for the whole or gain satisfaction from seeing the results of their input—or indeed learning from the experience.

This is compounded by constant changes in people's roles and poor career structures which contribute to the high turnover of staff and to distancing their input from the eventual outcome. Recognition and promotion within a department, with a clear sense of progression, is not the norm; people frequently leave their jobs after about two years going to another authority in order to proceed up a career ladder and get better pay; and if they don't leave their role is changed. Capital projects that change places generally take at least two and a half years to go through planning, design, funding and implementation phases before completion, so it is rare to have continuity of staff from beginning to end. Inadequate or no form of handover exacerbates problems and sets work back considerably at great cost in wasted time and staffing costs.

One comparatively modest project I worked on had seven different officers leading before finally one was given the role, started it again and finally saw it through to a successful outcome. This project was eventually completed in four years; it could have been completed in one, and not more than two. The frustration, loss of confidence and enthusiasm, resulting from these changes are costly; continuity is lost, much has to be repeated and accountability is diluted, with information also frequently being lost or ignored. This is particularly problematic for residents, and other stakeholders; building relationships and trust is hugely important for them and cannot be achieved if there is a constant change in personnel. Frequent staff changes also lead to inferior work being carried out, under pressure, at the last moment, driven by a need to spend and be seen to be doing something. When there has been a long wait anything is seen to be better than nothing and there is pressure to get something done regardless of quality or the initial integrity of a scheme.

At a different level there are many employees working at low grades, on the ground, who care passionately about the well being of the residents they serve but are powerless in the face of tiers of management, hierarchy and processes to effect simple, inexpensive change, let alone contribute to proposals for more strategic changes. They bear the brunt of complaints but have little opportunity to respond effectively. For instance it was easier, more effective and less frustrating or time consuming for me to go to a garden centre and buy £12 worth of bedding plants for a new central planter in a park that had just been redesigned than to endlessly go through more formal channels, with no-one willing or able to take responsibility or act. Similar examples of frustration are legion.

Such action is however effective as a one off but not sustainable. Leaving the planter empty for far too long was dispiriting for all; more importantly it also undermined the value of the recent investment in the park by restarting the cycle of neglect and decline. It would not have been noticed by senior managers based in departments far from the park in question and so would not have seemed important, but for those who had been involved in the park's transformation and who observed it regularly, residents in particular, it was an affront. Taking direct action was far easier and cheaper than spending time on constant emails or telephone calls and living with the frustration of witnessing a summer going by with no action. Although this might have been a quick fix it was no long term solution and there are not often people about who can, and will, take direct action. It has remained empty and arid for the last two years.

This example demonstrates the value of employing people who know an area well, frequent it, care for it, and who have the possibility of responding to its needs, people who, like residents, can see, and feel, the impact of things not being done. The employee with day to day care of this park felt constrained and unable to act. He had no budget, was aware of his powerlessness and of the fact that managers that might be sufficiently influential to act would not listen to him as he was too junior. Budgets are too inflexible and processes too far removed from individuals and issues to respond to need. Too often there is a separation between those who work with people, who understand their needs and care, and management that responds to numbers, statistics, quick fixes or the lure of prestige but not what is actually required.

Within the great scheme of things small issues such as the above are not of great importance. But there are hundreds of small issues in most places and, at a local level, they cause discomfort and distress compounded by the fact that trying to get them fixed is so labyrinthine that most people, both residents and officers, just give up, or a cheap and ugly temporary solution is found without the real issue being addressed.

Many managers are comfortable running systems and processes but they are not problem solvers and are terrified of passionate officers, who want to do a job. This characteristic was summed up by EC1 NDC's Chief Executive's comment referred to above when he yet again changed the criteria for releasing NDC funds. It was reiterated when I left having been responsible for co-ordinating significant change to an area that affected the lives of all the 12,000 residents as well as those who worked in, or visited, the area. I was told by a senior officer at the local authority that what had been achieved could not be continued because the 'processes were not correct'. A great deal was achieved in a comparatively short period of time, unique in the local authority's experience while resident satisfaction in the area has soared. The work as a whole received many awards, national and London wide, but what processes would have been correct were never clarified nor was consideration given to the fact that perhaps the 'processes' needed to be reconsidered or lessons learned, rather than the other way round.

The reorganisations taking place concurrently in the local authority never took the opportunity to discuss what was proving to be effective, just as earlier restructuring in the 1970s that I experienced when the 'Mackenzie men' (management consultants brought in to change public services in the 1970s) came in and failed to respond to experience. When I left the NDC outstanding work reverted to the council, was managed as it had been before the NDC.

In 2010 the strategy for work to the public spaces in the EC1 NDC area, and its implementation, received a Royal Town Planning Institute Award; credit was given to a long list of people who had had absolutely nothing to do with the thinking behind it, its implementation or its success, with no mention of those who had; with one exception they had all been moved on. A trivial, but symbolic, point; one that demonstrates the way in which employees are not valued; importance is given to a corporate approach that fails to acknowledge the role of individuals even when it is well known, and backed up by research, that people work better when they have some autonomy, responsibility/control and pride. Again, from discussion, this is a standard approach in many public services.

Privatising work in the public sector

Constant reorganisations and a focus on process are two ways in which public services have been influenced by the private sector, but as important is the way in which public service has been privatised. In terms of the environment much work is contracted out to private companies with a different ethos. This is true of both professional and maintenance work. Long gone are the days in which a park keeper has responsibility for looking after a park, nurturing its plants, getting to know regular users and making it feel safe and attractive; time after time this is requested by the public in frequent consultation and deflected. Functions are separated and carried out by a variety of private companies, employing many different people with limited responsibility, little linking up and constantly moving from place to place. In a park for instance to mention a few there are those who pick up litter, others who mow, those who patrol to give some security, others patrolling car parking or dogs, those looking after plants brought in from a private nursery and people whose task it is to work with the community. They are all spread thinly, duplicate and report problems relating to their task not the area as a whole, and all too rarely take practical action. The contract and monitoring culture is inflexible, mechanistic and not subject to dialogue, developing relationships and problem solving.

Similarly when there are opportunities for Planners to be proactive and initiate work on large sites or on an area basis it is all too often handed over to a consultant, developer, or private consortium, but not in such a way that there is a problem solving dialogue and the Planner is a partner and so feels involved in the eventual outcome. More frustratingly their role is one of control, they either accept or reject according to rigid and not necessarily appropriate criteria with little opportunity to engage, mould or indeed respond to suggestions. The opportunity to lead on, and find time and funding for, small, knit and stitch, interventions that make a huge impact at a local level are few indeed; they fall through the departmental net of local authorities and can't compete with the lure of a big project. This contract culture is set to get far worse in response to cuts in current staffing numbers; public service officers jobs are becoming more formulaic, controlling the private sector that delivers the service but not using judgement to respond to local need or individual circumstances.

What value evaluation?

The NDC programme as a whole invested heavily in monitoring, evaluation and publicity, giving this at least as much priority as developing projects while also shackling those of us working on projects with tedious, complex and pretty irrelevant forms to be filled in which were then processed in a mechanical manner to release funding. The information was standardised so it could be used for public documents evaluating the national programme overall; the result was bland reports. The information gathered was never designed to capture the essence of the work that was carried out to the public spaces as described above. Recognising this I was, in my last months, asked to prepare a report summarising the work that had taken place as part of the programme to improve the public spaces in the area, and to identify lessons learned. I was not allowed to present this work however or discuss it with officers who were to be responsible for continuing the work that remained in progress or, more importantly, with those who might in the future have funds, and the opportunity to plan for, and work on, improvements to other neigbourhoods.

Following my report a formal independent evaluation was commissioned, costing a substantial amount of money. This thorough document detailed much of what had been achieved, and while confirming the benefits of the work omitted all reference to the lessons learned, in particular the way in which it had been conceived and organised, or the focus on design. Like so many reports commissioned by local authorities that have no identified person to engage with them and to respond to them, both reports will, I suspect, fester on a shelf, be junked and lost to collective memory as officer churn continues apace. One of the key factors that made the public space programme a success was the web of relationships between all who were involved in the work. This emphasis on people and relationships is precisely what current working practices seek to avoid in the name of process, accountability, corporatism and so called 'professionalism'.

None of this is new. Changes do not get embedded and every so often a new initiative replaces the last with scant understanding or commitment to improvement emanating from a real analysis of both the strengths and weaknesses of a previous programme, but more of a knee jerk reaction to elements that were seen to have failed. This was true of the NDC programme which superseded the previous SRB (Single Regeneration Budget). On the positive side the time period was increased in response to previous experience but the NDC programme downplayed the importance of the physical environment. The SRB programme was seen to have failed to meet its potential as it was too short and focused too much on physical change as opposed to changing people's circumstances—the physical change it favoured was re-development and new buildings rather than a holistic approach as described above, but this distinction was not identified. Without recognising these nuances and limitations all programmes will continue to fail, to a greater or lesser extent, and remain as drops in an ocean rather than seriously changing the way in which services are delivered.

Localism, Neighbourhood Planning and some thoughts for the future

The pressures were great. I was determined to do as much as possible in the limited period of time available; much was achieved, way in excess of most local authority implementation. In retrospect it is a strong argument for a time limited programme; the time pressure was a key factor in making things happen, as was the use of independent design teams and having a clear focused programme, with an identified leader/co-ordinator.

Working with creative, problem solving designers was always a pleasure and contrasted with the bureaucracy of the NDC and council, despite the fact that many of the individuals in these organisations were wonderful people doing their best. It was not a comfortable period or experience however; layers of management at ECI were introduced that undermined autonomy, obstacles were constantly put in the way, petty harassment went on all the time while processes arbitrarily changed from week to week and had to be negotiated.

Regrettably many of the other NDCs also failed to live up to expectations. Where there was clear vision, continuity of personnel and determination they were able to indicate ways in which things could be done differently. The question still persists as to why it is so often difficult for work in public services to respond to need and enable those working within these services to feel they are being effective and that their contribution is worthwhile. With regard to making places work for people, and be enjoyable, reference has been made to many issues that mitigate against this, committing enough time and consistency of staffing being two.

Times are changing. The public sector is being squeezed, the rhetoric is all about 'localism' and 'neighbourhood planning' and again a 'bottom up approach' and the 'Big Society'. At one level this might be a cause for optimism and sound very like the approach described above. It is not new but could be seen as a different way of expressing the importance of public service in its broadest sense. Localism and neighbourhood planning are however focusing on new development, they could be a recipe for nimbyism, or for development, including homes, that are tacked on to existing places, not knitted into the area as a whole. Alternatively they could ensure that benefits are spread throughout a neighbourhood, that different areas link up seamlessly and the poor do not continue to be marginalised, kept from view, needing constant expenditure, but are fully integrated with the rest of society.

Lord Maurice Glasman has described new Labour's public service reforms as 'almost Maoist in their conception of zero managerial restructuring. Managerial, arrogant and ultimately doomed'. He has also said that 'Labour should know that unless the workforce is engaged and committed, change remains, in the worst sense of the word, aspirational'. But it is not just Labour: this approach has been growing in strength throughout the last 30–40 years regardless of which party was in power at a local or national level. This could however change; there is an opportunity to learn from what did indeed work and what did not.

The NDC programme nationally had huge problems as a result of a lack of definition about what was meant by it being 'resident-led'. A distrust of professional knowledge and expertise, the use of consultants and a lack of understanding about the difference between a designer and consultant were all part of the overall confusion about a 'bottom up, resident-led' approach. It persists in much current thinking and discussion of localism, neighbourhood plans and the Big Society; neither 'bottom up' not 'top down' work effectively, what is essential is mutual understanding and working together. Achieving lasting and positive change to an area is always painstakingly difficult. But the minimum conditions for success include:

- Effective local leadership
- The need to listen to and engage with local people to understand what they value and what is problematic
- Recognising the distinctions between understanding the problems in an area and having the skills and expertise to change it for the better
- Recognising the importance of developing and understanding a network of relationships
- Strong co-ordination and enough continuity in relationships to build up trust and maintain momentum.

Committed people taking responsibility and working together creatively in public services are crucial to improving neighbourhoods if combined with a substantial programme of professional development and training. A design-led problem solving approach could also help define a new role for ward councillors and their relationships with officers. When people see their efforts leading to positive change on the ground their motivation and sense of genuine public service will also increase.

POSTSCRIPT

In concluding my chapter on working in the public sector aiming to improve neighbourhoods, especially deprived neighbourhoods, I referred to two trends that were likely to affect the future. One was the increasing privatisation of work in the public sector, the use of consultants and handing work to private companies and consortia; the other was an increasing emphasis from government on 'Localism', 'Neighbourhood Plans' and 'Big Society'. Over the last year I have had direct experience of both and wanted to add a reference to this. Both trends have implications for each other, contradict each other, and affect those working in the public sector, especially those who retain a belief in, and commitment to, public service. I'll start with what I have observed of the privatisation of local authority services.

For a year I have been working, part time, in another area of deprivation in east London. The area is characterised by local authority housing, much of it large blocks of flats which, like the one described in the chapter above, was an NDC area and before that an SRB area. Despite receiving funding through these programmes, the neighbourhood has not significantly changed. The local authority had intended substantial redevelopment; when this was rejected in a ballot of residents in 2008 they changed tack and commissioned a Consortium made up of an RSL (Registered Social Landlord) developer and a building contractor employing architects to redevelop some blocks of flats and improve the rest of the housing stock, including the external areas. In so doing they have given the work to the private sector and handed over very substantial sums of public money with a complex contract that requires speedy delivery. The work is to be completed by 2013, with the Consortium being financially penalized if they do not make the deadline.

I have been employed by the Consortium, at the local authority planners' request, to help them transform the environment in a similar way to what had been achieved in the EC1 NDC area as the planners were unimpressed by initial proposals. The appointment has been resisted; it is seen to be too time consuming and so a threat to profit. The experience has however given me insights about the working of the private sector in carrying out work for the public sector. As is so often the case, the focus of the work has been on the buildings with the open space representing only a tiny proportion of the contracted cost; as such it is marginalised although, if done well, it will have a significant impact on residents' health, well-being, neighbourliness and feelings of belonging.

So as noted the planners were not satisfied with the proposals from the consortium but they were not responsible for the contract; this had been drawn up in conjunction with the local authority 'Housing Regeneration' department which is the client for the whole scheme. This Department had not seen the proposals let alone considered their potential. Their main concern was to ensure that the deadlines were met, money spent and accounted for; to this end I have observed many consultants as well as the Consortium being paid to deliver and monitor expenditure and the programme but not to consider the outcome. The Consortium is driven by the need to press on and ensure that whatever happens they should not be penalized for late delivery. As such they work in parallel with the housing regeneration department; they follow the letter of the contract even if it is clear it is inappropriate and could be varied.

Meanwhile local authority officers, whose numbers and skills base are being depleted, are too busy to give any time to ensuring that what is done is appropriate and will create an attractive and sustainable environment; like the Consortium they just want the job done which requires ensuring that nothing is either complex or controversial.

The planner who was responsible for my appointment was moved off the job the week after I started so I have been left with no-one wanting to change the direction of travel, with the contractor preventing me from engaging with the architect, this being seen as too costly and time consuming, the Consortium refusing to change anything without a direct instruction from the local authority and no-one in the local authority taking the time to engage in content, or give considered instructions; everyone is frustrated and the whole process absurdly time consuming and therefore costly.

As I have observed in other authorities the job is handed over, with the money, to the private sector without understanding that working in partnership is essential for a satisfactory outcome, as is some direction from management and local knowledge; instead too many local authorities rely on a formulaic, process driven approach. This, combined with the reduction of local authority employees, and the loss of skills and expertise, leaves the remaining officers ill equipped effectively to influence projects, makes their role more content free and project management orientated more stressful and less rewarding. Continuity, building relationships and trust between a wide range of people, and responding to a sense of place based on local knowledge are essential for positively changing neighbourhoods and indeed promoting 'localism'; they are all qualities that are increasingly marginalised and likely to be more so over the coming months.

'Localism' is however fundamental to the Planning Bill currently going through Parliament. I have also worked, in a paid advisory capacity, helping a village prepare a community-led plan. In a voluntary capacity, I have participated as a member of a group of concerned individuals, with professional expertise, aiming to encourage the small cathedral city where I live to take a holistic and planned, not piecemeal, approach to its future, to new housing development in particular. Both of these have been challenging but rewarding and exemplify all that 'Localism' is about, it responding to local need, opportunities and initiative. Whether this approach can succeed remains to be seen. It is however clear that this work will only have an impact if there are informed, dedicated and skilled people who have drive, leadership qualities, ability, resources and long term commitment, who can engage with a wide variety of people as well as the complicated statutory and political processes. It is asking a huge amount and might have an impact only in a few privileged places where there are such people and they can work together.

The contrast between these areas and the neighbourhoods I have described above is stark. This work is largely voluntary; the people involved are driven by a sense of public service quite different from what I have observed in the tiers of bureaucracy and management in the private sector where it is carrying out work on behalf of the public sector, or in the public sector itself when under pressure. More work is being given to the private sector, mostly to large monopolistic companies, and the job increasingly becomes one of managing with more and more bureaucratic controls. Meanwhile it becomes increasingly difficult for local firms, employing local people, to engage in dialogue and carry out work in the spirit of 'localism', which is fundamental at a neighbourhood level, in particular in deprived areas.

PART V

The Public Debate

Dan Carrier

From Heroes to Zeroes
How the Press report the work of public sector employees

If you take the news peddled in the popular press as simple fact, it would not be surprising if you got hot under the collar about how your taxes are spent. All too often there are stories about public sector employees doing a very bad job for wages funded by taxpayers. But huge cracks appear in such yarns once you examine such stories and the papers that print them. An ideological war is being waged by sections of the press against public services and public servants. There is no genuine discussion of the role of public service in today's society or of the performance of the majority of public servants.

In this climate, who would be a Union activist, representing hard working and poorly paid public employees?

Even for those so often painted as 'heroes' such as fire fighters, as soon as the Fire Brigade Union (the FBU) is mentioned, they are suddenly dangerous radicals intent on bringing down the state. Individual fire fighters are praised for their daily work of saving lives and battling fires — brave fireman rescues family from blaze, etc, etc — and then as soon as it comes to pay and conditions, the gloves are off.

The *Daily Mail*, as ever, fills its pages with rants against public sector workers and their union reps for such things as having second jobs, a media campaign that was stepped up after the FBU balloted its members for industrial action last year in reaction to changes in shift patterns and rota. The FBU saw these as cost cutting and that the changes would be dangerous. In particular the London Fire Brigade wanted to cut the night shift. Fire fighters argued that shorter night shifts could endanger people's lives as it would affect cover and at night fires tend to be worse as they are not discovered by householders so quickly.

But instead of reporting these issues calmly, the national press (with a few notable exceptions) failed to actually report what the dispute was about, and instead painted FBU members as dangerous radicals, who didn't know how lucky they were, happy to put the public at risk by calling for strikes. It led to industrial action in the summer and autumn of 2010, during which time the FBU was faced with a daily attack by sections of the media, who were in turn helped (according to the FBU) by the communications department of the fire brigade.

As a journalist who spent my teenage years working as a hospital porter, and was involved with the National Union of Public Employees before it was amalgamated with others to form Unison, I often find myself feeling deeply ashamed of the behaviour of journalists, due to their attacks on public sector workers via the newspapers they work for. Newspapers on the right love to get these workers in their sights on a regular basis, using individual stories to undermine entire professions.

This article describes the way public sector workers are attacked in print from the point of view of the workers and asks the question: why? When you trawl through archives it is hard not to think that the way public employees are portrayed has to be politically motivated. Public organisations are all too often depicted as inefficient behemoths, staffed by lazy workers more interested in their pay and conditions than putting in the hours for the good of all, all too often described as members of a closed shop union whose executives are champagne socialists, as bad as any fat cat bankers.

The FBU

London FBU representative Ben Sprung said he was often shocked at how the press turned their ire on his colleagues — especially considering the type of work they did.

'We felt we were always under attack from sections of the press,' recalls Mr Sprung, a fire fighter based in north London who is a union representative and was involved in trying to negotiate shift changes with the fire brigade. 'They were saying everything during the last dispute, such as attempts to negotiate a settlement whilst being threatened with mass sackings, was our fault.'

The way the press reported the work of fire fighters had some strange paradoxes, he states. The dispute came as moving testimonies about the work fire fighters did during the terrible events of the London bombings on the 7th of July, 2005, were made public at the 7/7 enquiry.

'They had reported acts of bravery our fire fighters had done, painting us individually as heroes,' recalls the FBU shop steward. 'But then during the dispute we felt that all the forces of the state were suddenly against us, from the government down. The London Fire Brigade had a communications department staffed by 40 people, paid for by the tax payer, and they were constantly briefing against us. We were aware they had good contacts with newspapers such as a *Daily Mail*, and suddenly the tone changed: we were no longer heroes but dangerous subversives who were willing to put people's lives at risk so we could get an extra few bob on the pay packet or some extra hours off to mow the lawn.'

So the same public sector workers who as individuals had been praised as heroes at the 7/7 enquiry and reported as such, were now being painted as militants willing to risk people's lives by going on strike, simply over what was portrayed as selfish reasons such as improving their own pay and conditions.

Mr Sprung revealed the union had made a series of Freedom of Information requests to access figures regarding the private firm used as strike breakers, Asset Co, who had a contract to provide fire services in the event of the strike. Unsurprisingly, says Mr Sprung, the fire brigade took as long as they could providing basic information that may have helped swing public opinion behind the firemen. Suspiciously, other statistics found their way into the public domain constantly as the dispute continued.

'The communications department was feeding friendly journalists a series of statistics which they felt could be used to rustle up stories against the FBU,' he says. 'It was a set up. There was collusion between the communications department and reporters.'

This led to a further paradox in union bashing. 'There were two issues they kept talking about, which had absolutely nothing to do with our industrial action or the dispute itself,' he recalls. One angle fed to the media was the fact that many firemen did not live in London, as if it meant they were country-seated lords of the manor, popping into town to work when they felt like it, and this was a reason they did not want their shifts changed.

'This basically ignored the fact that fire fighters are paid so badly that many can't afford to live near their central London bases,' he says, a point singularly ignored by so many who wrote about the dispute.

It got worse. 'Then there was the issue of fire fighters having second jobs,' he says.

Again, hostile reporting made out that the shift changes were being opposed for the selfish reason that fire fighters liked to have lucrative side jobs such as taxi drivers and this 'perk' would be lost if there were shift changes. This fundamentally ignored two things; firstly, the shift change, with a shorter night shift, could have actually made it easier for a fire fighter to find extra employment if they needed to, but more importantly, showed an attitude about the coverage which fire fighters still find it hard to fathom.

'Information was fed out about how many fire fighters have a second part time job,' says Mr Sprung. 'This story had nothing to do with our dispute but suddenly it became big news. But what shocked us was that if this was any one else and not FBU members, the right wing press would no doubt be praising us. They would be like oh, how hard working, they are struggling so much to make ends meet they are having to earn a second pay packet. Let's face it: it's not like any one would want to have two jobs. It's not a luxury but a necessity because of our pay. Do you think our families enjoy having us working on shifts, and then on days off still having to work? Yet they demonised us for working too hard!'

Mr Sprung said the second job issue has a knock on effect for the fire service in London — something that the press were told about but never reported. It is about fire training, something that the FBU have often said is not as good as it could be.

'We have many skilled fire fighters with experience in other trades — and you would be surprised how often we call on that expertise in dangerous situations,' he says.

'When we attend a flood, our fire service training might not be adequate, but on our crew there may well be someone who has experience as a plumber, so we use that. It is the same with electricity — all I have learnt about it hasn't really come from fire service training, but from working on the job with people who have previously been electricians. We all have skills that help each other out. This is never reported when we are criticised for being "greedy" and holding down part time work to make ends meet.'

Then the reporting of the FBU's conduct during the dispute also upset many members. 'We were accused of putting people's lives at risk,' he says. For a fire fighter who risks his own safety regularly to help others, this slur was a bitter pill to swallow, and hit morale.

'Our actions were never seen as about ensuring London had adequate fire cover,' says Mr Sprung. 'We were saying we do not want human resources officers who know little about the actual job to cut our cover at night and therefore put people's lives at risk. This was not made clear in papers and yes, it certainly affected our members. To make matters worse, we were branded yobs, and the fact we had picket lines made us easy targets.

'For example, we had two members run over by fire trucks, while there was not one arrest of any FBU member. With the case of two colleagues being run over, can you imagine what would have happened if it had been the other way round, if Asset Co workers had been hit by FBU men? It would have been all over *The Sun*. Instead it wasn't reported at all.'

But while all this may make for depressing reading, Mr Sprung says there has been a sliver of a silver lining. 'We feel our actions had an impact and will help keep London safe,' he says. 'It was not nice being vilified like this in the papers, but it has made our union stronger and more united.'

The RMT

The demonisation of the FBU is a scenario other public sector unions know all about, only too well.

In recent years one of the favoured groups to shackle in the tabloid stocks and throw rotten vegetables at has to be the Railway, Maritime and Transport Union (the RMT). It may simply have to do with the more rabid newspapers' demographics: home county Tories who commute are affected by industrial action on public transport, so whacking the people who may put readers out for an hour or two one morning makes sense to editors. It would explain, for example, why London newspapers such as the *Evening Standard* have for years loved to run 'commuter misery because of the hard left' style reports, even if there is no basis in fact.

The RMT has in some senses filled the role the National Union of Mineworkers played for the press in the 1980s. For Arthur Scargill, read Bob Crow. The public image of the RMT leader Mr Crow could hardly be worse. Whenever he appears in the press, it is almost always accompanied by a photograph of him that has caught him looking angry and aggressive—a decision to run pictures taken by a picture editor who is aware of exactly what their news desk wants.

And he is never quoted as speaking lucidly about the issues his members face at work, nor about Tube safety—something you would expect newspapers to care about in a land of common sense. No, instead, as a small but representative selection of headlines about the RMT show, whenever the RMT appears in the press it is in a wholly negative and personalised light. Examples abound: The *Daily Mail* and *The Sun* (perhaps unsurprisingly) are regular Crow baiters.

RMT press officer Geoff Martin is faced with the arduous task of putting reporters right, rebuffing stories and trying, in the face of endless hostile noise, to make sure the facts about issues such as Tube safety and workers conditions are aired publicly. 'I spend a lot of time speaking to reporters who have an editorial policy that is clearly against the RMT,' he says. '95 per cent of all papers I would say are hostile, but I have to try and get our case across.'

Bob Crowe is dubbed a 'yobbish union boss who earns £129,000 a year running the militant rail union'. For example Bob Crowe has been accused in one *Mail* headline of being threatened with being thrown out of a football match at the non-league game which his Union had sponsored due to a 'foul-mouthed rant'.

Mr Martin says this is par for the course. 'He is a working class bloke who went to a football match,' smiles Mr Martin at the ridiculousness of it all. 'There were no complaints from anyone there at the game or from the football club. He went into the boardroom afterwards. It was just a crazy story, but that is the environment we live in. We know what we are up against and we try to fight against it. If we were not successful they would not bother, and that is the fact of it. If we did not do good work for our members they would not come after us and it would not be such an issue for them. They do not like an assertive and successful working class trade union. It goes against what they want, which is subservience and knee bending. We are a challenge and a threat to them.'

The Sun also loves to get its claws into Mr Crow—and not always accurately. An apology had to be printed after some of their allegations about his pay and conditions were shown to be simply lies.

In one article headlined 'Comrade Crow's 12% pay increase: As millions suffer wage freezes, RMT's militant leader pockets £10,000'. (*The Sun*, 12 August, 2010)

It goes on to add: 'Since his election in 2002, the former communist has been known for his bullying style and lack of concern for the travelling public.'

Yet if you read releases by the RMT, concern for the travelling public is essentially at the heart of all their actions: yes, they do what any Trade Union should do—protect the rights of their members—but nobody has spoken out so much over issues like Tube safety and investment. They have acted as a valuable and well informed watch dog over our transport network—something desperately needed in an age where private companies carve up our systems of getting from A to B in an unending quest for profit, often at the expense of safety and services. This is a fact no paper ever comments on. Never mind—let us not let the facts get in the way of attacking the media's favourite self-created bogeyman, editors seem to say.

It gets worse. *The Sun* had to issue the following apology: 'An article on 15 September reported RMT General Secretary Bob Crow had a union-subsidised home and luxury car. In fact, Mr Crow's home has never been subsidised by the union and he does not own a car, union or otherwise, and champions public transport. We are happy to set the record straight and apologise to Mr Crow.'

Yet this did not calm down the attacks. *The Sun* was still at it: Under a title saying: 'Loathed: Rail union leader Bob Crow has been called the "most hated man in London"', the Sun quotes it's News International stable mate *The Sunday Times* who say 'militant union boss Bob Crow lives in a housing association home aimed at low-income families, despite enjoying a six-figure salary package', again, a story attacking the individual, not a calm critique of his union's policies.

It seems easier to accuse Bob Crow of making commuters lives a misery when his members hold the occasional one day strike — voted for by the membership and legal even under our country's draconian trade union laws — rather than look at the real issues, such as the lack of public investment in our transport infrastructure over the years, and the failure of the private and public finance partnerships that have been used to attempt to upgrade the creaking Tube system.

Yet still it goes on. *The Sun* took the fight right to Bob's front door — not content with attacking him personally in print, they stage managed a photo opportunity by parking a *Sun* logo'd bus in front of his home. Under a headline 'Hated union boss Bob Crow gets a taste of his own medicine from *The Sun* — after his two-day Tube strike brought misery to millions of Brits this week,' they claimed they had given '... Union Boss a taste of his own medicine.'

'Moaning Crow threw a hissy fit and called cops when we made him five minutes late for work. He flew into a rage after we parked our Sun bus outside his house in Woodford, East London, and walked in front of him as he tried to get to the Underground. We then stood in front of the entrance and asked him how it felt to be stopped from using the Tube. But the balding boss pathetically tried to claim to cops that we trod on his foot. The coward refused to talk to *The Sun*.' (*The Sun*, 13 June, 2009).

'They resorted to petty behaviour such as treading on Bob's toes to try and provoke him and get him to lash out,' recalls Mr Martin. 'But he is incredibly calm and simply did not respond. They have even followed him on holiday.'

This harassment in the attempt to create a negative news story is not a one off. 'Quite soon after I had started working here I came out of the office and there was a strike on the Victoria line,' recalls Mr Martin. 'There was a reporter and a photographer hassling people who came out.'

This is relentlessly hostile and provocative behaviour by journalists. Their hatred knows no bounds, and again does their readers a disservice by singularly failing to mention at all what his union may be campaigning for: in another 'exclusive', *The Sun* reports that Bob Crow — wait for it — had a go at karaoke, a disgraceful act, apparently, as at the same time as '... rail unions plot chaos.' The report states that at a Christmas party (or bash, as they put it) Mr Crow had the gall to stand up and sing a song. 'The hard-line RMT general secretary was cheered as he crooned Fly Me to the Moon at a union party,' they wrote.

Can you imagine? A union leader singing a song at a party? Disgraceful. It would be funny if it wasn't so damaging.

As Mr Martin recalls: 'They do like to drag up really arcane stories. Sometime you simply could not make it up. They even called me about it for a comment. The fact was he went to union Christmas party social function and then sang a song. He is the general secretary and some one said give us a song, Bob. That was it. On the back of that they ran a story.'

And it seems that newspaper reporters don't even need to be writing actually about Bob Crow to attack him: it's simply enough to be an acquaintance. In the *Mail*, a RMT official was arrested at a picket line — and was dubbed, of course as an ally of Bob's (who in an accompanying caption is described as 'Millwall fan Bob Crow showed his burly frame in a T-shirt while taking his dog, Castro, stroll near his Essex home,' painting a picture that will no doubt chill the hearts of its Middle England readers).

Photographs are regularly used to attack Mr Crow. One image speaks volumes about newsdesk attitudes as to what is and isn't a story when it comes to the RMT: the union leader was photographed by one of the many paps who like to trail him around, hoping for a picture of him picking his nose, carrying an umbrella that said 'Cuba' on it. 'It was as if Bob was plotting in the hills outside Havana, planning to march on London and impose martial law,' says Mr Martin.

'We have just had the 7/7 enquiry verdict and part of that praised the Tube staff and praised RMT members for their professionalism and courage,' says Mr Martin. 'Yet it is those staff whose jobs are under threat or have already been lost. The press seemed to want to ignore our role on that day and then they attack us when we express our worries over Tube safety. It means the myth of the RMT being a hostile force to the users of public transport gets trumpeted constantly.'

So why does this sorry state of affairs exist? It would be enough to make the most rational and accepting person feel there is some kind of damaging conspiracy against a legitimate trade union.

'The *Daily Mail* and *The Sun* recently ran a story that we were after "bribes" to work during the Olympics,' says Mr Martin. 'What exactly are they trying to say? That it is wrong for us to try and negotiate a deal regarding extra work for our members? The fact is they find our success in protecting the rights of our members galling.'

Mr Martin believes it has to be politically motivated. 'They do not want us to become a beacon for other working class unions and to show what can be done,' he says. 'Our successes for our members say

get organised and get in a Trade Union and you can benefit from it—
they do not like this message.'

Yet despite the constant rebuttals and the cheap snipes at Bob Crow
himself, Mr Martin believes they put up a good fight to get their
message across.' Our job is to look after our members, and to do all we
can to use all media channels to get our arguments across,' he says.
'The success of this can be measured by the fact, despite the negative
press, we are the fastest growing trade union in the country.'

At last also Mr Martin says that the fact the Tube service is seen as
being poor after years of under investment is no longer being blamed
on RMT members in the public's mind.

'The idea that bad public transport is somehow the RMT's fault is
now beginning to wear thin,' he says. 'Boris Johnson for a long time
avoided blame, but as the chairman of Transport for London, he
shouldn't be able to avoid this. We have tried to ensure Johnson is held
accountable. We had this situation where the Jubilee line would pack
up and he would say he was incandescent with rage that it had
happened, avoiding the uncomfortable fact that he is in charge of the
network.'

Criticism from the *Evening Standard* was a regular occurrence and
under the previous editorship of Veronica Wadley, the paper not only
ran attacks on the RMT, but campaigned to get Boris Johnson elected
over Ken Livingstone, who they saw as a friend of the RMT. 'Wadley
saw it as her role in life to get Boris Johnson elected,' Mr Martin says.

'The new editor, Geordie Greig, still shows that no love is lost for
the RMT, but what we have become better at is leaking internal
documents to prove our point about cuts and safety. We have people
who are looking around and researching internal reports at Transport
for London. The *Standard* and local news stations have been using it
and getting it out there—and that is moving the RMT out of a territory
that the hostile press had wanted to keep us in.'

What is behind the attacks on trades unions?

This state of affairs is a daily lament in many areas of trade unionism,
representing State employees. Unison officer George Binette, who
represents public workers in the London Borough of Camden, has
watched his fellow public sector workers have their professionalism
questioned and their roles belittled on a near daily basis.

'It is wrong to say there has ever been a halcyon age where there
was more balanced coverage,' says Mr Binette. 'But the situation has
certainly got worse. This is partly because of the triumph of Rupert
Murdoch, and the decline of the labour movement's press, and the
demise of the industrial and trade union correspondent. For example,

look at the case of the *Daily Mirror*. It is not what it was in the 1970s, the days of Paul Foot and John Pilger. That has long gone. There is now no real Red Top for working class people. It will occasionally support public sector workers, especially if they are ones who wear uniforms, but it is no longer a consistent ally.'

This view was echoed by Mr Martin for the RMT, who said *The Sun* was simply interested in giving their readers '... some tits, football and then off to the pub,' and had no interest in considering the type of work their readership did, nor in representing them in print in any way: a far cry from *The Sun*'s pre-Murdoch days, and its editorial stance, when it was known as the *Daily Herald*. Now it has a wholly different role in the media landscape—and Mr Binette believes that the right wing press is part of the neo-conservative attack on public services.

'I think the way the press reports the issues shows a concerted ideological effort against the public sector,' he says. 'There is highly concentrated media ownership at national level, and it is the same with the local press too. You find that reporters rely heavily on press releases and have very few resources now for proper investigative journalists.'

This means they go for easy stories, such as the occasional employment tribunal or investigation which can feature a public servant who has done something wrong. It quickly becomes the case that an individual's behaviour is used to taint an entire work force without any basis in fact.

'There is undoubtedly a strong sense of encouragement by owners and editors to bash the public sector work force at any given opportunity,' he adds. 'And public service broadcasting, packed with Oxbridge educated reporters who have only worked in the media industry and have no experience of other occupational spheres and are expected to write informed stories on them, is no better, says Binette.

'The BBC is increasingly simply a mouthpiece of the current government and its agenda seems to be basically a diluted version of the *Daily Mail*,' he claims.

'All of this means public sector workers do not get a fair crack. This is because of press ownership. We are looking at a media that works as an ideological state apparatus. Consecutive governments since the 1970s have been helped by the press who have consistently run down the public sector in the public's eyes. This is not a lefty conspiracy theory. They are printing an agenda that wants to see public services privatised and run by for profit companies.'

Mr Martin cites the demise of dedicated industrial correspondents, who not only had good links with unions but had a much better understanding of industrial relations and what the real issues were, for these petty attacks. 'When I first started nearly 30 years ago the industrial desk at national papers was seen as incredibly important' he says. 'This is no longer the case. Many do not have dedicated industrial reporters any more and it means the quality of reporting and the in-depth pieces have all but disappeared.'

In the past, industrial and trade union correspondents would have been more likely to get to the bottom of topics that the RMT have been in the headlines about. Recent issues have been over the loss of 800 more jobs on the Tube network and what this may mean for passenger safety. Yet, as with the FBU, the RMT find themselves attacked for simply flagging up issues that should matter to passengers.

Social workers

But while train drivers and fire fighters have been attacked in recent months, nothing can quite compare to the behaviour of the press when it comes to their favourite 'Nanny State Lefties', the tabloid's favourite bogeymen: social workers.

While social workers unions do not get the same treatment in the media as the RMT or the FBU—they appear anonymous, and are rarely quoted—individuals are attacked without mercy.

Ignore the fact that social workers have one of the hardest and most harrowing public sector jobs in the country, dealing with terrible cases, day in day out. Ignore the fact that GPs have reported social workers suffering from Post Traumatic Stress because of their work, or other research that shows social workers suffer personal problems: one such report found that they are more likely to split with their partners or have issues in their love lives, as they find it impossible to leave often harrowing day to day case loads when they finish for the night.

Ignore the fact that due to spending cuts their jobs have got a whole lot harder: not only do they sometimes lack the tools and staff they need, the increasing stresses of a society breaking down due to such issues as unemployment means their skills are more in demand than ever.

None of this is ever noted by those who write about them: to make matters worse, doing this vital work on small budgets, you stand a good risk of being personally vilified if anything, heaven forbid, should go wrong in anyway.

It is vital the press report evenly, honestly and accurately. It cannot be a public witch hunt, a trial by media, and does no one any good if it becomes so. It means a rational debate cannot be had, and therefore the real lessons are not learnt. Yet after a mother and two men were found responsible for the death of Baby P in August 2007, aged 17 months, the vitriol levelled at social workers who fail to protect children from their families reached a new crescendo.

It also highlighted a strange and bizarre paradox at the heart of press reporting when it comes to social workers. It seems, according to our newspapers, that when social workers intervene they are a meddling bunch of Guardianista do-gooders, wrecking happy family homes, and if they don't, they are incompetent never-do-wells who are directly responsible for child abuse.

The media often run stories about what they see as over-zealous interruptions into family affairs. This think piece comes from the *Daily Telegraph* on 21 May 2011.

'Vicky Haigh saves her baby from the clutches of the social workers,' it reads. 'A British woman has given birth in Ireland to stop Nottinghamshire social workers from seizing her child ...'

Then there is the thorny issue of how to report child protection cases. Of course the press must have the right to investigate and we rely on a free press to act as a watchdog. But there is often criticism of legal injunctions served to stop individual cases being reported in detail, and this is sometimes portrayed as being done because local authorities have something to hide. There is rarely an acknowledgement that injunctions are used to protect children from being identified under the jurisdiction of the courts.

A trawl through newspaper archives for stories on social workers underlines this damned if they do, damned if they don't approach. Recently, headlines such as: '... Social workers took our children away ... because of an incorrect hospital diagnosis,' and ' How social workers took away our children for 11 months without a shred of evidence,' and 'My baby had cancer but social workers falsely accused me of child abuse' have all been used.

Disturbing if true, but all too often newspapers use language that paints social workers as the villains of the piece, not as people working in a very complicated and tough field with the child's best interests at heart. A picture of a healthy and happy family ripped apart by social workers' incompetence and bad intentions provides a wonderful image and headline: that social workers are horribly under resourced and are dealing with some of the trickiest, most complex issues in today's society, often under strict terms of confidentiality so the real issues will never be aired in public, is routinely ignored.

Then there is the other side of this paradox: namely, social workers fail those they should be protecting, by making wrong diagnosis, not stepping in when they should, or ignoring evidence. Such horrific cases as Baby P and the Victoria Climbie enquiry highlight this.

Baby P is one of the most recent high profile cases that saw social workers attacked in print and in particular the scape-goating of Sharon Shoesmith, the Haringey social services chief who had previously had a long and successful career culminating in an invitation to her to take on the role at the department at Haringey.

No one can fail to be moved by the tragic story of Baby P and yes, it is of course important that any investigation is conducted in the full view of reporters. But it is all very well holding public servants to account, and report on issues in the public interest, but does this include personal attacks and attacks on the profession as a whole? The behaviour of the press – and, it has to be added, the knee jerk reaction by government ministers pampering to populism over the conduct of the head of Haringey's social services team – meant any reasoned investigation in the popular press of what went wrong, why it happened and how it can be fixed, went out the window.

Instead a witch hunt of over-worked, under-resourced and under-paid social workers has been a more populist route to take for many years. Stories headlined 'Toddler found starved to death … hadn't been seen by social workers for nearly a year' and 'Social workers "failed to act" on risks to toddler tortured to death' are representative.

A *Sun* editorial titled 'A Sorry Mess,' is a typical example of their approach to social workers. 'The appalling scandals caused by inept social workers just keep coming,' they stated. 'This time it's a known teenage sex offender placed into a loving foster family that included a boy of two and his nine-year-old sister … the culprits at the Vale of Glamorgan have, we are told, been "disciplined".'

Another headline in *The Sun*, referring to Baby P, was 'Blood on Their Hands,' while the *Daily Express* demanded: 'How many more children have to die?' *The Sun* then laid into social workers, calling them 'this disgusting lot' and then asked readers to sign a petition calling for wholesale sackings.

They want more than investigations and disciplines: they want heads on platters. Once more, we find *The Sun* is happy to exploit a terrible individual case to demean an entire profession. It also ignores the fundamental point that there are proper ways of going about holding professions to account: *The Sun* seems to think social workers operate in a vacuum, where they can intervene at will in others lives, for good or ill. It fails to point out that the regulatory body the General Social Care Council monitors and investigates. Instead, the paper paints itself as a champion, and it is put to them to demand sackings and achieve what they say is 'justice'.

Why is this the case? How can seemingly intelligent and well intentioned journalists act in this way? Critics could argue it may be because of the innate stupidity and bigotry of many right wing commentators. The work done by social workers sounds dangerously like 'nanny state' Socialism, a new fangled discipline born out of 1960s progressive universities and based on sociology, whose aims include improving the lot of the under classes at the cost of the tax payer.

Social workers are paid for by the state and are a bulwark against social meltdown—yet this means that rather than getting positive coverage, they are representatives of the meddling government. Their positive results cannot often be reported because of (quite rightly) privacy issues or protecting minors. So while fire-fighters can be seen bravely tackling blazes, police men foiling terror attacks, doctors providing miracle cures, teachers getting the odd working class kid into Oxbridge and while nurses are 'angels', social workers have no such ready store of media friendly triumphs to raise the coverage of their work.

The slow effect of good interventions by social workers can take years to be apparent. There is no magic wand they can wave. Yet when things go wrong it provides fuel for the brushwood under the stake. Can there be anything more harrowing than an abused child? We as a society want to find an easy enemy to blame, not wanting to face up to our collective responsibility for these tragic events, and social workers fit that easy-enemy bill neatly.

The way Sharon Shoesmith and her profession were treated means social workers say this case has affected the morale of the profession in general. One London based social worker, who did not want his name used, said since Baby P, he and his colleagues had been under perpetual stress. 'We have hard jobs, we are dedicated, we work with the country's most vulnerable people often in very difficult circumstances and without really the resources we need,' he said.

'This is no excuse for when things go wrong. They shouldn't and we are aware of how important it is that they don't. When mistakes are made, of course there needs to be a thorough and careful investigation so it does not happen again—any accusations of social workers not supporting 100 per cent this type of research, which will ultimately make us better at our jobs, is not a common sense way of looking at it. But the nature of reporting about our profession goes far and away over the boundaries of making any sense. Social workers as a profession face witch hunts. It makes you think that the reporters who write about us either have hidden agendas or just do not have any understanding of how social services work, what we do, how we are funded, and the cases that we have to look after.'

But, perhaps, now the profession is beginning to fight back. Prompted by the tragic events concerning the death of Baby P, the government formed the College of Social Work in 2009 to act as a professional body for social workers, in the same way the Royal College of Nursing or the Royal College of Physicians represent interest groups. It was in the findings of the Whitehall-run Social Work Task Force review of that year.

Press officer John Gaston now works to help the media write in a more balanced way about issues regarding social workers — and to ensure they have the information they need, and a professional association they can contact for advice, quotes and expertise.

'The idea was that the profession needed a central, dedicated organisation that could speak up for it,' says Mr Gaston. 'It would act to raise standards and as a leading voice for the profession, in the same way that doctors and nurses have colleges.'

There had not been a single body for social workers — the British Association of Social Work had existed for some time, but the government felt a more encompassing national body was needed.

Mr Gaston recognises the paradox that I have described and hopes things can change.

'Social workers get quite a conflicting press,' says Mr Gaston. 'There are a lot of myths about what they do and the type of people they are. The reporting is very contradictory. One section of the press pushes the first theory, while the second hammers the other.

'The *Telegraph* has a journalist who writes regularly about social workers snatching children, then you have *The Sun* taking the opposite view, that all social workers are incompetent, and they make mistakes that lead to tragedies. It is a very strange paradox and creates a confusing picture for the public. A lot of this is based on a lack of knowledge or research. It is easier to tell a story in simple and shocking terms to sell papers, rather than look at the larger picture and the issues involving the profession.'

Whichever part of the right wing press you study, it is clear that public sector workers are held up as bad examples of State power.

'There may be certain agendas in the press,' admits Mr Gaston. 'This could be down to the level in which the State can intervene in an individual's life: it is ideological.'

Perhaps unsurprisingly, the *Guardian* comes up in a good light: Mr Gaston says they tend to give a balanced view. 'Again, this may be based on the politics that prevail in the newsroom,' he says. 'They tend to value and understand the work the profession does.'

He believes that social workers also have to shoulder some blame, however, for this worrying state of affairs. He believes they have been forced to operate a closed-doors policy for the work they do: firstly, this has practical, child protection and confidentiality reasons, but it is also linked to the fact social workers read the criticism in the press and understandably want to have as little to do with journalists as they can.

'Part of the problem is that social workers are understandably defensive in the face of a hostile press,' he adds. 'It is because of the treatment they have received.'

It also comes down to the type of work they do: Mr Gaston points out that 1,000 of child protection social workers are helping people each and every day – 'but there is no story in the fact social workers do very good jobs each day,' he says.

But this hostile reporting can't help but make their working lives harder. Mr Gaston agrees that the reporting of the Baby P, and before that the Victoria Climbie, affair, seriously affected the morale of the profession. The public witch hunts over who was seemingly to blame for these two tragic events caused a fissure of despair amongst the profession. 'There were significant effects,' he says.

Despite this, there has not been a fall in numbers being recruited – new social work courses in universities have helped buoy up numbers – but retention has become a major issue after training is completed. Even more importantly, says Mr Gaston, the hostile reporting has had an effect on the ability of social workers to do their jobs effectively.

'It has hurt the public perception of what they do,' he says. 'This makes it more difficult for them to do their jobs effectively. People can be more hostile to social workers because of the negative stories they read. People do not have faith or confidence in social workers' services and therefore will not get the help they need.'

The answer as to how to deal with this unbalanced and inaccurate reporting has to be looked at as a long term aim. There can be no quick fix, especially as social workers, like so many other sections of the public sector, face an inherently hostile right wing press on a daily basis.

'We have to work with the media,' say Mr Gaston. 'We are now running media briefings for journalists, to explain what we are doing, and also to let reporters know how social workers feel about how they have been treated. It is about forging a better relationship, so journalists do not simply feel social workers are being defensive, but also so journalists are simply better informed. We hope to be able to give reporters channels they can use. The College is building up a bank of spokespeople so when the press has a story they know they can come to us, and we will have a team of expert spokespeople available to speak on behalf of the profession.'

This also means working closely with local authorities, says Mr Gaston, to ensure when issues come up they have the means to speak rationally and informatively about issues.

'We want to show positive stories and get social workers out there to help change peoples attitudes,' he added, and cited the role the press officers for the police service and doctors fulfilled, and how they worked: 'They do not sit about and hope they do not have to deal with the media,' he says.

'They put out comments and stories. Of course, the press can be looking for conflict and issues of failure and apportioning blame, but these services have built up relationships, so when things do go wrong, they have built up this level of goodwill. 'It means they do not get hammered to the same extent. Social workers have yet to do this, and this is why we are trying to encourage a more proactive relationship.'

The stark contrast with bodies such as nursing is obvious, says Mr Gaston. 'On nursing, there are failures, people get things wrong, but the public on the whole respect the profession. They know what nurses do and they value their work. However, most people do not ever meet a social worker or come into contact with them. Everything they know about the profession comes through the media. Whereas we all have experience dealing with doctors, teachers and nurses, it is very different with social workers despite the work they do being so valuable, working with the most vulnerable people in society.'

As well as the new national college, there is a campaign called Stand Up Now For Social Work: organised by magazine and website Community Care, they are calling for more support for social workers from the media, government and employers, as well as keeping a watching brief on the stories run by the national media on social workers.

It was prompted by *The Sun's* news coverage of the Baby P case, reacting to that campaign calling for all the social workers involved to be sacked: the newspaper petition garnered 1.2 million signatures. Social workers felt that this was inherently biased and ill informed. The Community Care website confirms that it is inevitable that this type of coverage, together with low levels of awareness about what social workers do, results in a low public opinion of social workers.

They say that these attitudes damage the profession's credibility in the eyes of those who use the services and other professions: it can also affect staff retention and recruitment. A Community Care poll of 250 readers found that 40 per cent felt media coverage of the case was affecting their practice and could adversely affect recruitment into the profession. Furthermore, Unison in Haringey said they had found social workers being verbally attacked by their clients regularly—egged on, they felt, by the media coverage. The sad effect of this is it could put vulnerable people at risk as fewer social workers are left to take on more cases, spending less time on each case.

What are the reporters up to?

Despite the actions of the government and the social work profession to try and turn the oil tanker of public opinion slowly round in the face of shock horror news headlines and a press happy to boast of their ideological opposition to the State, the future of reporting public sector workers does not seem rosy. While editors are after a quick fix to stick in tomorrow's edition, and reporters are employed to provide shocking headlines, there will always be an issue of press responsibility.

Perhaps the onus must be on individual reporters: there have been piecemeal complaints made for instance to the *Daily Star* and the *Daily Express* over accusations of racism for their coverage of the Gypsy community and Muslims in Britain and there have been campaigns to make individual reporters at these titles stand up in their news rooms and say: enough is enough. Perhaps what is needed is for some self-regulation when it comes to the coverage of public sector workers as well: perhaps this is something the National Union of Journalists (NUJ) should lobby their members over, and make the case for newspapers to stand up for the public sector.

NUJ President Jeremy Dear says he and his members are well aware of the issues.

'I do not think in general that the reporting is fair,' he says. 'That is not to deny there is some fair reporting in some sections of the media. But there are a lot of misconceptions regularly peddled: that the public sector workers get brilliant pay, massive pensions, long holidays and work short hours. The reality is very different from that.'

And he says some public workers regularly get a kicking from the newspapers. 'Civil servants particularly are vilified on a regular basis,' he states. 'They are portrayed as having non-jobs—but they are jobs that millions of people rely on to provide vital services.'

There are of course, says Mr Dear, public workers who stand up for themselves—but this just adds to the unfair treatment they receive. 'They really get attacked,' he says. 'In London, transport workers are particularly gone after.'

And he underlines the idea that individuals are painted as heroes but when they band together are seen as the crooks of the piece. 'They are called heroes for doing their jobs—nurses, fire fighters—but when it comes to asking that they be properly paid for their work, it becomes a completely different story. They are cast as shirkers.' He recalls the recent fire fighters dispute as a prime example of this.

The issues as to why this is the case are both complicated yet obvious: Mr Dear cites the ownership of the British media as a defining problem. 'Our papers are owned by big corporations and individuals who have a philosophy of believing in low taxes and a smaller state. They gratuitously use their publications to attack what they see as a state that is too big.'

He recalls working for union members at the BBC on pay and then receiving a call from journalists he knows personally, counts as friends and who are also union members—but work at the *Mail*, the *Mail on Sunday*, and the *Telegraph*.

'They said we hope you understand but we've been asked to write stories attacking the BBC journalists for asking for 2 per cent,' he says. 'This is while the directors at their papers are getting 10 per cent rises. This is a clear political agenda in many newspapers. They will always want stories like this—they could do exactly the same with the private sector, yet they never do.'

But can anything be done about this sorry state of affairs? Mr Dear believes it can be improved—and says that even at some of the worst offending papers, such as the *Express*, journalists can band together to fight these unbalanced and inaccurate reports.

'The *Express* actually has quite a strong union chapel,' he says. 'They have twice referred their own paper to the PCC (the Press Complaints Commission).'

The same applied to some of the terrible excesses at the *Daily Star*. There had been a plan mooted to run a page called the 'Daily Fatwa' on Page Three, featuring something called the 'Burkha Babes'—you can only imagine. Thankfully, despite the *Star* regularly running awful, racist stories, journalists finally stood up and said enough is enough, and that they would refuse to put the page together.

Mr Dear says, 'We have to encourage people to make sure they are not forced into a situation that is not just in breach of our own code of conduct but also that of the PCC.'

He recalls an example at the *Express* that he feels journalists could have spiked simply in terms of accuracy, as well as the inflammatory nature of the piece.

'They ran a story saying 1.6m Romas were entering Britain,' he recalls. 'This is patently absurd as there are only 1.6m Romas in the whole world.'

So why would they go with this? Mr Dear says the *Express* owner, Richard Desmond, is at least honest about why his paper runs such tales. 'He is honest and admitted why: he says simply sales go up by 30,000 when he runs headlines such as these. They are prepared to stretch the truth—or tell downright lies—just as they are prepared to use unlawful means to gain a competitive advantage.'

The answer is to educate journalists, and to encourage better discussion and stronger union voices in the newsrooms. 'We would also like to see it written in contracts that journalists can simply refuse an assignment if they asked to do something inaccurate or unbalanced. This has come to the fore because of the phone hacking scandal. They are under pressure from senior management to bring in stories and toe the line – but if union members stand together, this can be countered.'

As a journalist having worked in a series of newsrooms, I am often baffled by the motives of reporters: of course some are right wing and have agendas to promote, while others are simply willing to write anything they are asked to in order to earn a crust – but did any young person want to get into newspapers for these reasons? I have found from my experience of talking to scores of journalist students that they have the romantic idea of wielding the trusty sword of truth to hold those in power to account, of using language to further democracy by harvesting information, and to have a ring side seat on the events that make history.

I am encouraged by the stance of the NUJ, but it needs more than the Union to stand up and be counted. For real change, journalists need to look carefully every day at their work and that of their colleagues, and consider what they are writing about in terms of public interest and the public good – not just what satisfies the proprietors of their newspapers.

Following the hacking scandal, there has been talk of a Hippocratic oath for reporters – while this would have to go hand in hand with better legal regulation, it may be a good place to start for politically charged stories that denigrate public workers. The denigration of public service by the press must be checked before the imbalance in our society (public bad/private good) reaches a tipping point and cannot be saved.

POSTSCRIPT

It has been a monumental few months since I wrote my essay on the press and public service – and a period of time that looks likely to conclude with a new deal between the media and their readership for at least a generation.

The terms of this deal are still being worked out. It could result in a new ethical atmosphere of fair reporting or (and sadly more likely) some public apologies and then business as usual.

British journalism has lurched from one crisis another. We have seen the closure of the country's biggest selling Sunday tabloid, the *News of the World*, due to revelations regarding phone hacking. The extent of this illegal behaviour has shocked even those who know how low reporters can stoop in the quest for a story: hacking appalled the public, particularly as it moved from celebrities who have a hand in hand relationship with the red tops to the victims of violent crime and their families. The sheer scale has finally given politicians the guts they need to confront the behaviour of the press, and could potentially lead to a revamping on the Press Complaints Commission at the same time, taking it away from the silky-soft hands of self-regulation.

Watching Rupert Murdoch and his son James squirm as a select committee lead fiercely by Labour MP Tom Watson dragged them through painful evidence as to the criminal behaviour of their reporters felt like a crack in the levee. James Murdoch's return to the Commons Select Committee in November to be asked if he knew about phone hacking, and therefore condoned breaking the law, or didn't, and therefore was incompetent as a CEO, showed the Murdochs were not off the hook in terms of the way their organisations gathered stories.

This has helped create a public debate as to how the press behave, stating to a degree the obvious that they should not pay private investigators to snoop through personal data, not listen in to private phone calls, or bribe police officers for information (tip offs in the public interest yes, bribery, no).

But how could this help remind the press of their responsibility towards as fair and accurate reporting as possible when it comes to the public sphere? We have seen the continuing chasm between public servants and the press made clear this autumn: a strike over pensions slated for 30 November 2011 has again brought the usual reports on how selfish it is and disruptive it will be—and no mention has been made of the rights and wrongs of raiding funds, saved by public workers, to bail out the government. Very few people have made it clear that the strike is about the robbery of pension pots by the Treasury, savings put aside for old age. Instead it is public servants getting greedy again.

The Leveson Inquiry, whose remit is to look at the culture, practice and ethics of the press, may be a good place to start to tackle this. But will it be able to rein in this political bias and the accepted dogma reporters all too often spout, at the beck and call of their paymasters?

Possibly not: the closed shop nature of the media barons—with huge news companies like News International, Richard Desmond's Express group, Associated Newspapers and the Mirror group owning the vast majority of news providers—make it very hard to be positive about persuading the politically aligned behemoths to agree to play fair.

Perhaps the answer is twofold: Firstly, the responsibility for fair and accurate copy should ultimately fall on the shoulders of the reporter. They must look within themselves when they write a story, be aware that with their by-line on it, it is their moral judgement to make to ensure they are reporting fairly accurately. An example: if a reporter approaches a neo-liberal pressure group like the Taxpayers Alliance for a comment, they should also ask unions or left wing parties, think tanks and pressure groups for their views on the same question to provide balance. It can take many forms: after a tragic crash on the M5 in which many lost lives, the Institute of Advanced Motorists was asked to comment. Sadly the media didn't think of asking the many excellent experts available from the likes of Friends of the Earth to comment on how we can make our motorways safer — perhaps as they would discuss reducing the speed limit, using speed cameras to catch those who break the law, and encouraging people out of their cars and on to public transport — a news scenario that virtually none of the right wing newspapers are comfortable with reporting.

This reporter-led ethical stance sadly does not happen often enough. But it could. No editor can drag you over the coals for doing it, and if they take out your attempts to ensure various views are represented, then at least you can say you have tried.

The second and longer term way of combating this bias in reporting public services would be to fight for independent newspapers to survive — perhaps with the help of state funding. This could be in the form of local newspapers being turned into media trusts, along the same ownership model the *Guardian* newspaper is managed. This would mean instead of having a group of shareholders to answer to, a non-profit making trust would provide editorial guidance from above, and the profits could, like the John Lewis model, offer bonuses at the end of the year to the editorial staff. It could cut out the unfair reporting of public servants if the reporters do not get pressured to write biased stories by editors doing the job as 'yes men' to their billionaire bosses, who have personal interest reasons for promoting a low tax, laissez-faire body politic.